GLOBAL TRADE AND EUROPEAN WORKERS

Global Trade and European Workers

Edited by

Paul Brenton
Research Fellow
Centre for European Policy Studies
Brussels, Belgium

and

Jacques Pelkmans
Senior Research Fellow
Centre for European Policy Studies
Brussels, Belgium
and
Professor of Economics
University of Limburg
Maastricht, The Netherlands

Foreword by
Willem van der Geest
Research Director, EIAS

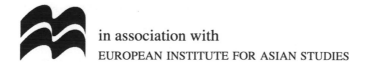

in association with
EUROPEAN INSTITUTE FOR ASIAN STUDIES

First published in Great Britain 1999 by
MACMILLAN PRESS LTD
Houndmills, Basingstoke, Hampshire RG21 6XS and London
Companies and representatives throughout the world

A catalogue record for this book is available from the British Library.

ISBN 0–333–72098–9

 First published in the United States of America 1999 by
ST. MARTIN'S PRESS, INC.,
Scholarly and Reference Division,
175 Fifth Avenue, New York, N.Y. 10010

ISBN 0–312–21686–6

Library of Congress Cataloging-in-Publication Data
Global trade and European workers / edited by Paul Brenton and Jacques
Pelkmans.
p.   cm.
Includes bibliographical references and index.
ISBN 0–312–21686–6
1. Foreign trade and employment—Europe.   2. Foreign trade and
employment—Great Britain.   3. Foreign trade and employment–
–Germany.   4. Foreign trade and employment—Asia.   5. Unemployment–
–Europe.   6. Wages—Asia.   I. Brenton, Paul.   II. Pelkmans,
Jacques.
HD5710.75.E85G55   1998
331'.094—dc21   98–7077
                                                                                                          CIP

Selection and editorial matter © Paul Brenton and Jacques Pelkmans 1999
Foreword © Willem van der Geest 1999
Chapter 1 © Jacques Pelkmans 1999
Chapter 2 © Paul Brenton 1999
Chapters 3 and 7 © Bob Anderton and Paul Brenton 1999
Chapters 4–6, 8 and 9 © Macmillan Press Ltd 1999

This book is printed on paper suitable for recycling and made from fully managed and
sustained forest sources.

10   9   8   7   6   5   4   3   2   1
08   07   06   05   04   03   02   01   00   99

Printed and bound in Great Britain by
Antony Rowe Ltd, Chippenham, Wiltshire

Contents

List of Figures

List of Tables

Foreword

High unemployment now appears to have become a structural feature in many of the OECD countries, in particular in Europe. Many young people entering the labour market find it extremely difficult to get started, whereas many of those presently employed no longer feel that their skill profiles are sought after. They experience a continuous threat of being laid off: keeping a job has become hard work. The 'normal' economic growth cycle – technical innovations leading to new economic opportunities, which in turn translate into further employment opportunities – appears to be wholly unable to deliver for Europe a level of employment which one may consider as anywhere near to full employment.

In this climate, it is not surprising that popular discussion perceives competitive imports from developing countries as a major threat and that corporate decisions to relocate industries and service providers to other parts of the world are the subject of intense criticism. It is often argued that 'outsourcing' and *delocalisation* harms Europe's work force and limits future employment, and this has become one of the delicate issues in the relationship between Europe and Asia. In this volume, the authors have sought to make a rigorous and impassioned analysis of these issues and to move away from the emotional, even at times racial, overtones of the debate.

Economic theory suggests that consumer welfare is enhanced if real purchasing power increases, for example through additional income or lower prices for goods and services. The ongoing process of globalisation means not only lower prices for imported goods but also a reduced demand for labour services in Europe. Though corporations and consumers stand to gain, the work force stands to lose. Increased profit opportunities occur but an increasing share of global investment resources is used outside Europe and the OECD. In response, labour market flexibility is called for but many in Europe believe that this amounts to little more than a wage cut through the back door.

The issue at the heart of the matter is whether enhanced consumer welfare will translate into new demand for goods and services which have a high domestic value added. Textiles may, perhaps, be manufactured in low-wage economies of Asia, but will high-tech, high-skill services continue to demand highly skilled specialists from

Europe and the OECD? In this sense, the global race should not simply be thought of as one between high-wage Europe and low-wage Asia, but rather as one where high skilled and highly responsive workers inside Europe continue to find new and innovative technologies ahead of anybody else. A failure to do so will inevitably lead to a loss of competitiveness, whereas the knee-jerk response of increased protection is likely only to postpone finding long-term and sustainable solutions.

The contributors to this volume bring to the fore an advanced and rigorous analysis of the determinants of trade flows between Asia and Europe and their impact on employment. They assess the impact of trade flows with Asia and note that many of the imported goods are not produced in Europe and hence are not directly competing with domestic suppliers and labour. Furthermore, rapidly increasing exports to Asia have offered significant economic and employment gains. However, evidence is also presented which shows that in various sectors the unskilled workers have been losing in both absolute and relative terms.

Public policy in Europe is facing a major challenge, requiring a greater emphasis on training, skill formation and the continuous upgrading of the skill profiles of the labour force. This is even more important if one realises that, after more than a decade of rapid growth in parts of South, South East and East Asia, technological and research competencies in these regions have substantially been upgraded. It is in these areas of skill formation and research and development (R&D) that supra-national initiatives at the European Union (EU) and OECD levels may prove particularly important – individuals, firms and national governments may tend to invest less than is socially optimal in these areas.

The Brussels-based European Institute for Asian Studies (EIAS) seeks to contribute to a better understanding of political and economic relations between Europe and Asia through briefings, seminars and research publications. The present volume has been the outcome of a collaborative project, sponsored by EIAS, involving researchers from across Europe under the direction of Paul Brenton and Jacques Pelkmans. It is hoped that this volume will inform the debate in Europe about appropriate and active public policy responses to Asia's phenomenal growth and, through this, contribute to welfare in both regions.

WILLEM VAN DER GEEST
Research Director, EIAS

Notes on the Contributors

Bob Anderton is a research fellow at the National Institute of Economic and Social Research (NIER).

Paul Brenton is a research fellow at the Centre for European Policy Studies (CEPS).

Olivier Cortes is a research fellow at the Centre d'Études Prospectives et d'Informations Internationales (CEPII).

Sébastien Jean is a research fellow at the Centre d'Études Prospectives et d'Informations Internationales (CEPII).

Matthias Lucke is head of the research team at the Kiel Institute of World Economics.

Richard Nahuis is affiliated with the Department of Economics and CentER, Tilburg University.

Jacques Pelkmans is a senior research fellow at the Centre for European Policy Studies (CEPS) and Professor of Economics at the University of Maastricht.

Dominique van der Mensbrugghe is a senior economist at the OECD Development Centre.

John Whalley is Professor of Economics at the Department of Economics University of Warwick and Department of Economics, the University of Western Ontario.

Randall Wigle is Professor of Economics at the Department of Business and Economics, Wilfried Laurier University.

1 Emerging Countries and Jobs and Wages in Europe: An Introduction

Jacques Pelkmans

1.1 TRADE AND DISTRIBUTION EFFECTS: SOME SUSPICIONS

Business between Asia and the European Union (EU) is booming. Economic interdependence between the two has been deepening rapidly since the early 1980s and has meanwhile spread over many sectors of economic activity. It has been accompanied by unilateral, bilateral and multilateral liberalisation of trade in goods, services and – selectively – direct investment, which, no doubt, has had a stimulating effect.[1] However, this success story and the implied structural adjustment are not always applauded in Europe. At times, it has been fiercely resisted. In the early 1980s when the EU economy suffered from high unemployment, stagflation, Euro-sclerosis (various deeply entrenched rigidities, identified as slowly paralysing the EU economy) and 'lost' competitiveness, the EU resorted to no less than ten voluntary export restraints *vis-à-vis* Japanese exports, some new restrictions at the Member States' level and a significant tightening of the third Multi-Fibre Arrangement (MFA) (1982–1986). The idea of a new GATT Round was also shot down by the EU in 1982.

In the early 1990s fears about the job losses caused by 'delocalisation' (relocation of labour-intensive parts of the production process to low-wage countries – by that time, not just Asia but also Central Europe or, for clothing, the Mediterranean, too) and by rapid growth of imports from NICs, new NICs and China were clearly on the rise. Although the policy climate had become distinctly less protectionist, there were strong sentiments that free trade had to be fair trade. At first, 'fair trade' referred to vague notions of reciprocity. Once the Asian countries, and other developing countries, had begun to open up their economies, and actively took part in the Uruguay Round, fair trade no longer referred primarily to trade barriers[2] but to the prevention of competitive advantages obtained via too low labour standards. As Chapter 9 of this book, by John Whalley and Randall Wigle, shows, policy actions by the developed economies against trade from countries with 'too low' labour standards would risk being extremely costly, while being counterproductive for the wages of workers in the South.

However, following the recessions in North America (1991–2) and in Europe (1992–3), a much more fundamental issue came to dominate the political debate. Labour union leaders and populist politicians began to question aloud whether more free trade and direct investments with the South were not against the interests of workers. The problem is fundamental because 'proper' labour standards would perhaps mitigate the perceived adverse effects for workers in the North, but not remove them. Of course, in the history of capitalism, trade with 'low-wage' economies has often been viewed with suspicion or fears by workers from high-wage countries. One might interpret the opposition to NAFTA, and the coincidence of the NAFTA debate with a US recession, simply as yet another manifestation of the fears of the part of the electorate of a loss of jobs. In the NAFTA debate the fears focused on relocation and swollen imports from Mexico, expected to be boosted by direct investments that otherwise might have come to the USA. However, the disenchantment in the USA with free trade was, and perhaps still is, more general and more systematic. The 1980s and 1990s saw an erosion of the long-standing free trade coalition in US domestic politics. With labour unions becoming increasingly sceptical about, if not hostile to free trade (for example, in clothing), and political party lines having become less clear, the leading lobbyists for freer trade in both goods and services became the US (and foreign) multinationals. This shift coincided with issues far more pervasive than labour standards – namely, the perception that free trade caused 'de-industrialisation' as well as an adverse distributional impact upon US workers. If this perception were to be correct, and worse still, could be extrapolated into the future, it would be alarming indeed. Before long, such adverse redistributional effects – once again, if correct – would have to be reversed by markets or transfers, or otherwise free trade would be doomed. The repercussions of the USA turning to protectionism *vis-à-vis* Asia and other low-wage economies would be very negative for the world economy. A major engine of growth for developing countries in Asia and elsewhere would be lost.

1.2   WERE US WORKERS ADVERSELY AFFECTED BY OPENNESS?

To be more precise about the US case, imports and (outward!) direct investments were asserted, by some, to be among the principal causes of three stylised facts:

1.2.1   De-industrialisation

The US found itself in a secular process of 'de-industrialisation'. This refers to a relative decline in the importance of manufacturing industry in total economic activity. Measured in industrial jobs, the decline was from 27.3 per cent of all jobs in 1970 to 17.4 per cent in 1990; measured in value added (as a percentage of GNP) it is down from 25 per cent in 1970 to 18.4 per cent in 1990.[3]

It is by no means obvious that de-industrialisation is caused, or mainly caused, by trade and FDI. First of all, the USA is a major exporter, too, and enjoys large inflows of FDI in industry. Moreover, it is well known that long-run development tends to be characterised by a secular shift to services. One (verifiable) explanation is that labour productivity increases in industry have consistently been higher than in services. This explains the relative decrease in jobs in industry, and helps to explain a slower rise in industrial product prices over the years. The latter, in turn, will lower the nominal value of industrial value added, and hence its share in GNP. The interesting question is, therefore, whether the relatively high increases in labour productivity are endogenous, and whether, and to what extent, this technological progress is prompted by imports. Any research about this question should not ignore the fact that cost competitiveness in exports may also be a forceful incentive to seek technological progress.

1.2.2   Stagnant Real Wage Level

The average real wage level in the USA appeared to be stagnant over decades. Indeed, the average American seemed to enjoy less prosperity than in 1970[4]. Such a stylised fact is a frustrating one for any economy, developed or developing, the more so in the leading economy in the world. Moreover, Japan and Western Europe continued to enjoy rising standards of living, thereby showing that stagnancy over several business cycles was not inevitable.

1.2.3 Real Wage Inequality

The greatest anxiety, however, was caused by a sharp increase in real wage inequality between workers of different skill levels, combined with a fall of real wages for the low skilled. Indeed, the real wage decline was so strong that Freeman (1995) speaks of 'immiseration' of low-skilled US workers. From 1979 to 1993 real hourly wages of males with (no more than) 12 years of schooling dropped by 20 per cent; when the low skilled were also inexperienced (young entrants), the drop was 30 per cent (Freeman, 1995, p. 18). Although one can observe modest increases in wage inequality (much less or not at all in household income inequality) in other OECD countries, the US case was extreme in many respects.[5]

Many potential causes of this immiseration have been explored, and only one of them is the increased openness of the US economy. There is widespread agreement that the relative demand for skilled workers in the USA has increased rapidly, particularly during the 1980s. Since imports from low-wage economies tend to be low-skilled labour-intensive, and hence compete (often sharply) with low-skilled labour-intensive import substitutes, this may be expected to exert downward pressure on low-skilled wages. Similarly, relocation of low-skilled labour-intensive production to low-wage economies or a reduction of output of low-skilled labour-intensive import substitutes – all else being equal – would reduce the demand for such labour, and hence imply an increase in the relative demand for skilled labour. Failing a matching change in supply, it would – still *ceteris paribus* – explain the rising wage inequality. Other potential causes include a skill-biased technological progress,[6] supply factors such as immigration and the increased labour force participation of women,[7] and institutional factors in the labour market.[8]

1.3 DOES OPENNESS TO TRADE INCREASE UNEMPLOYMENT IN EUROPE?

What about (Western) Europe? OECD-Europe is, broadly speaking, more egalitarian than the USA. There have been no dramatic examples of rising inequality in Western Europe, with the partial exception of the UK.[9] Yet, there is a mirror image of the US problem, concisely formulated by Freeman (1995, p. 19) as follows:

[I]n general, Europe has avoided an American level of inequality or changes in inequality, and wages at the bottom of the distribution rose rather than fell. By the early 1990s, workers in the bottom tiers of the wage distribution in Europe had higher compensation than did workers in the bottom tiers in the United States [Freeman, 1994]. Western Europe's problem was one of jobs, not of wages: the workers whose wages have fallen through the floor in the United States – the less skilled and (except in Germany) the young – were especially likely to be jobless in Europe.

Freeman continues:

[T]he rise in joblessness in Europe is thus the flip side of the rise in earnings inequality in the US. The two outcomes reflect the same phenomenon – relative decline in the demand against the less skilled that has overwhelmed the long-term trend decline in the relative supply of less-skilled workers. In the United States, where wages are highly flexible, the change in the supply–demand balance lowered the wages of the less skilled. In Europe, where institutions buttress the bottom parts of the wage distribution, the change produced unemployment. The question then is not simply why the United States and Europe experienced different labour market problems in the 1980s and 1990s, but what factors depressed the relative demand for low-skill in both economies.

Since 'institutions' in the labour market in Western Europe create and maintain a host of rigidities, labour market adjustments are slow or outright impossible. Among economists there is widespread agreement that European labour markets should be more 'flexible' for unemployment to fall significantly and structurally, rather than just cyclically. OECD and EU ministers echo this view in their own words but the actual changes in labour markets have been minimal, except in the UK.

The European debate on unemployment has identified a number of potential factors such as: real wage rigidity; a relatively high minimum wage; relatively high non-wage costs (acting as a 'tax' on labour); regulatory and institutional entry and exit restrictions in the labour market; the generous 'welfare state' undermining work incentives on the margin; a lack of intersectoral and interregional mobility of workers (in part, a consequence of the welfare state); insufficient overall structural adjustment (the EU concentrated relatively strongly on low-growth sectors with a secularly declining workforce); a lack of competitiveness of industry in the most competitive world markets; and, not least, since the mid-1980s,[10] a restrictive macroeconomic climate in the EMS and in preparation for EMU, in turn suppressing investment and consumption of durables.[11] There have been occasional references to trade and direct investment but this has rarely been seen as a prominent cause. Rather, some industrial sectors or segments of society associated specific job losses, or the threat of them, with moves to free(r) trade, which were then resisted. In a situation where unemployment rates hovered in many European countries in a 8 per cent–13 per cent band, the political economy of this response can hardly be surprising. Quite the contrary, the question is rather what political economy explains the EU's move to freer trade and deregulation. Indeed, European political leaders pride themselves about the shift away from protectionism via EC-1992, the opening up *vis-à-vis* Central Europe and the Uruguay Round in an era of high unemployment in the EU. The newly born ASEM summit – the Asia–Europe Meeting, first held in Bangkok on 1 and 2 March 1996[12] – explicitly confirmed at the highest political level that the EU was prepared to pursue trade liberalisation and facilitation as well as direct investment promotion and business alliances with the strongest low-wage economic zone, namely East Asia.

There is debate about possible job losses caused by trade and 'delocalisation' in Europe, but surely no groundswell or great popularity for assertions equivalent to Ross Perot's 'sucking sound'. This might be explained by Europe's willingness to provide large redistributional transfers – implicitly in the labour market by high minimum wages and explicitly via social security, the welfare state, rent control for social housing and low-cost health care for low-income groups. Another explanation, complementary to redistribution, is the laboratory effect of having a Union with a range of rather divergent policy records. The average EU unemployment rate of 10.9 per cent for 1996 exhibits a wide dispersion of country rates around the average: they range from 4.2 per cent for Austria, 6.2 per cent for Denmark, 6.8 per cent for the Netherlands, 7.3 per cent for Portugal and 8.3 per cent for the UK to 9.0 per cent for Germany, 12.3 per cent for France, 12.1 per cent for Italy and 22.0 per cent for Spain (this last rate is partly due to some peculiarities of social security).[13]

Since all EU Member States have exactly the same trade policy, it is hardly credible to see 'openness' as the main culprit. Nonetheless, immigration is more and more resisted, the EU is engaged in a quasi-permanent struggle to give workers, at the company level, the right to be informed about 'delocalisation', and the high share of low-skilled becoming structurally unemployed is widely viewed as a policy failure, with the risk of 'social exclusion' as a negative repercussion. Moreover, there is a perception that 'delocalisation' is not roughly compensated by inward FDI in Europe, since the former is thought to be strongly biased towards low-skilled-intensive products, whereas the latter is not.

1.4 INTRODUCING THE ECONOMIC DEBATE

In the early 1990s the debate about the impact of economic intercourse with Asia and other low-wage economies on jobs and wages was dominated by studies on the US case. Since Chapter 2 (by Paul Brenton) provides a systematic survey of the recent literature, the reader is advised to consume his rich menu. Suffice it to say here that there were three kinds of studies: those focusing on typical labour market aspects without any reference to economic openness to low-wage economies; those concluding that trade was one cause, among several, for the strong increase in the relative demand for high-skilled labour, based on so-called factor-content-of-trade analyses; and those rejecting factor-content techniques, instead concentrating on prices of relative low-skilled labour-intensive goods which suffered from strong import competition. As Brenton notes, studies diverged in their conclusions, but by 1994 a consensus seemed to emerge that trade was at most a small contributing factor.

However, it was a European economist, Adrian Wood (1994a) who challenged this basic result in essentially two ways. First, he holds that factor-content studies dramatically underestimate the actual impact of trade with low-wage economies on the low-skilled wages, while price-based studies suffer from the unavailability of appropriate data. Second, his book is not (only) about the USA but about the 'North', including extensive descriptive work on Europe. Focusing for a moment on the US main issue – increased wage inequality – Wood (1994a, 1995) concludes that the inequality increase which can be explained by US trade with Asia and other low-wage economies is about ten times as high as several leading studies had suggested before. Indeed, it might explain up to half or more of this inequality increase since 1980.

This challenge was not left unanswered. But it was mainly taken up in the USA. A number of the second-wave studies focused on methodology. Without anticipating how Brenton succeeds in disentangling some of the confusing elements of this debate, it is interesting to point out that the theoretical source of many studies is the well-known Heckscher–Ohlin–Samuelson (HOS) model. Brenton carefully, and step by step, explains how this elegant but highly restrictive model relates to the empirical studies on the possible trade impact on jobs and wages. As it turns out, the empirical methods used in a number of US studies are not consistent with HOS, even though the latter is, more often than not, the theoretical basis for the work. The methodological criticism is aimed at factor-content studies but has meanwhile spread to some other aspects. On the face of it, this criticism is justified. Whilst it is generally agreed that empirical analysis without a proper theoretical basis is a futile exercise, it is of course little better if the propositions to be verified empirically do not derive from the theory one claims to use. Upon further reflection, however, one may equally well hold that it has led some leading scholars astray. After all, the jobs and wages debate conveys the strong impression of a resurrection of the HOS model.[14]

Many economists have been trained in HOS because it is didactically useful for the classroom as it disciplines students' thinking, while serving as an elegant yet comprehensible general equilibrium approach to understanding interactions between key variables in the world economy. However, a huge empirical literature dating back to the 1960s and 1970s has shown that HOS is far too restrictive, and too simple, to explain actual trade flows properly. Read-

ers may remember the emergence of neo-factor proportions and
neo-technology approaches as amendments, to mention only two
well known ones.

Yet, in the current US jobs and wages debate one encounters
near-religious fights about fine points within the HOS framework,
without much emphasis (or, sometimes, any) on the restrictive assumptions of HOS itself. The results are bound to be sensitive to
changes in these (special) assumptions. The technical points are
set out by Brenton. At this stage, it is perhaps worthwhile quoting
Krugman (1995, pp. 4–5, 38):

[I]t is positively dismaying that . . . [economists] have adopted
the pose of guardians of the true tradition, defending theoretical purity against the barbarians . . . . What one does . . . [in the
classroom] is to perform a thought experiment . . . whose details
have been chosen to lay bare the mechanics of the model, not
necessarily to make sense of a real-world issue. Some theorists
seem, however, to have identified the canonical thought experiments with the model itself.

Some economists have recently attempted to look for explanations outside the HOS framework. For instance, Feenstra and Hanson
(1996) have found empirical evidence that outsourcing has played
a role in the sharp increase in US wage inequality. The scepticism
about the usefulness of HOS-based models for empirical research
is also supported by studies failing to find empirical evidence of
the mirror image of the rise of US wage inequality – a narrowing
of inequality between wages for different skill levels – in low-wage
economies (for example, Mexico) heavily exporting to the USA or
the 'North'.

1.5 THE VALUE-ADDED OF THIS BOOK

The present book responds to a number of challenges. First, empirical economic analysis on the possible impact of trade with Asia
and other low-wage economies on jobs and wages in Europe was
scant.[15] This volume offers five contributions to help fill this gap.
Second, in varying degrees, authors in this book have made an attempt to adapt HOS-type approaches, or avoid the restrictive textbook HOS model. Olivier Cortes and Sébastien Jean (in Chapter 5,

introducing imperfect competition with scale economies and product differentiation) and Bob Anderton and Paul Brenton (in Chapter 7, with an econometric study of outsourcing by UK firms) probably go the furthest in this respect. Third, the book comprises a mix of methodological approaches.

On the one hand, one should be prudent with partial equilibrium approaches, which, in some cases, have attracted considerable criticism in the US debate. At the other extreme, computable general equilibrium (CGE) models – no doubt, a useful and widely employed tool, with helpful insights for policy makers and others – do have drawbacks too. As is well known, CGE models are usually based on some heroic assumptions while elasticities and coefficients are calibrated rather than estimated econometrically. For these reasons, the editors of this book find it appropriate that the authors provide a variety of analytical approaches: detailed statistical analysis in Chapter 3 (by Bob Anderton and Paul Brenton), computable general equilibrium models in Chapters 5 (by Olivier Cortes and Sébastian Jean), Chapter 6 (by Richard Nahuis), Chapter 8 (by Dominique van der Mensbrugghe) and Chapter 9 (by John Whalley and Randall Wigle), as well as econometric approaches in Chapters 4 (by Matthias Lücke) and 7 (by Bob Anderton and Paul Brenton).

Fourth, unlike the US debate which is mainly about the recent past, several chapters attempt to understand the implications for jobs and wages in the long-run future, based on stylised scenarios. Not only are these exercises important to deepen our understanding of the possible redistributive implications of globalisation, they may also shed light on the controversy between Wood (1994a) and several other authors. Whereas some economists (who conclude that the trade impact thus far has been minor) have held that trade may have a greater impact in the future, Wood advocates a contrary view both on the recent past and on the long-run future. The argument for not expecting adverse effects in the North in the future is Wood's assertion that practically all relatively low-skilled labour-intensive products are no longer produced in Western Europe, North America and possibly even Japan.

That matters might well be more complicated is also shown in this volume. One characteristic of today's division of labour is outsourcing within multinationals or business alliances or even at arm's length, but in all cases in low-wage countries. Outsourcing is tantamount to a loss of low-skilled jobs, but it is little known how important the phenomenon is once all adjustments have taken place. Bob Anderton and Paul Brenton (in Chapter 7) incorporate outsourcing as a possible source of the sharp rise in wage inequality (between skilled and low skilled) which occurred in the UK in the first half of the 1980s.

The editors trust that the four different ways of adding value to this important economic debate will be helpful for economists in South and North, as well as policy makers. The book is organised as follows.

In Chapter 2 Paul Brenton provides a systematic survey of the relevant trade theory and empirical methods and results in this debate. Brenton's detached survey will surely prevent the reader from drawing rash conclusions from simple coincidences or ill-justified partial approaches in economic analysis. His chapter helps to put the near-religious controversies in the USA, flowing from the HOS basis of some research, into perspective. A major issue is whether (for example, labour-saving) technological progress, rather than trade, has caused the relative demand for the unskilled to decline. However, the words 'rather than' suggest that such progress would be exogenous whereas innovation in machinery and organisation may have been biased towards labour-saving because managers in import-competing industries were under strong pressure to stay competitive against imports from low-wage economies. Such endogenous technological progress is suggested by casual empiricism but it is not easy to model and verify properly. Brenton also pays attention to studies on direct investment – and, more specifically, outsourcing. The overall conclusion is that it is probable that three main causes can be identified for the predicament of the low-skilled in developed economies: competition with low-wage economies, technological progress and changes in the relative supply of skilled and unskilled labour.

In Chapter 3, Bob Anderton and Paul Brenton argue that recent empirical research has been unable to capture the sectoral mechanisms by which increased import competition from, say, the NICs may influence wage inequality – or, as the case may be, be a loss of jobs. The authors concentrate on the UK and Germany. They provide a detailed statistical analysis on a disaggregated basis of the relative prices of low-skilled-versus high-skilled-intensive products, relative wages and changes in trade shares. One result is that the experience of sectors typically treated as relatively low-skill-intensive is not uniform within a country, or indeed between Germany and the UK. Anderton and Brenton show that the impact of globalisation (they do look at outsourcing, too) is far more complicated than the standard trade model would suggest.

Matthias Lücke, in Chapter 4, also inspects the experiences of the UK and Germany. The author adapts two alternative modelling approaches from a very careful, HOS-based study by Baldwin and Cain (1997). The first focuses on the evolution of relative prices of skilled versus unskilled-labour-intensive goods; the second approach investigates changes in the pattern of trade specialisation which permit conclusions on relative factor endowments at home (i.e. the UK and Germany) compared to the rest of the world. Lücke, like Anderton and Brenton (see above), also finds the two countries to exhibit different responses, and fails to trace a single main cause for the deteriorating position of unskilled labour.

Olivier Cortes and Sébastien Jean, in Chapter 5, employ a CGE model with imperfect competition (scale and Cournot-type oligopolistic rivalry). They develop a sectoral approach by distinguishing fragmented and segmented industries with different degrees of product differentiation.[16] The shock representing a future deepening of economic interdependence with Asia and other low-wages economies is first assumed to be a doubling in the size of those emerging economies. This leads to a rise in the import penetration ratio from 1.6 per cent to only 3 per cent; wage inequality in the EU increases at most by 1 per cent. It takes a far bigger shock, still, for wage inequalities to increase by, for instance, 4 per cent, and even in this scenario the real wage of unskilled workers decreases at most by 0.5 per cent. Moreover, the overall economic benefits of this interdependence are considerable.

More pessimistic conclusions are reached with the help of another CGE model, by Richard Nahuis (Chapter 6). The author employs WorldScan, a multisector, multiregion, dynamic CGE model for the world economy, designed to support economic scenario studies of up to 25 to 35 years. The Nahuis study is a response to Krugman's (1995, p. 26)

> challenge to economists who claim that trade has had very large effect on wages: can they produce a general equilibrium model of the OECD, with plausible factor shares and elasticities of substitution, that is consistent both with their assertions and with the limited actual volume of trade?

Nahuis' results go against the chorus of studies concluding a minor impact. In asking what Krugman (1995) calls the 'but-for' question – what relative wages would have been *but for* the openness of OECD to non-OECD countries, so in effect a total elimination of trade with low-wage economies – Nahuis finds that trade is responsible for half of the rise in inequality for unskilled workers. This is the same impact as suggested by Wood (1994a, 1995). The complicated model makes it somewhat difficult to evaluate the analytical merits of this conclusion, but, clearly, it would be inappropriate to dismiss this strong result out of hand.

Bob Anderton and Paul Brenton in Chapter 7 focus on the aspects, largely neglected thus far, of outsourcing. There are two reasons for doing this. One is that most of the rise in inequality observed in the UK is concentrated in the first half of the 1980s, when sterling sharply appreciated. This raises the question whether the rise of sterling might have prompted a disproportionate increase in outsourcing. The other reason is that the few previous (US) studies on outsourcing have focused on the total import share of consumption in each industry, rather than the imports of inputs from low-wage economies only (which is what Anderton and Brenton do, on the basis of a disaggregated set of UK import data; however, the authors focus on selected sectors only). Their econometric analysis would suggest that outsourcing to low-wage countries, switching costs (that is, switching to imports is relatively less costly if price changes are large) and the high value of sterling in the early 1980s explain, in part, the sudden increase in inequality. Once outsourcing works smoothly, there is little reason to switch back, even if the exchange rate weakens.

Dominique van der Mensbrugghe, in Chapter 8, returns to a highly aggregated long-run scenario for free trade, and its implications for labour markets. The scenario is worked out with the CGE-type LINKAGE model, projecting the world economy in 2020. The study contrasts with that of Nahuis with respect to the former's assumptions of free trade and best-practice policy reforms and adjustments all around, designed as an ideal benchmark for policy reflection. The detailed results are not comparable between the two studies because the LINKAGE scenario does not for example distinguish skill levels. What tends to be easily ignored when focusing on the recent past is the prospect of future tight labour markets in the OECD economy, particularly in the EU. The OECD may also benefit from a favourable terms of trade effect. Thus real wages in the EU could rise perhaps 3 per cent–4 per cent on average per annum, assuming of course that the highly optimistic policy scenario comes true. Van der Mensbrugghe argues that, if OECD countries tackle skill problems in the labour force adequately, long-run equitable growth is entirely possible. It is crucial to see that this result is not a projection: rather, it represents a major challenge for policy makers.

Finally, Chapter 9 (by John Whalley and Randall Wigle) inspects, with the help of a CGE model, the impact of trade sanctions by the 'North', in response to a presumed failure of the South to implement 'proper' labour standards. The sanctions, in this model simulation, take the form of very stylised countervailing duties. This route of pursuing 'proper' labour standards is shown to be bad policy: the indirect effect is to depress the wages of the workers in the 'South' who supposedly were to be helped by labour standards; it also reduces trade of the North while world welfare falls.

The overall conclusion one may draw from this volume is that empirical research on this important theme is beginning to make headway, too, for the case of the EU. This research makes clear that the US debate, and its conclusions, cannot be literally transposed to Europe, and that simple HOS-based models are ill-suited. Indeed, the book contains empirical evidence to support this view.

However, our attempts to understand better the impact of trade and FDI with low-wage economies on jobs and wages in Europe has also shown how complicated the issue is, and how much need there is for disaggregated and painstaking empirical analysis. Given the EU's increasing openness, the argument to deepen and widen such research is a strong one.

Notes

1. For a survey with extensive trade data for 1980–93 (inclusive) and summaries of trade policies, see Pelkmans and Fukasaku (1995). For EU-Asia direct investment, see UNCTAD (1996) for a detailed report.
2. Although, of course, this did remain an issue. See, for instance, the policy paper by the European Commission, COM(96)53 on The global challenge of international trade: a market access strategy for the EU. Dumping is also often seen as unfair, but this is not a structural issue.
3. Data from Krugman and Lawrence (1993).
4. A year-by-year specification in Figure 1 of Baldwin and Cain (1997, p. 56) of average weekly real wages shows only mild fluctuations and

is practically flat; in 1992, the level is that of 1970. Of course, such averages hide the trends in relative wages, about which more below. However, one other stylised fact, neglected thus far in the trade debate, is also obscured by the overall average. While the real mean wages for males were about flat, real wages for women grew annually, on average, at 2.7 per cent from 1973 to 1993 (Gottschalk, 1997, p. 25).

5. For a very comprehensive, comparative survey of wage (earnings) inequality trends among OECD countries, as well as trends in household income inequality, see Gottschalk and Smeeding (1997).

6. See Johnson (1997) for a survey.

7. See Topel (1997) for a survey. Topel also asks the question whether human capital investment will mitigate rising inequality (via additional supply). On this, Topel suggests that the mitigating effect will be only among relatively high-wage workers.

8. See Fortin and Lemieux (1997) for a survey. The authors claim that one-third of the increase in inequality during the 1980s can be traced to three institutional changes in the USA: a declining real minimum wage, a decline in unionisation rate and economic deregulation. See also Gottschalk and Smeeding (1997).

9. On the UK, see Gregg and Machin (1994) and chapter 3 (by Bob Anderton and Paul Brenton), chapter 4 (by Matthias Lücke) and chapter 7 (by Bob Anderton and Paul Brenton) of this book. Note that the bottom decile of UK wage earners did not suffer a real deterioration. On other EU countries, see Gottschalk and Smeeding (1997).

10. Except shortly after Black Monday in October 1987.

11. See OECD Jobs Study (OECD, 1994) and European Commission (1997), especially Chapters 1 and 2. A major survey by Bean (1994) identifies other possible factors as well, such as, taxes. Unlike the OECD Jobs Study, Bean does not even include trade and FDI as possible causes of job losses.

12. ASEM consists of (the heads of states and government of) the seven ASEAN countries, Japan, China, South Korea, the 15 EU countries and the president of the European Commission. See for further background, purpose and development, Pelkmans and Shinkai (1997).

13. Data from European Commission (1997, p. 32)

14. Wood (1994b) even moves beyond the jobs and wages debate, and concludes (p. 20) 'that the H–O theory provides an accurate and illuminating description of a large part of the global pattern of trade'. Critical in his survey is that factors of production be 'restricted to inputs that are internationally immobile' e.g. skilled and unskilled labour. Wood considers capital as internationally mobile, hence it ought to be left out.

15. Notable exceptions are *The OECD Jobs Study* (1994, Chapter 3) and Messerlin (1995), on France, and the US comparison with Germany, in Lawrence (1994), besides the more descriptive approach of Wood (1994a).

16. First elaborated, in the context of the jobs and wages and trade debate, by Oliveira-Martins (1994).

...

References

Baldwin, R. and Cain, G. (1997) 'Trade and US relative wages: preliminary results', *Working Paper*, 5934, NBER.

Bean, C.R. (1994) 'European unemployment, a survey', *Journal of Economic Literature*, 32.

European Commission (1997) 'Annual economic report for 1997', *European Economy*, 63.

Feenstra, R. and Hanson, G. (1996) 'Globalisation, outsourcing, and wage inequality', *Working Paper*, 5110, NBER.

Fortin, N.M. and Lemieux, T. (1997), 'Institutional changes and rising wage inequality: is there a linkage?', *Journal of Economic Perspectives*, 11, 75–96.

Freeman, K. and Katz, L. (1994) 'Rising wage inequality: the US vs other advanced countries', in Freeman, R. (ed.) *Working Under Different Rules*, New York: Russel Sage Foundation, 29–62.

Freeman, R. (1994) 'How labour fares in advanced economies', in Freeman, R. (ed.) *Working Under Different Rules*, New York: Russel Sage Foundation, 1–28.

Freeman, R. (1995) 'Are your wages set in Beijing?', *Journal of Economic Perspectives*, 9, 115–23.

Gottschalk, P. (1997) 'Inequality, income growth and mobility: the basic facts', *Journal of Economic Perspectives*, 11, 21–40.

Gottschalk, P. and Smeeding, T.M. (1997) 'Cross-national comparisons of earnings and income inequality', *Journal of Economic Literature*, 35.

Gregg, P. and Machin, S. (1994) 'Is the rise in UK inequality different?', in Barrell, R. (ed.) *The UK Labour Market*, London: Sage.

Johnson, G.E. (1997) 'Changes in earnings inequality: the role of demand shifts', *Journal of Economic Perspectives*, 11, 41–54.

Krugman, P.R. (1995) 'Technology, trade and factor prices', *Working Paper*, 5355, NBER.

Krugman, P.R. and Lawrence, R.Z. (1993) 'Trade, jobs and wages', *Working Paper*, 4478, NBER.

Lawrence, R.A. (1994) 'Trade, multinationals and labour', *Working Paper*, 4836, NBER.

Messerlin, P.A. (1995) 'The impact of trade and capital movements on labour: evidence on the French case' *OECD Economic Studies*, 24, 89–124.

OECD (1994) *The OECD Jobs Study*, Paris, OECD.

Oliveira-Martins, J. (1994) 'Market structure, trade and industry wages', *OECD Economic Studies*, 22, 123.

Pelkmans, J. and Fukasaku, K. (1995) 'Evolving trade links between Europe and Asia: towards open continentalism?', in Fukasaku, K. (ed.), *Regional Cooperation and Integration in Asia*, Paris, OECD.

Pelkmans, J. and Shinkai, H. (eds), (1997) *The Promise of ASEM*, Brussels: European Institute for Asian Studies.

Topel, R.H. (1997) 'Factor propositions and relative wages: the supply-side determinants of wage inequality', *Journal of Economic Perspectives*, 11, 55–74.

UNCTAD (1996) *Investing in Asia's Dynamism: EU Direct Investment in Asia*, Geneva (in cooperation with the European Commission).

Wood, A. (1994a) *North–South Trade, Employment and Inequality*, Oxford: Clarendon Press.

Wood, A. (1994b) 'Give Heckscher and Ohlin a chance', *Weltwirtschaftliches Archiv*, 130, 20–47.

Wood, A. (1995) 'How trade hurt unskilled workers', *Journal of Economic Perspectives*, 9, 57–80.

2 Rising Trade and Falling Wages: A Review of the Theory and the Empirics

Paul Brenton

2.1 INTRODUCTION

Does trade impoverish unskilled workers in Western industrial countries? This is an emotive way of framing a question which has received a great deal of attention from economists in recent years: to what extent has trade with labour-abundant low-wage economies affected Western labour markets? Currently, it is imports from Asia which dominate discussions, although these issues are equally pertinent for trade with Eastern Europe, the countries of the CIS (Former Soviet Union), and Latin America. We are not the only ones to try and catch the eye in this way, Freeman (1995) rather provocatively asks: 'are your wages being set in Beijing?'

In this chapter, we ask whether economic theory and the available empirical evidence support the assertion that more openness to international trade – and, in particular, greater imports from low-wage countries – has contributed to increased unemployment and larger wage differentials in industrial countries. Much of the discussion has centred upon the USA, where the gap between the wages of skilled and those of unskilled workers has increased over a period in which imports from low-wage developing countries have greatly expanded (albeit from a very low base). Wage inequality has also increased significantly in the UK. Experience across countries is, however, not uniform. In continental Europe, in general, the gap between wages for skilled and unskilled workers has not increased markedly . A commonly heard argument for this is that rigidities in the labour markets of these countries have deflected the impact of greater competition from low-wage countries into higher unemployment rates for less skilled workers.

However, we must not, as politicians and others are sometimes apt to do, accept apparent associations – in this case between trade and inequality – on the basis of casual observation. Just because two events have occurred at the same time in no way implies that one must have caused the other. We need to be more scientific, particularly so when there are other possible causes of the phenomenon we seek to explain. In the 'trade and wages' debate the other principal suspects are technological advancement and changes in the relative supply of skilled and unskilled workers. To spoil the story somewhat, in the end it turns out that our economic theory implicates all three suspects and the role of the jury has become one of identifying, on the basis of empirical analysis, which one is most culpable.

Empirical analysis without an underlying theoretical base can be as vacuous as a theory with no empirical relevance. As Richardson (1995) remarks: 'a researcher could find correlations galore in the nexus of long-term trends in trade, technology, tastes and factor-supply growth – simple correlations, multiple correlations, in endless assortment. Only some are meaningful.' Unfortunately, much of the empirical work undertaken on this issue, nearly all of it on the USA, has not been based upon well specified economic models whose validity can then be tested using appropriate data and statistical techniques. Hence we cannot have much faith in the alleged causes and affects that these studies purport to identify (see Deardorff and Hakura, 1994).

Not all is gloomy. There is an increasing volume of literature, to which all the chapters in this book contribute, in which empirical analysis of the trade and wages and unemployment issue is well grounded in sound economic theory. After briefly reviewing the relevant theory, we proceed to summarise the current state of empirical analysis. This shows that we cannot derive unequivocal conclusions concerning the complicity of trade in widening wage inequality. Many studies rule out trade with low-wage countries as having had a significant impact on Western labour markets. However, a few studies, which cannot be ignored, conclude that trade has been the major protagonist. A final section presents some conclusions and briefly discusses the policy implications that can be derived from the previous analysis.

2.2 THE THEORY

Why do countries trade? The simple answer is because they benefit from doing so.[1] Economists since Adam Smith and David Ricardo have stressed that these gains from trade derive from countries being able to specialise in producing those products which they can make (relatively) efficiently compared to other countries – that is, those products in which they have a comparative advantage. It has long been recognised that even though the country as a whole will benefit, not all groups in society may gain from more open trade.[2] This explains why trade liberalisation is opposed by some. However, the gainers will, in principal, be able to compensate those who lose and still be better off themselves (trade offers potential Pareto improvements). So trade raises aggregate welfare but necessitates consideration of the internal distribution of the benefits. If there is no means for redistribution within a country then some people will lose from more open trade.

But what determines comparative advantage? Which products will a country specialise in producing with open trade? The workhorse of the economic analysis of international trade in the twentieth century has been the Heckscher–Ohlin–Samuelson (HOS) theorem. This explains comparative advantage in terms of the relative amounts of resources with which countries are endowed. Resources (land, capital, labour (of different types, such as low skilled and high skilled)) matter because they are used, in combination, to produce goods and services. The production of different goods requires the input of these resources in differing amounts Resources are scarce everywhere, but it is differences in endowments of resources across countries which provide the opportunity for beneficial trade, whereby countries exchange the products of different industries.

This theory has problems in explaining trade between similar industrial countries where the exchange of products within industries (intra-industry trade) dominates. It does, however, appear to be well suited to explaining trade between industrial and developing countries where endowments of resources differ substantially. To help explain the model, assume a very simple world where there are only two types of economic resource (skilled and unskilled labour),[3] two countries (one is industrial and has relatively more skilled than unskilled labour, the other is a developing country and is endowed with more unskilled than skilled labour), and two products (one, electronics, requires the input of relatively large amounts of skilled labour whilst production of the other – say, clothing – is intensive in the use of unskilled labour).

The industrial country will be relatively efficient at producing electronics whilst the developing country will have a comparative advantage in producing clothing. So in the absence of trade – due, say, to the presence of prohibitive trade barriers in both countries – electronics will be relatively cheap in the industrial country and clothing will be relatively cheap in the developing country. The removal of trade barriers permits consumers to buy from abroad more cheaply the good that is relatively expensive in the home market. So the industrial country will export electronics and import clothing. There will be greater specialisation in electronics in this country. In the developing country there will be specialisation in clothing. This shows the key prediction of the HOS theorem that countries will specialise in and export the good which uses intensively the factor with which they are relatively well endowed.

This theory is, however, based upon a rather strict set of assumptions. These are necessary to render the model tractable and to permit attention to be focused upon what is asserted to be the key determinant of trade – that is, differences in the endowments of factors of production across countries. The key assumptions are that:

- There is perfect competition in all product and factor markets
- Factors of production are able to move freely between industries within a country but cannot move between countries
- There are constant returns to scale (there are no cost advantages to firms from operating at a larger size)
- All countries use the same technology in producing goods and there is no technological advancement
- There are no factor intensity reversals (the production of, say, the unskilled intensive good uses relatively more unskilled labour than skilled labour whatever the wage rate for unskilled relative to that of skilled labour)
- Consumers everywhere have the same tastes so that only relative prices determine the relative demand for products.

Once any of these assumptions are relaxed then other causes of trade arise, in addition to differences between countries in the supply of basic factors of production. For example, the so-called 'new trade theory' has recently shown how the presence of economies of scale, product differentiation and imperfect competition can generate intra-industry trade between similar countries.

We return to the standard model. The removal of trade barriers affects domestic relative product prices in each country (even though international prices may not change).[4] Since consumers in the industrial country can purchase clothing more cheaply from abroad, the price of clothing relative to that of electronics falls in that country. These changes in relative product prices have a direct impact upon the real rewards of the factors of production (the two types of labour in our simple model).[5] This is formulated in the Stolper–Samuelson theorem as a rise in the relative price of a good will increase the real return to the factor used intensively in that industry. Hence an increase in the relative price of electronics in the industrial country will raise the real return to skilled labour in that country. In the developing country the real return to unskilled labour will rise. However, the welfare of unskilled labour in the industrial and skilled labour in the developing country will fall. The theorem also shows that the gap between the nominal wage paid to skilled labour and that paid to unskilled labour will widen in the industrial country but narrow in the developing country.

In this standard trade theory in which there is perfect competition in both product and factor markets and full employment, wages are determined by the value of the marginal product. That is the value of the output produced by the last worker to be employed and is given by the physical increase in output multiplied by the price of the product. The wage paid to unskilled labour in the clothing sector is equal to the amount of clothing produced by the last employed worker multiplied by the price at which that clothing can be sold. This illustrates an important issue: wages for the different types of labour are set on the margin. A relatively lower price for clothing reduces the wage rate paid to all unskilled workers in the industrial country. Note that the marginal product is a function of technology. Technological improvement, which is ruled out by assumption in the HOS model, raises productivity and hence wages. We return to this below.

Thus, the Stolper–Samuelson theorem shows that there is a direct link between relative prices in the domestic market and relative wages rates, a proposition which is amenable to empirical assessment. There is no direct role in the theory for changes in the quantity of trade or production. A prerequisite for trade to have influenced relative wages is that relative prices have changed. Indeed, relative prices and relative wages may change even when there is no change in imports and exports or in the level of output in each sector. If, for some reason, firms were unable to change the amounts of factors they used in production, then trade liberalisation would not lead to any changes in output and imports but it would still alter relative prices and relative wages.

If firms were able to change the quantity of their inputs then the output of the export industry would expand and that of the import-competing sector would decline. In the industrial country output of electronics will increase and that of clothing will decline. Resources will have to move *between sectors* from clothing to the production of electronics. In the developing country output of clothing will expand.

The change in relative factor prices will lead firms to make further changes in their use of the two types of labour. In the industrial country firms in both sectors will make greater use of, the now relatively cheaper, unskilled labour. Thus, trade liberalisation leads to *within-sector* changes in the relative demand for the different types of labour. This is necessary since the ratio of unskilled to skilled workers released by the declining clothing sector is higher than that required by the expanding electronics sector. The change in relative wages and the subsequent adjustments to the relative use of skilled and unskilled labour ensure that all resources are employed. Any constraints upon this adjustment mechanism may lead to resources being unemployed.

Within the strict confines of the assumptions upon which the HOS and Stolper–Samuelson theorems are based, changes in the world market (due to trade liberalisation or changing factor endowments) are the only possible cause of changing domestic relative product prices. However, once we relax these assumptions it is clear that trade may not be the only cause of changing product prices.

The HOS and the Stolper–Samuelson theorems assume, as noted above, that all countries have access to the same technology and that there is no technological advancement. Once these assumptions are relaxed we find other possible causes of changing product prices and changing relative wage rates.

Standard trade theory shows that the impact of technological change on relative wages depends upon whether the innovation occurs in the skill-intensive (electronics) or unskilled-intensive (clothing) sector. It does not matter whether the innovation is unskilled-labour or skilled-labour-saving but whether it is centred upon the skill-intensive or the unskilled-intensive sector. A technological improvement in the skill-intensive sector (electronics) will increase the demand for skilled labour by a greater amount than the increase in demand for unskilled labour. However, the declining unskilled-intensive sector (clothing) releases relatively more unskilled than skilled labour. The only way the electronics sector can absorb the unskilled labour is if its price falls. This also encourages the clothing sector to release less unskilled labour than it otherwise would have done. On the other hand, the wage of skilled labour rises and so inequality increases. Conversely, technological change which is biased towards the unskilled-intensive sector (clothing) will reduce the gap between skilled and unskilled wages. These changes in relative wages will lead to both between- and within-industry shifts in the relative use of skilled and unskilled labour, as occurs when trade alters relative product prices.

A feature that the Stolper–Samuelson and the sectorally-biased technology explanations have difficulty explaining is that the ratio of skilled to unskilled workers has increased in most industries. This is counter to what both these approaches would suggest, given that skilled labour has become relatively more expensive. As we shall discuss in more detail below, this has led many to conclude that technological advancement biased towards saving unskilled labour (factor bias) has been the principal cause of the decline in the relative conditions of unskilled workers in industrialised countries' labour markets. However, within the HOS model, this type of technological progress can affect relative wages only if it leads to changes in relative prices.

Krugman (1995) argues that the issue of the exogeneity of prices lies at the heart of the debate concerning the nature of technological change in the standard trade model. The conclusion that it is the sector bias that matters is derived from a strict application of the model to a small open economy and to a situation where the technological advance occurs only in this economy – that is, the technological improvement is 'unilateral'. When goods prices are fixed it is the sector bias of technological change that matters. Krugman argues that this is a useful classroom experiment to help explain the trade model. He argues, however, that it is not relevant to the current situation where technological change has been occurring simultaneously in all OECD countries, which together cannot be treated as having no influence upon world prices. Krugman shows that in a model in which technological change occurs in the world as a whole, and in which prices are endogeneously determined, it is the factor bias, not the sector bias, which determines the effect of technological change on factor prices. Sectorally biased technical change may lead to price movements which offset the initial impact on factor prices. We return the issue of technological change later in this chapter, and elsewhere in the volume (see, in particular, Chapter 6 by Richard Nahuis).

We conclude this brief review of the standard trade theory by stressing that the mechanism by which international trade – and in our particular context trade with developing countries – alters relative wages in industrial countries is by changing relative product prices. If the domestic prices of high-skill-intensive goods, such as electronics, have not risen relative to the prices of unskilled-labour-intensive goods (for example, clothing), then trade cannot have contributed to the increase in the gap between skilled and unskilled wages. Trade is not the only possible cause of changing relative product prices and of increasing inequality. An increase in the supply of unskilled workers in the industrial countries (due to the failure of the educational system) would push down the wages of the unskilled. Relative wages also depend upon technology. Even if product prices have changed, technology could have been the dominant influence upon wage inequality. Conversely, even if technology appears to have had a large impact upon inequality, trade may still have been an important influence. The relative impact of these factors thus requires careful empirical scrutiny.

2.3 EMPIRICAL ANALYSIS OF THE LINKS BETWEEN TRADE AND WAGES AND EMPLOYMENT

2.3.1 Factor-content Studies

Early research which sought to estimate the effect of trade on employment adopted an approach based upon measuring the factor content of trade. The amounts of different factors embodied in a country's exports are computed which, when multiplied by the increase in exports, gives the positive effect of trade on the demand for the different factors. The factor content of imports is then used to derive the quantities of the factors that would be employed if goods which are now imported were produced domestically. This is the negative effect of trade upon the demand for factors of production. These changes in the demand for labour are then used to impute the impact of trade on relative wages.

Note that this approach ignores the basic implications of textbook international trade theory discussed above – the key mechanism linking international and domestic markets is relative prices not changes in quantities. Krugman (1995), however, argues that the textbook simulation of a given change in goods prices on factor prices is not relevant to the problem at hand and that the real issue is to identify what relative prices would have been in OECD countries in the absence of trade with the NICs, the 'but for' question. The volume of trade, Krugman argues, is crucial to being able to identify these hypothetical relative prices.

In general studies using this approach suggest that the impact of trade on the demand for factors – and, in particular, unskilled labour – has been modest but not inconsequential. Most of the analysis has been based upon US experience. Borjas, Freeman and Katz (1992) find that trade did play a significant, but not the major, role, accounting for up to 15 per cent of the increase in wage inequality in the USA during the 1980s. Sachs and Schatz (1994) conclude that trade with developing countries did contribute to growing inequality for unskilled workers since increases in net imports (imports *minus* exports) were highest for sectors where large numbers of unskilled workers were employed relative to skilled workers. However, they qualify this by saying that the 'weight of the trade effect is uncertain'. Recent studies have suggested a similar conclusion for France: trade with low-wage economies has had, at most, a modest effect upon demand for unskilled labour (Messerlin, 1995; Cortes, Jean and Pisani-Ferry 1996).

These results are not too surprising given that, despite recent increases in the share of developing countries, the majority of industrial countries' imports of manufactures are provided by other industrial countries, who have similar endowments of skilled and unskilled labour and comparable wage rates. In 1994 less than one-fifth of total EU imports of manufactures (including trade between EU members) came from developing countries.

Underlying this approach is the application of the same factor-input coefficients (those of the importing country) in the computation of the factor content of both exports and imports. This implies that the goods produced by an industry are the same whether produced in the North or the South. Wood (1994) rejects this assumption and argues that many of the manufactured goods imported by the North do not have a direct domestic substitute, and so are non-competing. These goods are not produced in the North because the highly intensive use of unskilled labour makes them unprofitable. In other words, the factor input coefficients that have been used refer to types of goods which are not actually imported and which have much higher ratios of skilled to unskilled labour than would be used in the production of the types of goods that are actually imported.

Wood suggests that a more relevant approach is to compute the amounts of factors required in the North to produce non-competing imports from the South using the factor input coefficients of the South. For example, when computing the amounts of factors that would be required in the EU to produce the quantity of footwear currently imported from Asia, the amounts of unskilled and skilled labour and capital required to produce a unit of footwear in Asia should be used. However, these magnitudes then have to be adjusted to take account of the fact that unskilled labour is relatively more expensive in the North. That is, producers in the North would not use unskilled labour in the same proportion as in the South because of the relatively high price of unskilled labour in the North. Finally, since costs and prices are higher in the North the increase in the output of labour-intensive manufactures would be less than the level of imports.

Using this method suggests that trade liberalisation has had a major impact upon labour markets in Western economies. Wood estimates that increased trade between developed and developing countries has reduced the demand for labour in the manufacturing sector of the advanced countries by an amount equivalent to 12 per cent of employment in manufacturing. These calculations are around ten times greater than those based upon the factor input coefficients of the North, and this figure, it is claimed will be an underestimate, since it fails to take into account that increased trade with the South will encourage labour-saving technical innovation in the North.

However, there are a number of reasons to be very suspicious of these estimates. First, the assumption that imports of all manufactures, excepting processed primary products, are non-competing looks extreme. Baldwin (1994) notes that the constructors of input–output tables have to decide whether a particular import is a substitute for a domestically produced good: only 14 per cent of US imports were classified as non-competing for the 1977 and 1982 input–output tables.

A further issue relates to technology. If products from the South do not compete with those produced in the North why should producers in the North adopt new labour-saving technologies? It may rather be that producers in the North have access to better technology which raises the productivity of all factors of production relative to productivity in the South. If this is the case, then Wood's calculations will overstate the amount of labour that would be required if imports from the South were replaced by domestic production.

Finally, Wood has also been criticised for using low values of elasticities of substitution (around 0.5) in both production and consumption when making adjustments to allow for higher wages in industrial countries and for the lower demand that would result from higher prices if the goods were produced domestically. If these elasticities are assigned a value of unity, a value not inconsistent with econometric evidence, then Wood's estimates of the employment effects of increased trade with developing countries fall to levels comparable with those found by most other studies.

Studies using the factor-content of trade approach which have found a modest influence of trade on relative labour demand conclude that trade can have had only a relatively small influence upon relative wages. These studies often then conclude that technology must lie at the heart of rising inequality. The study by Wood, on the other hand, suggests that since trade has had a large effect on the demand for unskilled workers it must have had a pronounced effect upon earnings and inequality.

As we saw above, international trade theory shows that even if trade has not influenced relative factor demands it is wrong to conclude that it cannot have caused a change in relative factor rewards. Similarly, even if trade has had led to changes in relative factor demands there need not be any effect upon relative factor prices. In other words, standard trade theory shows that there is no specific relationship between the factor content of trade and relative factor prices.[6]

2.3.2   Tests of the Stolper–Samuelson Theorem

In the HOS model relative factor prices can change only as relative product prices vary. In a small country facing constant terms of trade, changes in trade flows will have no effect upon relative factor prices. In a large economy movements in domestic economic variables may offset a change in the international environment so that relative product prices and hence relative factor prices remain unchanged. Trade theory thus highlights the link between product prices and factor prices.

Lawrence and Slaughter (1993) examine movements in US import and export prices and find that, if anything, the price of skilled labour-intensive products fell relative to that of products using relatively large amounts of unskilled labour during the 1980s. They thus conclude that trade contributed to greater equality of wages in the US. Sachs and Schatz (1994) argue that the trend in the price of computers explains the decline in skilled-labour-intensive products. However, even when computers are removed there is no clear, statistically significant, relationship between changing prices and skill intensity in the USA. Lawrence (1994) reports data that suggest no evidence of relative price declines for unskilled-labour-intensive products in Germany and Japan.

Leamer (1996) suggests that the marginal US worker is employed in the clothing sector competing with workers undertaking the same tasks in China. Leamer finds that during the 1960s and 1980s the relative price of clothing was fairly static, but during the 1970s the relative price fell by over 30 per cent. These results are not inconsistent with those of Lawrence and Slaughter, who examined only the 1980s, but suggest that Stolper–Samuelson effects of trade were important in the USA in the 1970s. The problem is that increases in wage incquality in the USA appear to have been concentrated in the 1980s. According to Lawrence and Slaughter's (1993) data, the gap between the wages of skilled and unskilled workers declincd during the 1970s.[7]

Leamer (1996) argues that the effects of changing relative product prices may be delayed and that the full effects may only become apparent once sufficient time has elapsed to allow complete mobility of factors of production between sectors. Bhagwati (1997) counters that lack of adjustment should lead to a greater initial fall in relative wages which will be mitigated as labour moves to expanding sectors, so changes in relative wages should have been greater in the 1970s than in the 1980s.

The failure to find evidence of changes in relative prices consistent with trade being a source of rising inequality has not settled the debate. It has been argued that these studies have not used suitable price data. Others go further and suggest that such data are not available and use this in defence of the factor-content approach. Wood (1997, p. 73) states that

I regard the price data as being not contradictory, but just murky, because of fundamental problems with the data . . . conclusions should be based on the rest of the evidence, which supports the trade explanation.

The basic issue is one of measurement. Those sceptical of using relative prices to assess the impact of trade argue that the heterogeneity goods in standard statistical definitions of sectors and that changes in quality over time (which maybe correlated with the skill intensity of production) engender substantial errors into available price series. So, if subsectors within the industries which are studied are different – in terms of requiring different amounts of skilled and unskilled labour – then more open trade may reduce the prices of some goods but raise the prices of others, leaving the industry aggregate price unchanged. The implication of this is that much more detailed analysis is required and that much of the response to trade may be occurring within conventionally defined sectors rather than between them; we return to this issue below.

A feature of industrial economies which does not appear to fit well with the trade explanation of increasing inequality is the fact that the demand for unskilled workers relative to those with skills has declined across a whole range of industries in the industrial countries, not just those where there is a high degree of import penetration by developing countries. In the standard HOS model the decline in the relative price of unskilled labour will lead to the substitution of unskilled for skilled labour in all sectors including the skill-intensive export sector. In other words, if more open trade has led to a significant shift towards the skill-intensive sector it should also have contributed to a shift within sectors to the more intensive use of cheaper unskilled relative to skilled labour. There is no apparent reason why greater openness to international trade should lead to a decrease in the demand for unskilled workers in non-traded sectors, particularly if their relative wage has fallen. This has led many commentators to conclude that technological change must lie at the heart of explanations of labour market developments in OECD countries. Additional support for concentrating upon technology comes from studies which show that the relative wage of skilled labour has also increased in countries deemed to have an abundance of unskilled labour, contrary to what the basic Stolper–Samuelson theory suggests (see Hanson and Harrison, 1995, on Mexico, for example).

As we saw above, standard trade theory shows that with regard to relative wages it is the sectoral bias of technological change that matters. Technical progress concentrated upon the skill-intensive sector leads to a rise in the relative wage of skilled labour. However, there is no reason why this, too, should lead to an increase in the ratio of (now cheaper) unskilled workers to skilled workers in the unskilled labour-intensive sector. We observe the opposite. A number of economists have therefore argued that this economy-wide increase in the relative use of skilled labour can be explained only by technological progress which occurs in all sectors but which is biased towards saving unskilled labour (for example, computers replacing workers). They then proceed to state that, by default, this type of technological change must be the cause of the increase in inequality for unskilled workers in industrial countries.

Unskilled labour-saving technical progress has undoubtedly occurred in industrial countries over the past two or three decades. The issue is whether this is the primary cause of rising wage inequality. Economic theory shows us that this form of technical progress can affect relative wages only if it leads to changes in relative product prices. Such technical progress which occurs to the same extent in both sectors will lead to within-industry shifts away from the use of unskilled relative to skilled labour. The maintenance of full employment then requires that the output of the unskilled-labour-intensive sector rises relative to the output of the skill-intensive sector. If the country is large these changes will influence the international prices of the two goods. The relative price of the unskilled-labour-intensive good will fall relative to the price of the skill-intensive good. This change in product prices will tend to reduce the relative wage of unskilled labour.

However, we have not observed the relative prices changes that this approach requires. Further, we should also have seen an increase in the output of unskilled-intensive goods relative to skill-intensive goods. However, it is the skill-intensive goods which appear to have experienced relative expansion. Thus, we end up by concluding that technological change must have taken a particular form if it has led to increased inequality and at the same time caused an increase in the ratio of skilled to unskilled workers in all sectors: technical progress must have led to the saving of unskilled labour in all sectors but must have occurred to a greater extent in the skill-intensive sectors.

In industrial countries in the past 20 years there has been a substantial increase in the supply of skilled labour relative to unskilled workers. This increase in the endowment of skilled workers should have contributed to a fall in the price of the skill-intensive good and a fall in the return to skilled relative to unskilled labour. Baldwin (1994) suggests that if unskilled labour-saving technological progress has been concentrated in the skill-intensive sector this could explain why the relative wage of skilled workers has risen despite a fall in the relative price of skill-intensive products. However, the terms of trade improvement (implying a rise in the relative price of skill-intensive goods) experienced by the USA and the EU during periods of the 1980s does not fit with this explanation. Baldwin concludes that international competition must be introduced as an explanation for this relative price change. So, the fall in the relative wage of unskilled labour is due partly to technical progress being biased towards the skill-intensive sector and partly to the fall in the relative price of the unskilled-labour-intensive good due to increased international trade.

Wood (1995) suggests that attributing all of the economy-wide increase in skill intensity to technological improvement is misleading and that trade may have played an important role in this development. Again the argument arises from problems of defining and precisely measuring an industry. If the categories which are commonly assessed include activities which differ in their skill requirements, then more open trade could lead to the decline of the unskilled-intensive activities and the expansion of skill intensive activities within the sector. At the sectoral level this would be reflected in an increase in the relative employment of skilled labour even in the absence of technical progress.

A comprehensive analysis of the increase in wage inequality and the rise in the unemployment rates of unskilled workers, within the HOS framework thus requires that the separate effects of the increase in the supply of different types of workers, the improvement in technology and international trade are carefully disentangled. We have yet to reach a consensus, on the basis of empirical analysis, of the relative magnitude of the various possible contributors to increasing inequality and unemployment for unskilled workers, and so the conclusion of Leamer (1994) that the jury still remains out on this issue, continues to be pertinent. The evidence made available so far does not have sufficient force for the jury to allocate the weight of blame to any of the usual suspects.

2.4 ALTERNATIVE APPROACHES

The studies discussed above have been rooted within the fairly rigid framework of standard neo-classical trade theory. As we have argued, it is important to have a theory upon which to base analysis of trade issues and the HOS model provides one framework from which to proceed. However, the HOS model and the Stolper–Samuelson theorem are predicated upon a range of rather restrictive assumptions and there is little empirical support for the general applicability of the model. Indeed, for much of the past 40 years trade economists have been busy seeking to extend, redefine or even supplant the HOS model. It is thus a little surprising that the model has in many cases been unquestioningly rehabilitated for the purpose of analysing the impact of trade on relative wages. This unerring reliance on this model has led the search for the impact of trade on relative labour demand and relative wages to concentrate upon identifying changes in relative sectoral prices and movements of skilled and unskilled labour between sectors. A number of authors have recently started to consider the impact of trade on factor demand and factor prices in different frameworks.

Feenstra and Hanson (1996) argue that the basic issue of how firms respond to import competition has been overlooked. They suggest that an important response in the USA has been an increase in outsourcing, whereby intermediate inputs are imported from low-wage countries. Globalisation thus tends to fragment production into different discernible activities, some of which are then undertaken overseas. Firms in industrial countries facing increased competition from developing countries allocate unskilled-intensive activities to these low-wage economies. Although these activities are intensive in the use of unskilled labour in the industrial countries, they may be skilled-labour-intensive in the developing countries, so that the relative demand for skilled labour rises in both regions. In this case, however, an increase in trade will be associated with a shift towards more employment of skilled labour within industries, rather than between industries as is commonly presumed. In their empirical work, Feenstra and Hanson suggest that this outsourcing may account for up to 50 per cent of the rise in the relative demand for skilled labour that occurred in the 1980s in US manufacturing industries.

Markusen and Venables (1996) show how the activities of multinational firms may also play a role in explaining the increase in inequality between skilled and unskilled workers in industrial countries. In their theoretical model they show that when countries have differing relative endowments of factors of production, the entry of multinational firms increases the ratio of skilled to unskilled wages in the rich skilled-labour-abundant country. This is because the multinationals locate their headquarters in the initially rich country and this increases the demand for skilled labour. Production, which requires mainly unskilled labour, is shifted overseas. Further, as countries become more similar in terms of both relative and absolute (size) endowments the ratio of skilled to unskilled wages rises in the large skilled-labour-abundant country. However, it is also demonstrated that in this environment trade barriers in the rich country favour skilled labour in that country. Empirical work which addresses the impact of multinationals on relative wages is clearly required. Initial studies for the USA (see Brainard and Riker, 1997) tend to suggest that the activities of multinational firms have not had a great impact on the domestic labour market.

The view that intra-sectoral effects of trade are important is reinforced by a recent study by Bernard and Jensen (1997) who find that the relative performance of exporting and non-exporting plants within sectors can explain a large proportion of the increase in the use of skilled labour relative to unskilled labour and much of the widening gap in wages in the USA. Exporting firms within a sector were found to employ more skilled workers relative to unskilled workers than non-exporting firms. Exporting firms grew more rapidly than non-exporting firms in the 1980s and this led to an increase in the skill intensity within each sector. Further, during this period skill intensities increased within exporting plants. Adjustment to trade here takes the form of shifts of resources (and plants) from non-exporting activities to exporting, primarily within sectors.

Finally, in addition to the issue of defining the level of industrial activity at which comparative advantage is determined, Bhagwati (1997) suggests that greater volatility in comparative advantage has occurred from greater internationalisation of markets. In contrast to the standard HOS model, where there are no changes in comparative advantage, Bhagwati contends that there are now more footloose industries, such that, countries may suddenly lose their comparative advantage in a particular product or sector.[8] This in turn will generate greater degrees of labour turnover, with perhaps an increase in frictional unemployment. Since skilled workers are more likely to be able to transfer to other jobs they will presumably suffer less from this than unskilled workers, and this may be reflected in greater wage inequality.

These recent studies tend to suggest that analysis based upon strict application of the standard HOS model and Stolper–Samuelson theorem may miss the intricacies of the way firms and industries in OECD countries respond to increasing competition from low-wage countries. We are not yet, however, able to form a clear view of whether these alternative approaches will further implicate trade as a source of rising inequality in Western labour markets or whether they will provide compelling evidence for the defence. It may actually be that we will never be able to answer the question of the role of trade in rising inequality in such black and white terms.

2.5 CONCLUSIONS AND IMPLICATIONS FOR POLICY IN THE EU

The problems of declining employment opportunities for unskilled workers and rising wage inequality have not led to the response of widespread trade protection. The analysis above confirms that there is no strong evidence by which to unambiguously conclude that trade has been the fundamental factor causing these trends. Even if it were, trade protection would not be appropriate. The fact that declining employment for unskilled labour has led to the persistent unemployment of a proportion of such workers suggests problems with the efficient working of labour markets.

Most economists advocate the removal of restrictions which constrain the ability of the labour market to work and suggest that there is a role for governments in increasing the supply of skilled labour. This can be achieved through investment in education and in training and re-training programmes. Some economists argue for greater redistribution of income from skilled to unskilled workers to offset, in part, the increase in wage inequality. Finally, there may be a case for intervention to stimulate technological innovation. Because of problems relating to securing a reasonable return on investments in R&D, firms may provide less than the socially optimal amount of funds for such activities. Further, in fragmented market structures there may be socially wasteful duplication of research effort.

Many of these arguments have been accepted by the Commission as reflected in the White Paper 'Growth, competitiveness and

employment' (CEC, 1993) This rejects protectionism as a suitable
policy but stresses the need for the liberalisation of labour markets, investment in education and training and policy towards technology. The Commission has adopted horizontal policies which are
designed to affect the inputs used across industries and has rejected vertical policies which target the outputs of particular sectors. The latter policies have failed in the past to provide solutions
to the problems of falling employment and declining relative wages
for the unskilled.

Notes

1. Gains from trade cannot be guaranteed if there are distortions in the
   economy. For example, if trade liberalisation generates greater imports
   of a product which emits pollution in the act of consumption, such as
   motor vehicles, then the benefits from freer trade may be offset by the
   costs of more pollution. However, if appropriate policies are used to
   tackle the distortion – here, taxes on the use of fuels – then trade will
   be unambiguously beneficial. Difficulties arise if such policies are not
   available.
2. In situations where economies of scale are important and countries
   are similar then everyone may gain from trade (see Helpman and
   Krugman, 1985).
3. Wood (1994) argues that this approach is relevant to the analysis of
   trade in manufactured goods between industrial and developing countries since capital is internationally mobile and so can be ignored. Trade
   is determined only by endowments of internationally immobile factors
   of production.
4. Domestic product prices could also change in this model if relative
   factor supplies were to change. For example, population growth in the
   developing country would increase the relative endowment of unskilled
   labour there, enabling it to raise output and exports of clothing. This
   in turn would lead to a fall in the relative price of clothing on the
   world market and on the domestic market in the industrial country.
5. The real return to a factor of production measures the amount of both
   goods that can be purchased with the actual (nominal) wage that is
   paid.
6. Factor contents can approximate changes in relative factor prices but
   only under particular circumstances, such as, homothetic preferences
   (see Deardorff and Staiger, 1988 and, for an elaboration, Krugman,
   1995).
7. There are, however, some doubts concerning the data on inequality.
   The data for the USA which are typically used distinguish between
   production and non-production workers which are taken to be equivalent to unskilled and skilled workers. Leamer (1994) notes that this

categorisation may be inappropriate since supervisors and product development personnel are included under production workers, while sales, delivery and clerical workers are defined as non-production employees.
8. This may also occur if there are factor-intensity reversals, such that, a good which initially required relatively large amounts of skilled labour in production could now be produced with unskilled labour-intensive techniques.

References

Baldwin, R. (1994) 'The effects of trade and foreign direct investment on employment and relative wages', *OECD Economic Studies*, 23, 7–54.
Bernard, A. and Jensen, J. (1997) 'Exporters, skill upgrading, and the wage gap', *Journal of International Economics*, 42, 3–31.
Bhagwati, J. (1997) 'Trade and wages: a malign relationship', in Kuyvenhoven, A., Memedovic, O. and Molle, W. (eds), *Globalization of Labour Markets*, Kluwer, 31–65.
Borjas, G., Freeman, R. and Katz, L. (1992) 'On the labour market effects of immigration and trade', in Borjas, G. and Freeman, R. (eds), *Immigration and The Work Force*, Cambridge, MA: NBER, 213–44.
Brainard, S.L. and Riker, D. (1997) 'Are US multinationals exporting US Jobs?', *Working Paper*, 5958, NBER.
CEC (1993) 'Growth, competitiveness and employment', *Bulletin of the European Communities*, Supplement 6/93.
Cortes, O., Jean, S. and Pisani-Ferry, J. (1996) 'Trade with emerging countries and the labour market: the french case', *Working Document*, 96–04, CEPII.
Deardorff, A.V. and Hakura, D.S. (1994) 'Trade and Wages – What are the Questions?', in Bhagwati, J. and Kosters, M.H. (eds), *Trade and Wages. Levelling wages Down?*, Washington, DC: AEI Press, 76–107.
Deardorff, A. and Staiger, R. (1988) 'An interpretation of the factor content of trade', *Journal of International Economics*, 24, 97–107.
Feenstra, R. and Hanson G. (1996) 'Globalization, outsourcing, and wage inequality', *Working Paper*, 5424, NBER.
Freeman, R. (1995) 'Are your wages set in Beijing?', *Journal of Economic Perspectives*, 9, 15–23.
Hanson, G. and Harrison, A. (1995) 'Trade, technology and wage inequality', *Working Paper*, 5110, NBER.
Herpman, E. and Krugman, P.R. (1985) *Market Structure and Foreign Trade*, Cambridge, MA: MIT Press.
Krugman, P. (1995) 'Technology, trade and factor prices', *Working Paper*, 5355, NBER.
Krugman, P. and Lawrence, R. (1993) 'Trade, jobs and wages', *Working Paper*, 4478, NBER.
Lawrence, R. (1994) 'Trade, multinationals, and labour', *Working Paper*, 4836, NBER.
Lawrence, R. and Slaughter, M. (1993) 'International trade and American

wages in the 1980s; giant sucking sound or small hiccup', *Brookings Papers on Economic Activity: Microeconomics*, 2, 161–226.

Leamer, E. (1994) 'Trade, wages and revolving door ideas', *Working Paper*, 4716, NBER.

Leamer, E. (1996) 'In search of Stolper–Samuelson Effects on US Wages', *Working Paper*, 5427, NBER.

Markusen, J. and Venables, A. (1996) 'Multinational production, skilled labour, and real wages', *Working Paper*, 5483, NBER.

Messerlin, P.A. (1995) 'The impact of trade and capital movements on labour: evidence on the French case', *OECD Economic Studies*, 24, 89–124.

OECD (1992) *Structural Change and Industrial Performance: A Seven-country Growth Decomposition Study*, Paris: OECD.

Oliveira-Martins, J. (1994) 'Market structure, trade and industry wages', *OECD Economic Studies*, 22, 1–23.

Richardson, J.D. (1995) 'Income inequality and trade: how to think, what to conclude', *Journal of Economic Perspectives*, 9, 33–55.

Sachs, J. and Shatz, H. (1994) 'Trade and jobs in US manufacturing', *Brookings Papers on Economic Activity*, 1, 1–84.

Wood, A. (1994) *North–South Trade, Employment and Inequality*, Oxford: Clarendon Press.

Wood, A. (1995) 'How trade hurt unskilled workers', *Journal of Economic Perspectives*, 9, 57–80.

Wood, A. (1997) 'Comment of Bhagwati', in Kuyvenhoven, A., Memedovic, O. and Molle, W. (eds), *Globalization of Labour Markets*, Dordrecht: Kluwer, 71–74.

3 Trade with the NICs and Wage Inequality: Evidence from the UK and Germany

Bob Anderton and Paul Brenton*

3.1 INTRODUCTION

Most research to date into the causes of the substantial increase in wage inequality in the UK concludes that increased competition from low-wage Newly-Industrialising Countries (NICs) has had very little impact on either the employment or relative wages of un-skilled workers.[1] But everyday experience suggests the reverse.[2]

We argue in this chapter that previous research may not have been able to demonstrate these links because the aggregate nature of the data used, combined with an approach which tends to ignore the implications of standard trade theory, does not capture the sectoral nature of the mechanisms by which increased import competition from the NICs may influence wage inequality. With a new 'wave' of rapidly emerging low-wage NICs, such as China and the new democracies of Eastern Europe, set to increase their share of world trade, it is vital that the full impact of trade on labour markets in the industrialised countries is fully understood.

This chapter investigates the impact of increased competition with the NICs and other low-wage sources of import demand on the relative wages of the unskilled, particularly in the UK, using a descriptive disaggregated sectoral analysis. The impact of the NICs on labour markets in Germany is also considered with the objective of improving our knowledge of how some nations have succeeded in minimising the impact of trade, or other factors, on the relative wages and employment of the less skilled.

The chapter begins by providing a brief overview of the key issues and the principal features of existing studies. We then provide

39

a basic but detailed investigation of sectoral data relating to relative prices, relative wages and changes in trade shares, using the standard trade theory framework of the Stolper–Samuelson theorem to provide a basis by which to analyse changes between/across low-skill and high-skill sectors. Such preliminary analysis has often been taken for granted in previous studies and, as a result, key insights regarding the impact of trade on labour markets may have been overlooked. In particular, we draw attention to our key result that the outcomes for sectors typically defined as 'low skill' are not uniform *within* a country. Further, a given sector exhibits different performance *across* countries.

We then proceed to look at the relative wages and employment of less-skilled workers *within* sectors and see how they have changed over time. We check to see whether such movements correspond with changes in import shares and import prices due to increased competition from low-wage suppliers, using the framework provided by the more recently proposed theory of outsourcing. A more detailed statistical analysis of outsourcing is contained in Chapter 7.

3.2   TRADE AND WAGES: THE ISSUES

Over the past two decades wage inequality has increased markedly in some countries, but not in others.[3] Part of the explanation for the increase in inequality seems to be a shift in demand towards higher-skilled workers. Two explanations are frequently offered for such a demand shift. Firstly, that labour-saving technical progress has reduced the relative demand for unskilled workers. Secondly, that increased international trade with the NICs, that is, nations with an abundant supply of low-skill and low-wage labour, has decreased the demand for low-skilled workers in the advanced industrialised countries. It is argued that imports of goods produced by the NICs have replaced domestic production of low-skill products in the advanced countries (see, for example, Wood, 1994).

One framework for analysing the mechanisms by which trade may influence wages is the Heckscher–Ohlin–Samuelson (HOS) model incorporating the Stolper–Samuelson theorem. In this model, high-skilled workers are assumed to be abundant in the advanced countries and low-skill workers abundant in the NICs. Sachs and Shatz (1996) explain that, if trade opens up between these two regions, then the theorem predicts the following three major effects: (I) the advanced industrialised countries will *export* high-skilled-intensive manufactures and *import* low-skilled-intensive manufactures; (II) the *price* of low-skilled-intensive manufactures will decline relative to high-skilled-intensive manufactures in the advanced countries; (III) the *wages* of low-skilled workers relative to that of high-skilled workers will decline in the advanced industrialised countries.

This theorem emphasises the connection between relative output prices and relative wages: the relative wage of unskilled labour falls if and only if the relative price of low-skilled-intensive output declines.[4] If empirical evidence can be found which shows that the relative price of low-skilled traded goods has declined, and that the sectoral patterns of movements in relative prices are consistent with the sectoral changes in relative wages predicted by Stolper–Samuelson, this will provide strong *prima facie* evidence in support of the hypothesis that trade has influenced wage inequality. This is what we initially seek to investigate in this chapter.

Sachs and Shatz (1996) show that the price of low-skilled-intensive output in the USA fell sharply relative to the price of high-skilled-intensive output and find that this is consistent with the evolution of wage inequality in the USA. However, little work has been done on relative prices for other countries. Indeed, the majority of research on the impact of trade on UK labour markets has largely ignored the mechanisms suggested by standard trade theory as to how trade prices may influence inequality, and has therefore neglected to conduct a detailed analysis of movements in the price of low-skill-intensive products relative to high-skill-intensive goods. In addition, research on the UK has tended to use *aggregate* trade data (see, for example, Haskel, 1996; Machin, Ryan and van Reenen, 1996), whereas *highly disaggregated* trade data are far more appropriate given the sectoral nature of the mechanisms by which relative trade prices may influence wage inequality.

Another reason for using highly disaggregated data for evaluating the impact of trade on wage inequality is that the *magnitude* of the above effects depends on the degree to which the traded goods are *differentiated* (see Helpman and Krugman, 1985). In sectors where competition is based on product differentiation, an increased exposure to trade with the NICs will have little impact on relative prices and wages whereas sectors characterised by homogeneous products are more likely to exhibit large changes in relative product and factor prices in response to trade effects. Oliveira-Martins

(1994) provides some evidence that import penetration from the NICs decreases wages in sectors making homogeneous products relative to wages in sectors producing differentiated products. One objective of the chapter is therefore to investigate the impact of increased competition with the NICs on the relative wages of the unskilled by conducting a highly disaggregated sectoral analysis using the Stolper–Samuelson framework.

This standard trade theory approach places emphasis on the way in which greater international competition affects the prices, wages and employment levels of certain sectors (exporters) relative to other sectors (import-competing), thus focusing upon shifts between industrial sectors. Recently, however, attention has also been given to the apparent increase in inequality between skilled and unskilled workers *within* sectors. One explanation (see Feenstra and Hanson, 1995) is that firms in Western industrial countries, in the face of more intense international competition, have 'outsourced' to lower-wage countries those parts of the production process that require the largest input of unskilled labour. This shift in the source of supply of intermediate inputs leads to an increase in the relative demand for skilled labour within industries in industrial countries. In the final section of this chapter we look for evidence of these within-sector shifts in relative wages and discuss whether the trade data support the idea that outsourcing has been an important mechanism by which trade with low-wage countries has influenced Western labour markets.

3.3   TRADE AND WAGE INEQUALITY: WHAT CAN THE DATA TELL US?

3.3.1   Analysis Across Sectors

The basic argument from the Stolper–Samuelson theory regarding the influence of trade on wage inequality is that changes in relative wages are caused by changes in relative product prices which in turn are related to changes in import prices and world supplies. Here we start with a simple analysis of trends in the data to check whether such effects are apparent for the UK and Germany since 1970.

We begin by looking at relative prices in the domestic market. Given the Stolper–Samuelson theorem, we expect that the price of low-skilled-intensive products will have fallen relative to the price of high-skilled-intensive products. Figure 3.1 for the UK, and Figure 3.2 for Germany, show the evolution of the price of value added for certain industrial sectors relative to the average price of value added for manufacturing as a whole.[5] The sectors chosen are among those typically treated as being intensive in the use of unskilled labour (textiles, clothing, leather products, footwear, wood products and furniture) and those usually referred to as skill-intensive (electrical machinery, non-electrical machinery, professional goods).[6]

Three main conclusions tend to emerge from these figures. First, relative product prices were much more variable in the 1970s. If globalisation is behind the changes in the relative prices shown here then its impact has waned in the 1980s. Leamer (1996) finds a similar feature for the clothing sector in the USA. This is in contrast to the perception, borne out by data for the USA and the UK, that inequality increased much more sharply in the 1980s than in previous periods. As we shall see below, the increase in the share of UK imports accounted for by the NICs occurred primarily in the 1980s. Thus, a clear link between rising imports from low-wage countries and relative price movements in not apparent from our simple inspection of the data.

Secondly, within each country, experience across sectors typically classed as intensive in the use of low-skilled labour or sectors intensive in the use of high-skilled labour is not common. Taking the UK as an example, the relative price of clothing products, typically seen as low-skill-intensive, fell dramatically during the 1970s, then stabilised in the early 1980s and actually increased in the late 1980s and early 1990s. A very similar pattern is apparent for textiles. However, for leather products and footwear, also classed as low-skill-intensive, a quite different evolution of relative prices emerges: relative stability in the early and mid-1970s, an increase in relative price in the late 1970s and early 1980s followed by a decline in the relative price in the mid-1980s. There is subsequently a recovery in the relative price in the late 1980s, occurring slightly earlier for footwear. The evolution of relative prices also varies for sectors typically treated as skill-intensive, for example, non-electrical machinery and electrical machinery. Similar conclusions are reached from analysis of the data for Germany.

The final point to emerge from this analysis is that the experience of sectors classed as high- or low-skill does not appear to be common across countries. For example, the change in the relative

Figure 3.1   UK: price of value added relative to total manufacturing, 1970–92

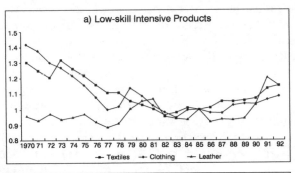

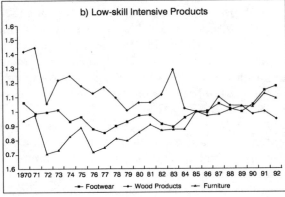

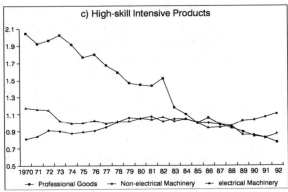

Figure 3.2 Germany: price of value added relative to total manufacturing, 1970–92

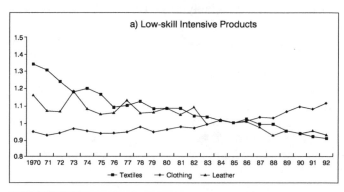

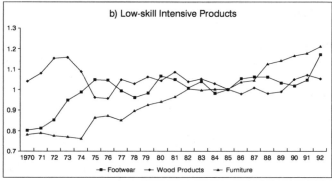

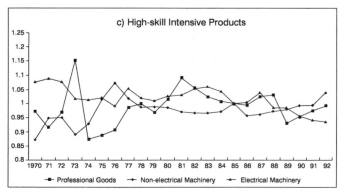

price of clothing is quite different in the UK compared to Germany. The large fall in the relative price that occurred in the UK in the 1970s did not take place in Germany. The relative price of footwear increased appreciably in Germany in the 1970s but not in the UK.

One explanation for different relative price movements for Germany and the UK may be that the degree of product differentiation between the goods produced by the NICs and those manufactured by Germany is substantial, due to *quality* differences (even though the goods are classified as belonging to the same industrial category – International Standard Industrial Classification (ISIC)), whereas the goods manufactured by the NICs and the UK may be fairly homogeneous. For example, Jarvis and Prais (1995) claim that superior vocational training results in higher-quality German products relative to British products; and Nickell and Bell (1996) argue that such a training system has enabled relatively low-skilled workers in Germany to avoid the relative declines in both wages and employment experienced by similar workers in the UK and USA. Hence, the degree of product differentiation *vis-à-vis* the manufactures of the NICs and Germany, relative to the degree of product differentiation between the manufactures of the NICs and the UK, may help to explain why movements in wage inequality in Germany are relatively small in comparison to the UK (and may explain differences in the relative domestic price movements of high- and low-skill products in Germany and the UK).

We thus conclude that it may not be relevant to group together into single aggregates sectors traditionally treated as unskilled-intensive or as skilled-intensive. Furthermore, detailed individual country analysis is required to provide a complete picture of the impact of globalisation. Finally, analysis which does not include the 1970s will miss most of the action regarding changing relative prices. This then begs the question as to why the impact of globalisation has become such an important issue in the late 1980s and 1990s and was not high on the agenda in the 1970s.

Having shown that there have been important changes in relative prices in the UK and Germany we proceed to briefly look at the evolution of relative wages for some of the sectors. Initially we have simply compared average wages across all employees in a sector with the average in manufacturing as a whole. Figure 3.3 for the UK and Figure 3.4 for Germany show the evolution of relative wages and relative prices for four unskilled-intensive sectors; textiles,

47

Figure 3.3 Relative wages and relative prices in UK low-skill sectors, 1970–92

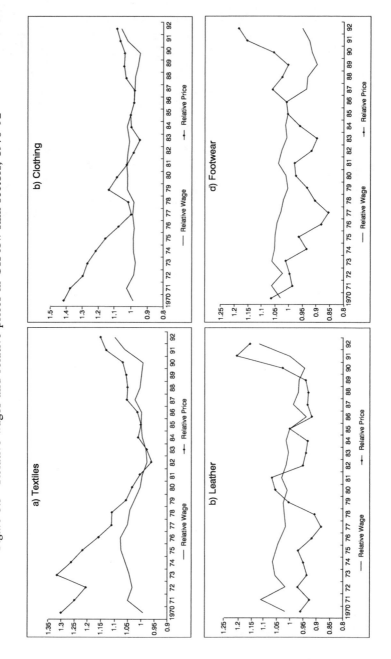

48

Figure 3.4 Relative wages and relative prices in German low-skill sectors, 1970–92

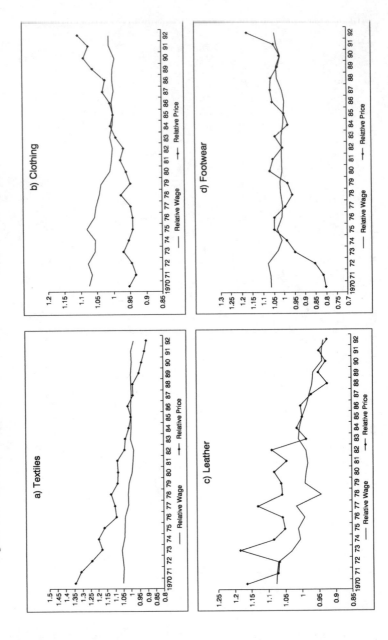

clothing, leather, and footwear. Very tentatively these figures suggest that relative wages have been much more stable than relative prices.[7] It is also visually difficult to detect strong positive correlations between the two series. The exceptions are perhaps textiles in the UK and leather in Germany. We attempted a slightly more formal statistical analysis by checking to see if there was any evidence that changes in relative prices had 'Granger-caused' movements in relative wages in these sectors. With the exception of leather products in Germany we found no evidence of causality running from relative prices to relative wages.

Changes in average wages may vary between sectors due to differences in the evolution of the wage received by different skill groups and following changes to the mix of skilled and unskilled workers employed.[8] Our data on average wages cannot distinguish between these two separate effects. However, the observed stability in relative average wages combined with fairly large movements in relative prices indicate the possible complexity of the story regarding the impact of globalisation. For example, domestic firms may have responded to more intense international competition by shifting into the production of higher-quality, higher-value products which typically require a higher proportion of skilled workers than the production of more standardised manufactures, which will, in turn, affect both average wages and prices.

So far in our analysis, changes in UK and German domestic prices of unskilled-labour-intensive products relative to skilled-intensive products do not provide strong support for the Stolper–Samuelson view of the way in which trade influences the domestic labour market. However, as authors such as Wood (1994) have suggested, it may be that the classification of industries that we and others have used is not suitable for identifying the precise impact of trade. The simple treatment of broad sectors as unskilled- or skilled-labour intensive will not be relevant if there is significant product heterogeneity within each sector. Within the textiles sector there may be products that are produced with relatively more skilled than unskilled labour in addition to unskilled-labour-intensive products.

Given that the (available) domestic prices may not be suitable for assessing the role of trade our next step is to analyse the behaviour of relative import prices, which can be computed at more detailed sectoral levels. In principle, it is import prices which translate increasing world supplies, or falling trade barriers, into changes in relative domestic prices. Thus, we investigate whether the price of imports of low-skill products has fallen relative to the price of imports of skill-intensive products. First, however, we establish the degree to which the share of low-wage countries in the imports of Germany and the UK has changed over time.

Our data set identifies three different groups of low-wage economies: the NICs (Hong Kong, South Korea, Singapore and Taiwan); former COMECON countries; and the Rest of the World (ROW).[9] Table 3.1 and Table 3.2 show the share of each of these country groups together with an aggregate of industrial countries, expressed as a percentage of the total imports of the UK and Germany in 1970, 1980 and 1993. The tables focus upon the six low-skill-intensive and three skilled intensive sectors which have been studied in the previous sections.[10]

The trade data permit analysis at a more detailed level of the ISIC industrial classification than is possible with the value-added data. This is useful given our previous discussion of the possibility of product heterogeneity within broad sectors, a feature which receives some support in Tables 3.1 and 3.2 from the variation in performance between 4-digit sectors within an overall 3-digit industry group. For example, look at the share of the various groups of countries in UK imports of textiles. For sector 3211 the share of the NICs in UK imports has fallen throughout the 1970s and 1980s. The share of the former COMECON countries also fell in both periods but principally in the 1970s. The share of the ROW fell in the 1970s but increased dramatically in the 1980s from 12 per cent of the total to over 31 per cent in 1993. The final columns of Table 3.1 show that the share of industrial countries in UK imports of 3211 increased in the 1970s but fell back in the 1980s. In contrast the NICs and the ROW increased their share of UK imports of 3213 in both the 1970s and the 1980s, mainly at the expense of COMECON suppliers in the 1970s and industrial countries in the 1980s.

In general, the data for the UK suggest that for most sectors increasing import penetration in the 1970s was accompanied by a rising share of imports for industrial countries. This may reflect the impact of UK accession to the EC in 1973 and the redirection of the source of UK imports away from Commonwealth countries towards industrialised European countries. Typically, increases in the share of UK imports in the 1970s for one group of low-wage economies came at the expense of another group of low-wage countries. In contrast, in the 1980s rising import penetration in the UK

has typically occurred together with a rising share of low-wage countries in imports at the expense of industrial countries. It is important to note that the declining share of industrial countries in UK
imports in the 1980s occurred across most sectors, even those classed
as skilled-intensive. Increased competition from the low-wage countries has not been confined to low-skill-intensive products, but the
increase in share for skill-intensive products has occurred at much
lower levels of import penetration.

The situation for Germany is more mixed, but if anything the
data suggest a quite different evolution of market shares to the
UK with the share of industrial countries in German imports declining in the 1970s. For some sectors this increase in the share for
low-wage countries continued throughout the 1980s. However, for
a number of sectors the industrial countries increased their share
of German imports in the 1980s. Consequently, in a similar fashion
to relative product prices and relative wages, there is little unifor-
mity across the UK and Germany regarding the evolution of the
trade shares of low-wage sources of imports.

Given the increasing importance of low-wage countries as a source
of imports, particularly in the UK in the 1980s, we now seek to
assess the impact of changing trade shares on the price of imports.[11]
To do this requires a comparison of the actual outcome with an
appropriate counterfactual or anti-monde. In this case, the alternative scenario should show what would have happened if the increased supply of exports from low-wage countries had not occurred.
Below we attempt a fairly crude analysis of what would have happened to import prices if the share of low-wage countries had remained constant. But first we quickly look at *actual* changes in the
import price of unskilled-intensive products relative to skilled-
intensive products.

The first two columns of Table 3.3 for each country show the
percentage change in the price of imports of each product during
the 1970s and during the period 1980 to 1993. These data again
reflect different evolutions for different categories within broad
sectors, such as, textiles. Both German and UK import prices of
carpets and rugs (3214) have consistently grown at a slower rate
than the import prices of other products falling within the broad
textiles category.

Generally, these data show that the import prices of skilled-
intensive products (machinery) grew faster than the import prices
of unskilled-labour-intensive products in the 1980s. This is particularly

Table 3.1 Shares of UK imports, 1970–93

	NICs			ROW			COMECON			Industrial (Ind) countries			Change for ind countries	
	1970	1980	1993	1970	1980	1993	1970	1980	1993	1970	1980	1993	1970–80	1980–93
Textiles														
3211	9.4	7.1	3.1	18.3	11.8	31.2	16.4	8.1	7.4	55.8	73.0	58.4	17.2	−14.6
3212	14.2	8.8	8.5	5.6	8.1	31.3	33.3	31.4	21.1	46.9	51.8	39.1	4.9	−12.6
3213	0.5	6.1	9.8	1.2	4.6	29.3	24.1	13.5	11.9	74.3	75.8	49.0	1.5	−26.8
3214	0.3	0.2	0.2	42.0	17.3	22.1	3.9	3.6	3.5	53.8	79.0	74.2	25.2	−4.7
3215	2.2	3.0	3.9	3.5	4.7	11.3	2.9	16.0	7.2	91.4	76.3	77.7	−15.2	1.4
3219	0.6	1.0	1.1	5.2	3.1	19.9	13.1	10.5	8.5	81.1	85.4	70.6	4.3	−14.9
Clothing														
3220	41.6	35.1	22.5	5.0	17.6	41.0	13.7	5.4	7.1	39.7	41.9	29.4	2.2	−12.5
Leather														
3231	0.0	0.6	1.4	49.7	32.4	33.8	7.3	6.3	2.1	42.9	60.7	62.7	17.9	2.0
3232	1.5	2.9	8.8	21.5	1.3	16.9	11.8	18.0	23.1	65.2	77.8	51.2	12.6	−26.7
3233	20.5	52.4	43.9	10.3	16.0	32.1	8.0	3.3	1.2	61.3	28.4	22.8	−32.9	−5.6
Footwear														
3240	20.2	10.2	10.2	6.0	9.6	30.1	10.7	4.6	1.0	63.1	75.7	58.7	12.6	−16.9
Wood Products														
3311	1.8	4.5	2.3	12.2	11.9	39.9	35.9	33.0	14.2	50.0	50.6	43.5	0.6	−7.0
3312	1.8	6.2	16.6	5.2	40.7	63.4	5.6	5.8	1.4	87.5	47.4	18.6	−40.1	−28.8
3319	2.1	10.8	21.6	4.1	11.6	28.8	20.7	6.9	4.3	73.1	70.7	45.2	−2.4	−25.4
Furniture														
3320	1.2	4.1	6.0	5.8	6.6	18.9	15.3	9.7	7.7	77.8	79.6	67.4	1.9	−12.2

Non-electrical Machinery														
3821	0.0	1.3	1.3	3.4	9.8	32.3	10.0	9.6	7.4	86.6	79.3	59.1	−7.3	−20.2
3822	0.0	0.0	0.0	0.5	0.6	14.1	8.7	6.5	7.1	90.7	92.9	78.7	2.1	−14.2
3823	0.2	0.7	3.3	0.8	1.0	16.1	17.4	16.5	11.5	81.6	81.8	69.2	0.2	−12.6
3824	0.0	0.2	0.9	0.9	1.0	16.2	15.9	13.2	11.9	83.1	85.6	71.0	2.5	−14.6
3825	0.6	1.2	12.7	1.0	2.1	21.9	7.7	6.0	2.2	90.6	90.7	63.2	0.0	−27.5
3829	0.0	1.2	2.8	1.3	1.5	17.6	16.6	10.1	7.1	82.0	87.2	72.5	5.2	−14.7
Electrical Machinery														
3831	1.8	3.0	6.1	2.2	2.2	20.0	15.5	7.4	8.7	80.6	87.4	65.2	6.9	−22.2
3832	3.8	14.2	10.3	2.3	3.1	26.9	14.4	4.6	4.3	79.5	78.1	58.5	−1.5	−19.6
3833	0.2	2.6	12.5	0.3	0.4	8.5	15.2	6.9	4.8	84.4	90.1	74.2	5.7	−15.9
3839	2.5	3.9	5.3	2.2	1.5	16.0	8.3	6.4	6.5	87.1	88.3	72.1	1.2	−16.2
Professional Goods														
3851	0.2	0.9	1.7	5.0	8.6	29.9	10.9	7.2	10.6	83.9	83.4	57.8	−0.5	−25.6
3852	2.1	4.9	5.8	1.9	1.3	17.7	9.7	4.8	2.8	86.3	89.0	73.7	2.7	−15.3
3853	0.5	33.5	25.8	0.3	2.1	19.1	59.9	20.2	33.9	39.3	44.1	21.2	4.9	−22.9

Table 3.2 Shares of German imports, 1970–93

	NICs			ROW			COMECON			Industrial (Ind) countries			Change for ind countries	
	1970	1980	1993	1970	1980	1993	1970	1980	1993	1970	1980	1993	1970–80	1980–93
Textiles														
3211	0.9	2.1	1.9	5.4	13.0	16.4	6.6	10.8	3.5	87.1	74.2	78.3	−12.9	4.1
3212	3.2	9.1	3.3	9.8	13.2	21.5	23.7	22.1	10.7	63.3	55.6	64.5	−7.7	8.8
3213	1.9	7.6	8.1	0.8	7.0	14.3	6.7	13.0	6.6	90.6	72.3	71.0	−18.3	−1.4
3214	0.2	0.3	0.0	45.5	38.0	53.7	1.2	2.9	1.1	53.2	58.8	45.2	5.7	−13.6
3215	0.2	2.5	5.3	19.8	51.0	19.7	9.0	10.8	7.9	71.0	35.7	67.0	−35.3	31.3
3219	0.0	0.7	1.0	13.3	4.1	14.6	6.8	10.2	2.0	79.8	85.0	82.4	5.2	−2.6
Clothing														
3220	12.7	21.4	9.8	7.8	21.1	35.2	4.4	5.1	11.5	75.2	52.4	43.5	−22.7	−9.0
Leather														
3231	0.0	0.6	0.6	23.3	16.9	18.4	2.2	7.0	8.5	74.5	75.5	72.5	1.0	−3.1
3232	0.0	0.6	6.0	11.3	23.8	26.1	8.0	3.1	10.9	80.6	72.5	57.0	−8.1	−15.5
3233	9.1	41.0	12.1	5.4	12.3	57.4	3.0	3.0	3.4	82.5	43.7	27.1	−38.8	−16.6
Footwear														
3240	2.8	7.0	4.1	4.6	7.0	23.9	3.8	10.4	10.2	88.8	75.6	61.9	−13.2	−13.7
Wood Products														
3311	0.1	2.7	1.3	11.9	12.0	19.3	35.6	36.2	8.3	52.4	49.1	71.1	−3.3	22.1
3312	9.8	11.7	1.6	26.0	40.4	49.8	5.3	7.2	26.5	58.9	40.8	22.1	−18.1	−18.6
3319	1.3	9.2	3.5	9.6	8.5	22.6	7.4	13.8	21.1	81.8	68.5	52.8	−13.3	−15.7
Furniture														
3320	0.2	1.5	2.3	5.2	5.6	10.2	7.1	17.7	20.0	87.4	75.2	67.5	−12.2	−7.7

Non-electrical Machinery

3821	0.0	0.2	0.3	4.1	10.1	24.3	20.5	15.1	2.0	75.4	74.6	73.5	-0.7	-1.1
3822	0.0	0.0	0.0	0.2	0.7	15.3	7.2	15.7	5.1	92.6	83.6	79.5	-9.0	-4.1
3823	0.0	1.0	2.1	2.2	1.2	10.6	31.7	33.4	3.2	66.2	64.4	84.1	-1.8	19.7
3824	0.0	0.4	0.9	0.5	0.7	8.6	21.4	24.2	2.4	78.1	74.7	88.0	-3.3	13.3
3825	0.0	2.4	15.4	1.8	1.1	24.1	9.1	5.3	0.0	89.1	91.3	60.4	2.1	-30.8
3829	0.1	1.0	1.9	1.1	2.7	12.0	17.1	19.2	3.0	81.6	77.2	83.2	-4.5	6.0

Electrical Machinery

3831	0.1	3.0	5.2	1.6	2.9	13.6	18.5	24.5	4.8	79.8	69.6	76.4	-10.2	6.8
3832	2.1	10.0	10.3	1.6	2.8	22.0	6.7	10.0	0.6	89.6	77.3	67.0	-12.3	-10.3
3833	0.0	1.7	3.7	3.5	7.6	12.9	5.2	9.1	7.5	91.2	81.5	75.8	-9.7	-5.7
3839	0.7	4.8	13.1	0.8	4.3	13.1	12.2	15.5	6.0	86.3	75.4	67.8	-10.9	-7.6

Professional Goods

3851	0.1	0.7	1.2	0.8	2.1	24.6	17.8	21.6	1.9	81.3	75.6	72.4	-5.7	-3.3
3852	1.0	4.9	6.8	2.6	5.4	14.8	6.8	7.1	0.7	89.6	82.5	77.7	-7.1	-4.8
3853	0.8	36.8	24.0	0.1	1.9	13.1	57.0	33.0	0.7	42.1	28.3	62.2	-13.8	33.9

Table 3.3 Actual and counterfactual import price increases: UK and Germany, 1970s–1980s

	Germany actual price increases		Counterfactual*		UK actual price increases		Counterfactual*	
	1970s	1980s	1970s	1980s	1970s**	1980s	1970s**	1980s
Textiles								
3211	85.9	40.2	0.6	1.1	109.7	17.1	−13.3	13.5
3212	104.2	80.4	5.7	−15.9	151.4	12.4	−12.2	19.7
3213	70.5	62.9	−10.5	0.7	75.6	42.9	−19.3	13.2
3214	52.8	31.1	19.9	−20.7	49.3	5.5	42.6	22.3
3215	101.7	83.0	−17.7	−10.5	119.5	62.1	0.1	−6.7
3219	167.2	41.2	−29.8	−19.9	93.3	47.0	−26.1	−2.4
Clothing								
3220	85.3	24.1	4.5	12.4	60.0	14.8	6.0	11.7
Leather								
3231	100.4	21.3	−9.2	27.1	65.8	102.3	6.3	−35.6
3232	74.5	19.7	−5.5	7.7	−45.6	−30.9	388.7	−5.9
3233	79.7	3.4	18.0	21.0	−103.5	37.5	−71.9	7.8
Footwear								
3240	78.5	72.5	0.4	9.3	142.0	74.5	39.0	9.9
Wood Products								
3311	113.1	75.6	−8.3	0.3	166.4	−1.3	10.9	−5.8
3312	87.2	48.2	−2.7	6.0	104.0	144.0	−52.9	−51.0
3319	103.4	−23.0	35.2	52.2	−1.3	36.6	−71.4	21.2
Furniture								
3320	81.3	27.3	5.5	13.8	74.8	−8.5	−8.2	43.5

Non-electrical Machinery								
3821	128.3	108.4	1.4	3.4	4.9	156.0	10.2	−20.8
3822	106.5	54.9	−5.9	4.7	104.9	75.5	2.2	0.7
3823	115.1	77.8	−9.7	−4.6	84.6	65.7	1.2	5.4
3824	92.5	66.2	2.7	0.3	89.1	81.6	2.4	4.5
3825	119.9	45.7	−13.5	37.1	72.5	83.7	9.8	7.5
3829	92.3	77.8	0.9	4.0	64.6	79.9	4.7	7.3
Electrical Machinery								
3831	85.5	76.9	−8.0	6.1	50.7	68.0	3.9	13.9
3832	55.1	95.8	3.6	−5.0	−39.2	76.8	−64.1	2.2
3833	95.5	72.2	−14.1	−3.0	92.6	44.5	−4.4	7.1
3839	85.7	76.0	5.5	7.7	49.8	48.0	6.4	9.6

Notes:
* The number of percentage points the aggregate import price index would have been higher or lower (−) if the geo-graphical structure of imports had remained the same as in the first year of the respective decade.
** For certain products for the UK the first observation used is 1973 to avoid problems arising from the pre-metrification of quantities.

pronounced for the UK, but much less so for Germany. There is no clear evidence that the relative import price of unskilled-labour intensive products declined in the 1970s. Thus, changes in the relative prices of high-skill and low-skill imports are consistent with the increase in wage inequality in the UK in the 1980s, but our key question is whether the low-wage countries are responsible for this fall in the relative import price of unskilled-intensive products.

One way of capturing what would have happened to trade and product prices if the supply of goods from low-wage economies had not increased is to construct an appropriately specified computable general equilibrium model (CGE) and apply a suitable counterfactual. One disadvantage of such an approach is that the number and detail of sectors permissible is limited. These models may not be able to capture the within broad industrial sector effects and responses which the analysis above suggests may be important.

Here we propose a much more simple approach but one which does allow for a fairly detailed sectoral analysis. We attempt to compare the evolution of the import price for each sector with what would have happened if the share of the different country suppliers of imports had remained constant. The basic assumption, supported by the data, is that the price of imports, even for quite narrowly defined products, varies between different sources. This suggests that, even for fairly standardised products, product differentiation and differences in quality may be important. So a shift in the demand for imports towards higher-priced sources – as a result, for example, of an increase in consumers' income – will lead to an increase in the aggregate import price index for the sector even if actual prices do not change. We thus attempt to separate out from the sectoral import price index changes due to movements in import shares and changes due to movements in actual prices. We then show what would have happened to the aggregate price index if shares had remained the same as in 1970 and then at 1980 levels.

However, this approach cannot capture the full impact on the prices of traded goods of increasing world supplies due to greater output in low-wage countries. It is possible for import prices of unskilled-intensive products to fall as a result of developments in low-wage countries even though their share of a particular country's imports do not change. Thus, our analysis cannot provide

unambiguous evidence of the role of low-wage countries in influencing the import prices of industrial countries. However, the results are informative because the approach allows us to assess the
extent to which increases in the price of imports of low-skill products have been constrained by a shift in demand towards cheaper
sources of supply. A more detailed technical description of the
approach adopted is contained in Appendix 3.1.

Table 3.3 shows the total proportionate change in the unit value
index in the 1970s and 1980s for Germany and the UK for each
4-digit ISIC group within our nine low-skill and skilled-intensive
sectors (results for all 4-digit ISIC groups are presented in Anderton
and Brenton, 1996). The next columns then show the extent to
which the unit value index would have been higher or lower if the
mix of supplying countries had remained unchanged from the initial year of the decade.[12] For example, the table shows that for
German imports of clothing (3220) the overall import price index
actually rose by 85 per cent in the 1970s and by 24 per cent in the
period 1980–93. The next two columns show that, if the mix of
import supplying countries of clothing to Germany had not changed
during the 1970s, the overall import price index would have been
4 percentage points higher at the end of the decade (that is, the
index would have increased by 89 per cent). For the 1980s the import price index would have been 12 percentage points higher.

According this analysis, the shift in the import bundle towards
low-cost suppliers had a much greater impact in the 1980s than in
the 1970s. For a number of low-skill sectors import prices would
have been considerably higher if low-wage countries had not increased their share of UK and German imports. The UK import
price of furniture, for example, would have been almost 50 per
cent higher at the end of the 1980s if trade shares had not changed
during the decade. However, the results are not uniform across
low-skill sectors. For example, the industrial countries increased
their share of UK imports of tanneries and leather finishing (3231)
in both the 1970s and the 1980s, hence, as Table 3.3 shows, the
overall import price for this group would have been lower if import shares had not changed.

There are also signs that changes in the country composition of
imports played a role in explaining the evolution of the overall
import prices of skill-intensive sectors (3821–3839) during the 1980s.
In most cases, particularly in the UK, the import price index
would have been higher if trade shares had not changed. This

reflects the declining share of industrial countries in UK imports of engineering products during the 1980s. So, even for apparently skilled-intensive sectors trade movements towards low-wage countries appear to have depressed import prices. However, the constraining effect on import prices of higher import shares for low-wage countries appears to be much greater for low-skill sectors than for the high-skill sectors.

This rather simple analysis of the basic data suggests against making broad pronouncements across countries and across sectors with respect to the impact of trade with the NICs on the relative wages and employment for the unskilled in Europe. If anything our analysis points to the need for more detailed analysis *within* broad sectors such as textiles or clothing, but also within sectors such as engineering, which are normally assumed to be skilled-intensive. It may be that much of the adjustment to trade with low-wage economies is occurring within sectors. International specialisation is increasingly being defined at more specific industrial categories, and one can easily find high-skill niches within broad sectors typically treated as low-skill-intensive. The focus of previous work has been on changes occurring between broad sectors and, hence, may not have been able to identify the key adjustments to rising imports from low-wage economies.[13] We now turn to a more detailed analysis of this issue, taking the UK as our example.

3.3.2 Analysis of the Impact of Trade within Sectors

Research on inequality in the UK clearly shows that the major declines in the relative wages and employment of the less skilled have occurred *within* sectors (see Gregg and Machin, 1994). Consequently, in this section we look at developments within two UK sectors (textiles, which we continue to treat as low-skill-intensive, and non-electrical machinery production, which we define as high-skill-intensive). Figure 3.5 shows the ratio of the average wage paid to the lowest-decile earners relative to the highest-decile earners for the textiles and non-electrical machinery sectors.[14] The figure shows a strong increase in wage inequality beginning around the end of the 1970s and continuing until beyond the mid-1980s before coming to a halt and partially abating in the early 1990s. The figure also shows that the differential between the high and low earners is larger for textiles in comparison to non-electrical machinery.[15]

Using a different database, Figures 3.6 and 3.7 show the wage bill and employment shares for non-production workers for the same two UK sectors (production workers are deemed to represent the less skilled and non-production workers are defined as high skilled).[16] Figures 3.6 and 3.7 clearly show that a substantial part of the decline in the economic fortunes of the less skilled in the UK occurred in the first half of the 1980s. The figures also support our assumption that non-electrical machinery contains a higher proportion of skilled workers relative to textiles as the share of non-production workers in the latter sector was approximately half that of non-electrical machinery at the start of the 1970s.

One implication of the Stolper–Samuelson theorem is that, given the predicted fall in the relative wage of low-skilled workers, all sectors will increase the proportion of low-skilled workers employed relative to high-skilled workers. This prediction is clearly at odds with the increased share of employment for non-production workers in both textiles and non-electrical machinery in the UK, as shown in Figures 3.6 and 3.7. In contrast, the phenomenon of the simultaneous decline in both relative wages and employment of the low skilled is consistent with more recent theories, such as that of outsourcing (Feenstra and Hanson, 1995).

Given the different skill intensities of the two sectors, which may reflect the average quality of production in the sectors, it may be interesting to investigate the *relative* change in the economic fortunes of the less skilled in these two sectors. Figure 3.8 therefore shows the wages of the lowest quartile (decile) in textiles relative to the lowest quartile (decile) in non-electrical machinery and it is clear that, from around 1979–84, the wages of the less skilled in textiles deteriorated to a greater extent than the less skilled in non-electrical machinery. We find a similar deterioration in the share of employment of production workers in textiles relative to non-electrical machinery.

Looking again at Tables 3.1 and 3.3 we see a fairly strong correlation between the above movements in the relative employment and wages of the less skilled in our two sectors and changes in import shares and import prices. Table 3.1 shows that both the UK textiles and non-electrical machinery sectors experienced substantial increases in the share of UK imports coming from the lower-wage countries in the 1980s, which may explain the decline in the relative employment and wages of the less skilled within these sectors during the 1980s in the UK. But the magnitude of the increase

Figure 3.5   Relative wages within UK textiles and non-electrical machinery, 1974–94 (ratio of the wages paid to the lowest decile of workers to those paid to highest decile within each sector)

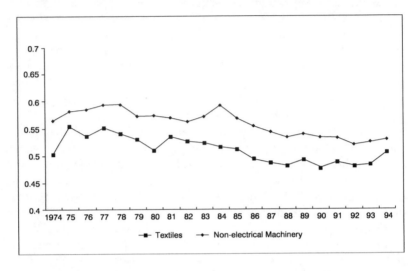

Figure 3.6   Employment and wages of skilled labour within UK textiles, 1970–86

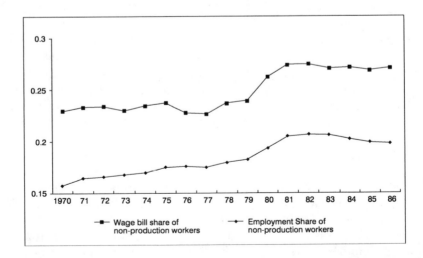

Figure 3.7   Employment and wages of skilled labour within UK
non-electrical machinery, 1970–86

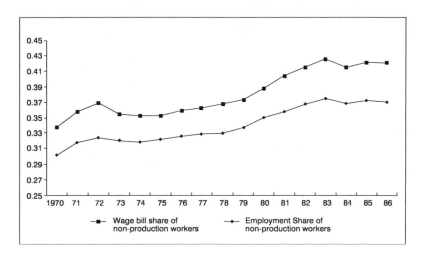

Figure 3.8   Relative wages between UK textile and non-electrical
machinery sectors, 1974–94

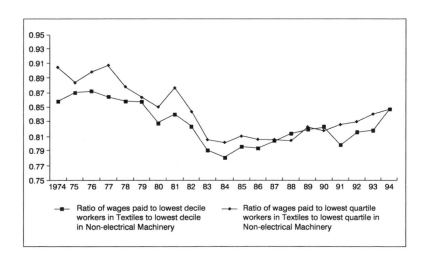

in UK imports supplied by the non-industrialised countries in the 1980s is similar for both sectors and does not explain the relatively greater deterioration in the economic fortunes of the less skilled in Textiles. However, Table 3.3 not only shows that without this shift towards lower-wage import suppliers, import prices in both sectors would have been higher than if the import supplier mix had remained the same, it also shows that import prices would have been higher by a greater amount in textiles in comparison to non-electrical machinery.

Hence the greater downward pressure on import prices in UK textiles caused by the switch to lower-wage import suppliers may explain why the wages and employment of the less skilled in textiles deteriorated more than the same category of workers in non-electrical machinery. Furthermore, the high-skill-intensive nature of UK non-electrical machinery production probably results in higher-quality products relative to the UK low-skill-intensive textile sector which, in turn, may result in the non-electrical machinery sector being far less prone to low-skill/low-price/low-quality competition from lower-wage economies (which may be one reason for the smaller decline in non-electrical machinery import prices relative to textiles after a similar increase in both sectors in the share of low-wage import suppliers). This again suggests that the evolution of inequality varies across sectors, and that a full investigation of the causes of inequality requires a highly detailed sectoral approach.

3.4   CONCLUSIONS

Standard trade theory, which stresses that adjustment to greater international competition occurs in the form of a reallocation of resources between sectors, shows that trade can be the cause of increases in wage inequality only if relative product prices have changed. This study shows that information on product prices for broad industrial sectors is not supportive of trade having had a major impact on wage inequality in the UK and Germany. This result is also consistent with most studies of relative price movements in the USA.

However, we found that the relative price of imports of unskilled-labour-intensive products did fall in the UK in the 1980s. We conducted a simple experiment which showed that if low-wage countries had not increased their share of UK imports then the import prices of low-skilled products would have been higher. Interestingly, we also found that even for skilled sectors, such as machinery, trade with the NICs and other low-wage countries has depressed import prices, but by much less than that for unskilled-intensive products. We also found, from a number of indicators, that economic outcomes within broad sectors usually defined as low-skill-intensive, such as textiles, are far from homogeneous.

The above findings all suggest that the impact of globalisation is much more complicated than the standard trade model would suggest. We need to look more deeply *within* sectors at how firms respond to increased international competition. The final section of this chapter showed that unskilled workers in the UK textiles sector have fared badly relative to unskilled workers in the non-electrical machinery sector. Our analysis of UK imports, which showed that the increasing import share of low-wage countries depressed the price of imports of textiles to a greater extent than the price of imports of non-electrical machinery, is consistent with trade playing a role in this development.

APPENDIX 3.1 THE DECOMPOSITION OF IMPORT PRICES

Here we describe the methodology underlying the separation of trends in import prices into that component due to increasing shares of trade from low-wage countries and that due to general movements in import prices. In practice, import prices are measured by unit values. A unit-value price index for a particular sector will be an average across all supplying countries. This index will fall if there is a substitution from high-to-low value sources, all else held fixed. Chinloy (1980) among others, has shown how the impact of this recomposition of the import bundle can be separated out from actual price changes using Divisia index numbers. The idea has been applied by Aw and Roberts (1986) to show the impact of quantitative restrictions (QRs) in terms of promoting substitution within the import bundle towards higher-priced products and sources. They show that the difference between changes in the unit-value index and the discrete-time Divisia price index (Tornqvist index) can be attributed to the changing mix of suppliers.

More formally, the aggregate unit value index is defined by

$$P_j(t) = \frac{\sum_{i=1}^{n} V_{ij}}{\sum_{i=1}^{n} Q_{ij}}$$

where v is the bilateral value of imports of a 4-digit ISIC category, j, in year t from country i, and Q is the corresponding volume of imports. The change in the aggregate unit value index is measured by

$$\Delta \ln P(t) = \ln P(t) - \ln P(t - 1)$$

The Tornqvist price index for this group is defined by

$$\Delta \ln P_j^* (t) = \sum_{i=1}^{n} s_{ij} (t) \, \Delta \ln P_{ij} (t)$$

where

$$s_{ij} (t) = 0.5 \left[\frac{V_{ij} (t)}{\sum_{i=1}^{n} V_{ij}(t)} + \frac{V_{ij} (t - 1)}{\sum_{i=1}^{n} V_{ij}(t - 1)} \right]$$

and

$$\Delta \ln P_{ij}(t) = \ln \left(\frac{V_{ij}(t)}{Q_{ij}(t)} \right) - \ln \left(\frac{V_{ij}(t - 1)}{Q_{ij}(t - 1)} \right)$$

The change in the overall import price index due to the changing mix of imports among different country suppliers is given by the difference between the unit-value index and the Tornqvist index

$$\Delta R_j(t) = \Delta P_j(t) - \Delta P_j^*(t)$$

Notes

* Part of Anderton's research in this paper was financed by the British Academy
1. The work of Wood (1994) is one obvious major exception.
2. For example: the decline in the relative wages of the low skilled in the UK has coincided with a world-wide increase in both foreign direct investment (FDI) and the quantity of goods manufactured in low-wage countries (perhaps reflecting the increasing ease with which multinational corporations are able to relocate production to low-wage countries); shipyards and coal mines have closed down in the UK while these industries flourish in the NICs; we see rapid growth of UK imports from the NICs across virtually all categories of low-wage products; and we know that manufacturing employment in the UK fell by more than 25 per cent in the early 1980s at the same time that imports from the NICs increased dramatically (see Anderton, 1996).
3. By wage inequality we mean the differential between the wages of unskilled relative to skilled workers. Gregg and Machin (1994) show that wage inequality has grown rapidly in the UK and US in recent years.

4. It should be mentioned that there are other links between trade and wages that are not covered by this framework where the relative wages of unskilled workers may fall *without* the relative price of low-skilled output in the advanced countries declining.
5. We calculate relative measures of *value-added* domestic prices as wholesale prices are distorted by the inclusion of import prices. These data are from the OECD STAN database.
6. Analysis of additional sectors which reinforces the points made here is described in Anderton and Brenton (1996)
7. This is not surprising given that trade unions will probably attempt to limit the growth of wage differentials between industries.
8. Wages may differ between sectors for other reasons – such as, economic rents, compensation for different degrees of danger, and returns to effort. If these factors vary over time they will affect the evolution of relative wage rates.
9. The ROW group includes China and other Asian economies, Latin American countries, African countries and unfortunately, Australia and New Zealand. However, since we concentrate upon trade in manufactures the inclusion of the latter two countries should not have a significant effect upon the analysis.
10. Again, data for a wider range of sectors are presented in Anderton and Brenton (1996)
11. As data on the actual prices of imports are unavailable, in common with other studies, we use unit values (value per unit of volume) to proxy import prices.
12. In other words, the table shows the difference between the unit value index and the Tornqvist index, as described in Appendix 3.1.
13. Smith (1997), using a disaggregated CGE model, similarly concludes that analysis that assumes that goods produced within a broad sector are homogeneous will 'miss much of the impact of trade on the relative fortunes of skilled and unskilled workers in advanced economies'.
14. Data source: *UK New Earnings Survey*.
15. This differential does not seem to reflect differences in trade union coverage as both industries have very similar union densities. Hence the relatively higher differential between low and high earners for textiles may reflect a higher skill differential *within* textiles in comparison to non-electrical machinery.
16. Data source: *UK Census of Production* (which covers a slightly different sample period, more of the 1970s but less of the 1980s).

References

Anderton, R. (1996) 'Trade performance and the role of R&D, patents, investment and hysteresis: an analysis of disaggregated import volumes for the UK, Germany and Italy', *Discussion Paper*, 101, National Institute of Economic and Social Research.
Anderton, R. and Brenton, P. (1996) 'What has been the contribution of

trade with the NICs to adverse relative wage movements for the un-skilled in Europe?' paper presented at the conference 'Europe and Asia: The Impact of Trade with Low-Wage Economies on Employment and Relative Wages in the EU', Brussels: EIAS (December).

Aw, B.Y. and Roberts, M. (1986) 'Measuring quality change in quota-constrained import markets: the case of US footwear', *Journal of International Economics*, 21, 45–60.

Brenton, P. and Winters, L.A. (1992) 'Estimates of bilateral trade elasticities and their implications for the modelling of 1992', *Discussion Paper*, 717, Centre for Economic Policy Research.

Chinloy, P. (1980) 'Sources of quality change in labour input', *American Economic Review*, 70, 108–19.

Feenstra, R. and Hanson, G. (1995) 'Foreign investment, outsourcing and relative wages', *Working Paper*, 5121, NBER.

Gregg, P. and Machin, S. (1994) 'Is the rise in UK inequality different?', in Barrell, R. (ed.) *The UK Labour Market*, London: Sage.

Haskel, J. (1996) 'Small firms, contracting-out, computers and wage inequality: evidence from UK manufacturing', *Discussion Paper*, 1490, Centre for Economic Policy Research.

Helpman, E. and Krugman, P. (1985) *Market Structure and Foreign Trade*, Cambridge, MA: MIT Press.

Jarvis, V. and Prais, S. (1995), 'The quality of manufactured products in Britain and Germany', *Discussion Paper*. 88, National Institute of Economic and Social Research.

Leamer, E. (1994) 'Trade, wages and revolving door ideas', *Working Paper*, 4716, NBER.

Leamer, E (1996) 'In search of Stolper–Samuelson effects on US wages', *Working Paper*, 5427, NBER.

Machin, S., Ryan, A. and van Reenen, J. (1996) 'Technology and changes in skill structure: evidence from an international panel of industries', *Discussion Paper*, 1434, Centre for Economic Policy Research.

Nickell, S. and Bell, B. (1996) 'Changes in the distribution of wages and unemployment in OECD countries', *American Economic Review, Papers and Proceedings*, 86, 302–8.

Oliveira-Martins, J. (1994) 'Market structure, trade and industry wages', *OECD Economic Studies*, 22, 1023.

Sachs, J. and Shatz, H. (1996) 'US trade with developing countries and wage inequality', *American Economic Review, Papers and Proceedings*, 86, 234–9.

Smith, A (1997) 'The labour market effects of international trade: a computable general equilibrium model', University of Sussex, mimeo.

Wood, A. (1994), *North–South Trade, Employment and Inequality* Oxford: Clarendon Press.

4 Trade with Low-income Countries and the Relative Wages and Employment Opportunities of the Unskilled: An Exploratory Analysis for West Germany and the UK

Matthias Lücke*

4.1 INTRODUCTION

Since the early 1970s, European imports of manufactures from developing countries, especially from East and South-East Asia, have grown rapidly. The production of many of these imports requires relatively large amounts of unskilled labour. At the same time, the wage rate for unskilled labour has declined relative to skilled labour in some European countries while elsewhere in Europe unemployment among the unskilled has increased substantially.[1] Several recent studies, including in particular Wood (1994), have argued that these trends are linked and that it was growing imports from Asia and other lower-income countries that made the unskilled in many industrialised countries worse off.

There has ensued a lively debate on this 'trade impact' hypothesis, involving a wide variety of conceptual, methodological and data-related questions.[2] To date, most of the debate has been based on empirical evidence for the USA. However, relative wages and employment opportunities are probably affected not only by international developments but also by a host of national institutions and policies. This chapter, which is intended to open the way for a comparative study of several OECD countries, presents preliminary evidence on the link between international trade and the labour market in West Germany and the UK since 1970.

The trade impact hypothesis, as formulated by Wood (1994), is based on a three-factor Heckscher-Ohlin–Samuelson (HOS) trade model with internationally mobile physical capital and immobile skilled and unskilled labour. As imports from developing countries replace domestic production of unskilled-labour-intensive manufactures in industrialised countries, demand for unskilled labour falls. When labour markets are flexible, such as in the USA and increasingly in the UK, reduced demand for unskilled labour leads to a widening wage differential of skilled over unskilled labour, when full employment is maintained. When the relative wages of skilled and unskilled labour are prevented from adjusting to the change in relative demand, as is often asserted happens in West Germany and other continental EU countries, the result is growing unemployment of unskilled labour.

Although the trade impact hypothesis is plausible *a priori*, the magnitude of the Stolper–Samuelson effect, possible alternative causes of the deteriorating position of unskilled labour, and various methodological issues are controversial. In this chapter, I account for this conceptual and methodological uncertainty by using two alternative modelling approaches adapted from Baldwin and Cain (1997) to assess the strength of the trade impact on the labour market. The two approaches make assumptions of varying stringency, and consequently shed light on the sensitivity of conclusions to the underlying assumptions.

The first approach investigates the evolution of the relative prices of skilled- versus unskilled-labour-intensive goods and represents a direct test of the trade impact hypothesis. However, the results can be interpreted in a straightforward manner only if certain strong assumptions are satisfied, such as infinitely price-elastic world demand for the domestic output (small-country case) and the instantaneous adjustment of the output mix and factor input ratios to changing relative product and factor prices. The second approach investigates changes in the pattern of trade specialisation to draw conclusions on *relative* factor endowments at home compared with the rest of the world. Additional information is then required to determine what changes in *absolute* endowments at home or abroad (for example, immigration or a growing global supply of unskilled labour) brought about the inferred changes in relative endowments.

In Section 4.2 below, I prepare the ground for the empirical analysis by discussing several conceptual issues that have been raised by recent papers on the link between international trade and the labour market. I start by demonstrating how an increasing global supply of unskilled-labour-intensive goods interacts with technical progress on factor prices and output in a simple HOS model of a small open economy. Specifically, I argue that technical progress should be, and can be, included *explicitly* in the estimated model (Section 4.2.1). I then introduce the econometric approaches used in the analysis (Section 4.2.2). Section 4.3 presents the regression results. Section 4.4 concludes and discusses possible directions for future research.

4.2 CONCEPTUAL ISSUES

4.2.1 Trade, Technical Progress and Factor Prices in a Simple HOS Model

This section discusses the link between trade, technical progress, and factor prices in the framework of a simple 'two-by-two' HOS model for a small open economy. Possible extensions of the model to more realistic dimensions (more than two factors, more goods than factors) will be discussed in section 4.2.2. The small-country assumption means that product prices are determined solely by world demand and supply; this implies infinitely price-elastic demand for the home country's output. The production side of the economy may be described on the basis of the assumption that both factors of production (henceforth to be called unskilled labour and human capital (skilled labour) for convenience) are fully employed. Furthermore, the production functions of both industries (to be called clothing and machinery) are of the Cobb–Douglas type so that factor prices multiplied by factor inputs sum to output in each industry (zero-profit condition). Production of clothing uses unskilled labour more intensively than human capital. Machinery is human-capital-intensive.

In a comparative-static interpretation, the model may be written in relative rates of change and (exogenous) technical progress may be allowed to affect factor input coefficients. (4.1) and (4.2) then describe the difference between two equilibria, assuming that the differences in variables are small:[3]

$$\lambda(\hat{Q}_C - \hat{Q}_M) = (\hat{L} - \hat{H}) + (\pi_L - \pi_H) + \delta(\hat{w}_L - \hat{w}_H) \qquad (4.1)$$

$$\theta(\hat{w}_L - \hat{w}_H) = (\hat{p}_C - \hat{p}_M) + (\pi_C - \pi_M) \qquad (4.2)$$

where

λ, δ, θ	Positive constants (cf. Jones, 1970 for details)
$\hat{x}$	Percentage change in x
Q_C	Clothing output
Q_M	Machinery output
L	Stock of unskilled labour
H	Stock of human capital
w_L	Unskilled wage
w_H	Return to human capital
π_L, π_H	Increase in effective (productivity-adjusted) factor stocks through technical progress
π_C, π_M	Percentage change in total factor productivity through technical progress
p_C, p_M	Price of clothing/machinery

(4.1) and (4.2) show that a decrease in the relative price of clothing in the world market ($\hat{p}_C - \hat{p}_M < 0$) – for example, due to increased supply from developing countries – leads to a new equilibrium that differs from the former in three important ways. First, according to (4.2), the unskilled wage declines relative to the return to human capital: $\hat{w}_H - \hat{w}_L < 0$. Second, according to (4.1), clothing output decreases and machinery output increases. Third, because of the reduction of the unskilled wage, production in both sectors becomes more unskilled-labour-intensive. This is achieved by transferring human capital and unskilled labour from clothing to machinery production in such proportion that in clothing production the amount of human capital is reduced by a greater proportion than unskilled labour and in machinery production the amount of human capital is increased by a smaller proportion than unskilled labour.

Technical progress affects both effective (i.e. productivity-adjusted) factor endowments at the national level (π_L and π_H in (4.1)) and total factor productivity at the sectoral level (π_C and π_M in (4.2)). The impact of technology-induced changes in effective factor endowments ($\pi_L - \pi_H$) is equivalent to changes in actual endowments, e.g. through migration ($\hat{L} - \hat{H}$). The impact of sectoral total factor productivity growth ($\pi_C - \pi_M$) is equivalent to changes in the relative product price ($\hat{p}_C - \hat{p}_M$). Note that if the small-country assumption holds and the economy produces both goods, the relative wage is determined solely by world market product prices and sectoral total factor productivity – changes in effective factor endowments, either through technical progress or through actual changes in stocks, are accommodated through intersectoral factor mobility and changes in the output mix. This is the factor price equalisation theorem emphasised, *inter alia*, by Leamer (1995). Immigration of predominantly unskilled labour ($\hat{L} > \hat{H}$), for example, leads to an increase in clothing production ($\hat{Q}_C > \hat{Q}_M$) in accordance with (4.1), but leaves relative factor prices unaffected (4.2).[4]

These observations explain why the factor content of trade – for example, increasing OECD net imports of unskilled labour in the form of imported manufactures (Wood, 1994) – may not reveal much about the causes of shifts in relative factor prices. If the factor price equalisation theorem holds – as it should as long as the economy is not completely specialised in the production of one good – then the output mix and the amount of trade may change without any change in relative factor prices. It follows that if the entry of developing countries into the international division of labour had a measurable impact on the relative wage, then this must have been transmitted through goods prices, not through trade alone.

Several studies based implicitly on (4.2) seek to identify the effects of trade or of technical progress on relative factor prices, mainly in the USA. Baldwin and Cain (1997) abstract from technical progress and assume that all changes in product prices reflect changes in the international division of labour. Hence they calculate the (hypothetical) changes in relative factor prices that follow from the (given) changes in product prices and compare these to the actual changes in factor prices. Conversely, Leamer (1994) seeks to isolate the impact of technical progress by calculating the (hypothetical) changes in relative factor prices that follow from the (given) rates of total factor productivity growth.

In this chapter, I take the view that technical progress is essentially a world-wide phenomenon. As a first approximation, it can be assumed to occur at similar rates at home and abroad. Hence a firm in an industry with especially rapid technical progress will normally face a declining relative price for its output in the world market; at the same time, however, its production costs per unit of output decline due to the growth in total factor productivity. If we assume further that demand is homothetic, then expenditure shares are constant and a decline in the output price leads to a compensating increase in the quantity demanded. As a result, there may be no need for any reallocation of factors of production and total factor productivity (TFP) growth may have no impact on labour demand after compensating product price changes are accounted for. Quite plausibly, the sum of the relative changes in output prices and total factor productivity may then be looked upon as reflecting the impact of factors other than technical progress on the domestic labour market.[5]

4.2.2   Dimensionality Issues and Econometric Models

For the purpose of the empirical analysis, the two-by-two model in Section 4.1 needs to be replaced by a framework that allows for more than two factors of production and for more goods than factors. To avoid data problems related to the measurement of the stocks of natural resources and agricultural land, the present empirical analysis is limited to broadly defined manufactures, including food processing and metallurgy.[6] Assuming further that all material inputs are freely traded internationally, it is plausible to consider unskilled labour, human and physical capital as the relevant factors of production and to measure output by gross value added.

In a three-factor, multiproduct framework, a country produces a range of goods whose factor intensities are similar to its relative factor endowments ('Leamer triangles').[7] Changes in a country's factor endowments lead to a different output mix, but do not affect factor prices as long as the country produces the same set of goods. This is equivalent to incomplete specialisation in the two-by-two model and applies even when factors of production are not substitutable but used in fixed proportions (Leamer, 1994, p. 11). However, if relative factor endowments change substantially – for example, through sustained human or physical capital accumulation – then the country may produce a different set of goods and relative factor prices may change as a result. This is equivalent to the shift from incomplete to complete specialisation in the two-by-two model.

Even such an extended model predicts that most countries produce a far smaller set of manufactures than they actually do. On the one hand, this may result from non-tradable activities subsumed in some manufacturing sectors. On the other, this observation may reflect the heterogeneity of most manufactures which implies that firms operate under monopolistic competition.[8] Hence, if faced with increasing import pressure, firms may maintain their output prices by specialising in high-value-added product varieties. Even within a given industry, the quality attributes of domestic production may then be very different from those of imports from low-wage countries. Another implication of monopolistic competition is that although the domestic output price may not change in response to increased import competition, firms may still have to reduce their output. Therefore, factors of production need to be reallocated to other sectors and factor prices need to adjust just as in the case of actual output price changes.

Given these conceptual and data-related uncertainties, the present empirical analysis follows the example of Baldwin and Cain (1997) in taking a two-pronged approach. First, the zero-profit condition in a multiindustry framework is used to establish which (hypothetical) changes in factor prices would have been consistent with the changes in product (i.e. value added) prices and TFP over consecutive five-year periods since 1970. This is essentially an extension of (4.2) to a three-factor, multiproduct framework. The zero-profit condition for industry i may be written as

$$p_i = a_{Li}w_L + a_{Hi}w_H + a_{Ki}w_K \qquad (4.3)$$

where

a_{Li}, a_{Hi}, a_{Ki}	Factor input coefficients
w_K	Return to physical capital
i	Industry index

(4.3) may be written in relative rates of change to give the link between product price changes, the growth of TFP, and the implied changes of relative factor prices. Outsourcing may be accounted for by introducing a new input which represents those material inputs or externally purchased services (a_x) which are purchased at the end of the period of observation (i.e. at time 1) to replace activities which were still part of the industry's value-added chain at the beginning of the period of observation (i.e. at time 0).[9] By taking differences and dividing through by p_i we obtain:

$$\hat{p}_l = \sum_k \theta_{kl}^{(0)} \cdot \hat{w}_k + \sum_k \theta_{kl}^{(0)} \hat{a}_{kl} + \sum \theta_{kl}^{(0)} \hat{a}_{kl}\hat{w}_k + a_{xl}^{(1)} \cdot p_x^{(1)} / p_l^{(0)} \qquad (4.4)$$

where
$k = L,H,K$
$\theta_{Li}, \theta_{Hi}, \theta_{Ki}$ Shares of factors of production in gross value added
$\hat{y} = (y^{(1)} - y^{(0)}) / y^{(0)}$.
The change in factor input coefficients may be rewritten as

$$\hat{a}_{ki} = (\hat{R}_{ki} - \hat{Q}_i) / (1 + \hat{Q}_i) \qquad (4.5)$$

where
R_{ki} Input of factor k in production of good i
Q_i Output of good i
It follows that

$$\sum_k \theta_{ki}^{(0)} \hat{a}_{ki} = -\pi_i' \qquad (4.6)$$

with

$$\pi_i' = \left(\hat{Q}_i - \sum_k \theta_{ki}^{(0)}\hat{R}_{ki} \right) / (1 + \hat{Q}_i) \qquad (4.7)$$

Thus defined, π_i' may be interpreted as the growth rate of TFP in the production of product i in discrete time. By substituting (4.7) and (4.5) into (4.4) we obtain:

$$\hat{p}_i + \pi_i' - dv = \sum \hat{w}_k \cdot \theta_{ki}^{(0)} (1 + \hat{a}_{ki}) = \sum \hat{w}_k \cdot \theta_{ki}' \qquad (4.8)$$

with
$\theta_{ki}' = \theta_{ki}^{(0)} (1 + \hat{a}_{ki})$
$dv_i = a_{xi}^{(1)} \cdot p_x^{(1)} / p_i^{(0)}$ (outsourcing)
    (4.8) is written in discrete time because the econometric analysis is based on relative changes in variables over five-year periods that are not necessarily small in the sense that the equivalent of (4.8) in continuous time represents an acceptable approximation. Although (4.8) is an identity, it may not hold exactly in reality for a variety of reasons such as measurement errors, etc.[10] Hence I regress the sums of price changes and TFP growth rates in each sector on factor shares. The resulting coefficients are the hypothetical changes in factor prices that would be consistent with the given product price changes. Furthermore, (4.8) may be rewritten slightly

to obtain a direct estimate of the difference between the rates of change of unskilled wages and of the return to human capital. The econometric model thus becomes

$$\hat{p}_i + \pi_i' - dv_i = \beta_1(\theta_{Li}' + \theta_{Hi}' + \theta_{Ki}') + \beta_2\theta_{Hi}' + \beta_3\theta_{Ki}' + u_i \quad (4.9)$$

where
$\beta_1 = \hat{w}_L$
$\beta_2 = \hat{w}_H - \hat{w}_L$
$\beta_3 = \hat{w}_K - \hat{w}_L$
u_i Error term

A positive and significant estimate of β_2 implies that relative product prices have shifted so as to depress the unskilled wage relative to the return to human capital. To the extent to which domestic value-added price changes result from changes in world (rather than domestic) demand and supply, such a finding would support the trade impact hypothesis. If the estimate of β_2 is not positive and significant, several possible explanations need to be considered. For example, with an inflexible wage structure (as in Germany) and product differentiation, the model may be inappropriate because production and employment rather than product prices adjust to growing competitive pressure from developing country producers. At the same time, the zero-profit condition could still be assumed to hold because domestic prices do not imply a shift in relative factor prices, nor is such a shift actually observed.

With a flexible wage structure (as, increasingly, in the UK) and a growing observed skill differential in wages, the absence of a significant positive β_2 coefficient raises potentially more difficult questions. First, the zero-profit condition may not hold in reality even over the chosen, relative long period of observation, so that output prices can move relatively independently of factor prices. This possible explanation is not very plausible, but would invalidate the analytical approach. Second, there may be serious data or conceptual problems that prevent us from observing the (existing) link between output and factor prices. For example, the calculation of the underlying value-added price indices or the adjustment of price changes for outsourcing may be incorrect. The appropriate response in this case would be a more detailed analysis of relative price changes.

The econometric model in (4.9) may appear counterintuitive because the exogenous variables (world market prices and TFP growth) are on the left-hand side of (4.9) whereas the dependent variables (implied factor price changes) are on the right-hand side. Note, however, that we are interested in finding those values of (β_1, β_2 and β_3) that 'minimise the difference between' (intuitively speaking) the sum of the products on the right-hand side of (4.8) and the sum of changes in product prices and total factor productivity on the left-hand side. This is exactly what the least-squares method does. Furthermore, observations are weighted by each sector's value added to account for the fact that output prices in large sectors have a greater impact on economy-wide factor prices than output prices in small sectors.

An alternative approach to assessing the impact of increasing trade with developing countries on developed country labour markets has also been proposed by Baldwin and Cain (1997). Rather than describing small changes in variables over time, (4.4) may also be thought of as describing small differences in product and factor prices between two countries under autarky (say, between the home country and the Rest of the World (ROW)). Further, it is likely that even under actual trading conditions, product prices are not completely equalised across countries because of transportation costs, product differentiation, etc. In this case, positive net exports of a given sector imply a lower product price at home than abroad under autarky. Relative product prices are related to relative factor prices under autarky and, by implication, to relative factor endowments according to (4.4). Abstracting from possible differences in value-added chains within industries ($dv = 0$) and from technological differences across countries ($\pi_i' = 0$), a cross-section regression of net exports on factor shares should therefore reveal the ranking of relative factor prices under autarky and, by implication, the ranking of relative factor endowments at home and abroad. These considerations lead to the following econometric model:

$$NX_{i,t} = \beta_{L,t}\theta_{Li,t} + \beta_{H,t}\theta_{Hi,t} + \beta_{K,t}\theta_{Ki,t} + u_{i,t} \tag{4.10}$$

(4.10) may be rewritten so that estimated coefficients relate directly to the endowments with human and physical capital relative to unskilled labour (using $\theta_{Li,t} + \theta_{Hi,t} + \theta_{Ki,t} = 1$):

$$NX_{i,t} = \beta_{L,t} + (\beta_{H,t} - \beta_{L,t})\,\theta_{Hi,t} + (\beta_{K,t} - \beta_{L,t})\theta_{Ki,t} + u_{i,t} \tag{4.11}$$

For example, a positive and significant estimate of ($\beta_{H,t} - \beta_{L,t}$) implies that the home country is well endowed with human capital relative to unskilled labour, compared with the rest of the world.

The trade impact hypothesis suggests that, in the industrialised countries, $(\beta_{H,t} - \beta_{L,t})$ increases over time: As the supply of unskilled labour increases in the rest of the world, industrialised countries become *relatively* better endowed with human capital relative to unskilled labour. A similar hypothesis may be formulated for physical capital. Both hypotheses may be tested in a second-stage regression of the form

$$(\beta_{H,t} - \beta_{L,t}) = \alpha_H + \gamma_H T + v_{Ht} \tag{4.12}$$

$$(\beta_{K,t} - \beta_{L,t}) = \alpha_K + \gamma_K T + v_{Kt} \tag{4.13}$$

where
T Time trend $(1970 = 0)$
v_{Ht}, v_{Kt} Error terms
Combining the first and second stages into a variable coefficient model, the econometric model may be written as

$$NX_{i,t} = CONST + D_{71} + \ldots + D_{92} + \alpha_H \theta_{Hi,t} + \gamma_H(T \cdot \theta_{Hi,t})$$
$$+ \alpha_K \theta_{Ki,t} + \gamma_k(T \cdot \theta_{Ki,t}) + z_{it} \tag{4.14}$$

where the variables have the following interpretation:
$z_{i,t}$ Error term
$CONST$ β_L in 1970
$CONST + D_t$ β_L for t later than 1970
α_H $(\beta_H - \beta_L)$ in 1970
γ_H Annual change in $(\beta_H - \beta_L)$
α_K $(\beta_K - \beta_L)$ in 1970
γ_K Annual change in $(\beta_K - \beta_L)$

Thus a positive and significant estimate of γ_H would be consistent with, but would not constitute positive proof of, the trade impact hypothesis. Further information would be needed to assess where the divergence in relative factor endowments between the home country and the rest of the world originated. An increase in the home country's endowment with human capital relative to unskilled labour compared with the rest of the world for example, could result from better education and training at home as well as from a growing stock of unskilled labour in the rest of the world.

The possible advantage of this approach is that it does not rely on observed value-added prices, which may be difficult to interpret, especially in the presence of product differentiation between domestic and foreign goods.

4.3   SECTORAL PRODUCT PRICES AND TRADE PATTERNS IN WEST GERMANY AND THE UK SINCE 1970

4.3.1   Definitions of Variables and Data Sources

The analysis is based on national accounts data for German manufacturing and on the OECD STAN database for UK industry and trade data.[11] Manufacturing is defined widely to include food processing and metallurgy. At this level of aggregation, data are available for roughly 30 industries whose size varies widely. Although it would be desirable to use more disaggregated data (if only for a sensitivity analysis), this is impossible because capital stock data by branch of industry which are required for the calculation of total factor productivity are not available at a lower level of aggregation.

The input of human capital is measured on the basis of the assumption that the compensation received by each person engaged reflects remuneration both for unskilled labour services and for human capital services. Thus my definition of 'human capital' includes formal education as well as training on the job as both are reflected in wages. Alternative definitions of human capital, such as the number of persons engaged with a certain minimum duration of training, take care only of formal education and neglect learning by doing which is potentially equally important. The stock of unskilled labour is therefore defined as the total number of persons engaged. The unskilled wage in West Germany is proxied by two-thirds of the compensation received by a salaried employee without vocational training and with only minimal training on the job. In the UK, the unskilled wage is proxied by the average earnings of the bottom 10 per cent of wage earners. The total remuneration of human capital employed in production is then defined as that portion of employee compensation (adjusted for the hypothetical compensation paid to owner-managers) that exceeds the hypothetical compensation of unskilled labour. The total remuneration of human capital is deflated by the difference between the compensation of highly qualified employees (top 10 per cent of wage earners in the UK) and the hypothetical unskilled wage to obtain a proxy for the volume of human capital employed in production.

Output is defined as gross value added. Accordingly, the compensation of the three factors of production is calculated as follows: for unskilled labour, it is the number of persons engaged times hypothetical compensation; for human capital, total compensation of the persons engaged *minus* the compensation of unskilled labour; for physical capital, the difference between gross value added and the compensation of unskilled labour and human capital. Output prices are value-added prices that relate to the goods actually produced domestically rather than non-competing imports that are no longer produced at home.

4.3.2 Changes in Product Prices and TFP

Tables 4.1 and 4.2 report estimates of (4.9) for West Germany and the UK for consecutive five-year periods since 1970. The regression model according to (4.9) is equivalent to regressing $\hat{p}$ on the adjusted factor income shares (θ'_L, θ'_H and θ'_K), TFP (π') and the outsourcing effect (dv), under the restrictions that the coefficient of π' is equal to (-1) and the coefficient of dv equal to 1.[12] Since both π' and dv are subject to measurement problems, these restrictions are tested explicitly. Model I without either π' or dv provides a point of reference for all the other estimates. A comparison of these results with Model II demonstrates that accounting for the impact of technical progress (π') on output prices affects the estimates of the skill differential ($\hat{w}_H - \hat{w}_L$) considerably. The results of the Wald-test for the estimated coefficient of π' demonstrate that the estimate is often not significantly different from (-1) so that the restriction imposed in Model III appears acceptable.

Similarly, the inclusion of dv influences some estimates considerably (Model IV). However, many of the estimated coefficients of dv deviate considerably from the expected value of 1 (Wald-test). This is unsurprising because dv is only a rough estimate of the extent of outsourcing. Developing more detailed estimates, for example on the basis of input–output tables, therefore appears promising (see Feenstra and Hanson, 1996).

The estimates summarised in Tables 4.1 and 4.2 offer little support for the hypothesis that output price changes adjusted for TFP growth tended to depress the price of unskilled labour relative to human capital. In the case of Germany, significant positive estimates

Table 4.1 Regression results for relative value-added prices: Germany, 1970–91 (weighted least squares)

Period	Model	LHS variable	$\theta'_L + \theta'_H + \theta'_K$ $(\hat{w}_L)$	θ'_H $(\hat{w}_H - \hat{w}_L)$	θ'_K $(\hat{w}_K - \hat{w}_L)$	π'	dv	Wald-test[a] (F-statistic)	$\bar{R}^2$ (weighted)[b]	Mean of dep. variable (un-weighted)
1970–5	I	$\hat{p}$	-0.13	0.71	0.58				0.89***	0.28
	II	$\hat{p}$	0.51*	-0.03	-0.29	-1.27***		1.5	0.95***	0.28
	III	$(\hat{p} + \pi)$	0.38	0.13	-0.10	-1.09***			0.94***	0.33
	IV	$\hat{p}$	0.10	0.84**	-0.05		1.30***	0.8	0.97***	0.28
	V	$(\hat{p} + \pi + dv)$	0.13	0.72**	0.07				0.97***	0.33
1975–80	I	$\hat{p}$	0.23	-0.04	0.02				0.76***	0.21
	II	$\hat{p}$	0.52**	-0.44	-0.18	-0.84***		0.7	0.85***	0.21
	III	$(\hat{p} + \pi)$	0.58***	-0.51	-0.22	-0.86***			0.90***	0.27
	IV	$\hat{p}$	0.53***	-0.44	-0.20		0.07	2.5	0.85***	0.21
	V	$(\hat{p} + \pi + dv)$	0.64***	-0.47	-0.36				0.91***	0.26
1980–5	I	$\hat{p}$	-0.09	0.50***	0.25**				0.93***	0.14
	II	$\hat{p}$	-0.11	0.61***	0.28***	-0.36***		60.1***	0.95***	0.14
	III	$(\hat{p} + \pi)$	-0.15	0.79***	0.33**	-0.42***			0.93***	0.23
	IV	$\hat{p}$	-0.06	0.49***	0.23***		0.29***	44.7***	0.96***	0.14
	V	$(\hat{p} + \pi + dv)$	0.03	0.31	0.16				0.88***	0.17

1985–91								
I	$\hat{p}$	0.76**	−1.18**	−0.24				0.74***	0.17
II	$\hat{p}$	0.68***	−0.75***	−0.39***	−1.18***		2.4	0.94***	0.17
III	$(\hat{p} + \pi)$	0.69***	−0.82***	−0.37**				0.90***	0.28
IV	$\hat{p}$	0.68***	−0.76***	−0.40***	−1.18***	0.09	21.6***	0.94***	0.17
V	$(\hat{p} + \pi + dv)$	0.64**	−0.76*	−0.33				0.72***	0.28

Notes:

***, **, * Significantly different from 0 at the $\alpha = 0.01$, $\alpha = 0.05$, $\alpha = 0.10$ level.

[a] Tests the hypothesis that the coefficient of π' is equal to (−1) and that the coefficient of dv (Model (V)) is equal to 1.

[b] The significance level relates to the F-test of the hypothesis that all coefficients are jointly 0.

Source: Data, see text; own calculations.

Table 4.2 Regression results for relative value-added prices: UK, 1970–89 (weighted least squares)

Period	Model	LHS variable	RHS variables					Wald-test[a] (F-statistic)	$\bar{R}^2$ (weighted)[b]	Mean of dep. variable (un-weighted)
			$\theta'_L + \theta'_H + \theta'_K$ ($\hat{w}_L$)	θ'_H ($\hat{w}_H - \hat{w}_L$)	θ'_K ($\hat{w}_K - \hat{w}_L$)	π'	dv			
1970–5	I	$\hat{p}$	1.11*	−0.25	−0.61				0.87***	1.02
	II	$\hat{p}$	0.88	0.05	−0.46	−0.80		0.2	0.88***	1.02
	III	$(\hat{p} + \pi)$	0.82	0.13	−0.42				0.86***	1.01
	IV	$\hat{p}$	1.04**	−0.12	−0.74	−1.69***	0.69***	4.8**	0.91***	1.02
	V	$(\hat{p} + \pi + dv)$	1.42**	−0.61	−1.08				0.90***	1.00
1975–80	I	$\hat{p}$	1.08***	0.10	−0.08				0.97***	1.05
	II	$\hat{p}$	1.20***	−0.18	−0.18	−0.83**	0.3		0.98***	1.05
	III	$(\hat{p} + \pi)$	1.23***	−0.24	−0.20				0.97***	1.08
	IV	$\hat{p}$	0.86***	0.41	0.17	−0.91***	0.92***	0.2	0.99***	1.05
	V	$(\hat{p} + \pi + dv)$	0.84***	0.43*	0.19				0.99***	1.05
1980–85	I	$\hat{p}$	−0.44*	1.39***	0.97***				0.88***	0.30
	II	$\hat{p}$	−0.24	1.16**	0.65	−0.22		9.1***	0.91***	0.49
	III	$(\hat{p} + \pi)$	0.50*	0.33	−0.14				0.88***	0.30
	IV	$\hat{p}$	−0.28	1.20**	0.65	−0.06	−0.30	3.8**	0.88***	0.30
	V	$(\hat{p} + \pi + dv)$	0.13	0.75*	0.39				0.89***	0.48

1985–89								
I	$\hat{p}$	0.19	−0.06	0.17			0.82***	0.16
II	$\hat{p}$	0.17	0.15	0.13			0.83***	0.16
III	$(\hat{p} + \pi)$	0.15	0.48	0.07	−0.40	6.2**	0.90***	0.33
IV	$\hat{p}$	0.12	0.39	0.24	−1.00***	0.56***	0.91***	0.16
V	$(\hat{p} + \pi + dv)$	0.10	0.32	0.38*		9.8***	0.92***	0.31

Notes:

***, **, * Significantly different from 0 at the $\alpha = 0.01$, $\alpha = 0.05$, $\alpha = 0.10$ level.

[a] Tests the hypothesis that the coefficient of π' is equal to (-1) and that the coefficient of dv (Model (V)) is equal to 1.

[b] The significance level relates to the F-test of the hypothesis that all coefficients are jointly 0.

Source: Data, see text; own calculations.

of $(\hat{w}_H - \hat{w}_L)$ that are not sensitive to model specification are found only for the 1980–5 period. The coefficient for the 1970–5 period becomes significant only for Models IV and V. Quite unexpectedly, a significant, robust, negative estimate of $(\hat{w}_H - \hat{w}_L)$ is obtained for the 1985–91 period. If the trade impact hypothesis were correct, however, the estimates of $(\hat{w}_H - \hat{w}_L)$ should be consistently positive throughout the 1970s and 1980s.

The econometric analysis of trade specialisation in the following section can be expected to shed light on the question of whether the present, indifferent finding is due to widespread monopolistic competition with inflexible wage structures that causes quantities, rather than prices to adjust. Besides, it is conceivable that the very high absolute values of the estimates of $(\hat{w}_H - \hat{w}_L)$ for the 1980–5 and 1985–91 periods result from collinearity among the explanatory variables (about which nothing can be done, given the structure of the econometric model). For example, the estimates for 1980–5 imply that the return to human capital should have increased by 50 to 70 percentage points *more* than the unskilled wage, whereas the sum of product prices and TFP rose only by little more than 20 per cent during the same period. To the extent to which the estimates are affected by multicollinearity, few conclusions can be drawn either from the positive values for 1980–5 or from the negative ones for 1985–91.

In the case of the UK, significant positive estimates of $(\hat{w}_H - \hat{w}_L)$ are found for the 1980–5 period (Models I, II, IV, V) and for the 1975–80 period (Model V only). Even for the 1980–5 period, however, the coefficient estimates of the factor income shares do not appear very robust because their size varies widely. Furthermore, this is the only period for which all coefficients of π' and dv are insignificant. Again, this may be due to collinearity among the explanatory variables or other special factors that permit few conclusions to be drawn from these findings.

It seems noteworthy, nevertheless, that for the 1980s, nearly all estimates of $(\hat{w}_H - \hat{w}_L)$ are positive (though insignificant for the 1985–9 period), whereas for the 1970s the picture is very mixed in each subperiod. This is consistent with the evolution of the skill differential in UK earnings (top decile over bottom decile) which remained fairly constant during the 1970s but has risen markedly since the early 1980s. More detailed studies of sectoral price developments and of the precise form of outsourcing need to be undertaken to confirm the link between changes in value-added prices (corrected for TFP growth and outsourcing) and the rising skill differential since 1980. Furthermore, more analysis is needed to assess the extent to which changes in output prices, TFP, and the extent of outsourcing can be attributed to growing trade with low-income countries rather than to domestic developments. With these weighty qualifications, the findings are at least consistent with the hypothesis that UK value-added prices have moved to depress unskilled wages at least partly in response to growing trade with lower-income countries.

4.3.3 Changes in Net Exports and Factor Prices

Estimates of (4.14) are presented in Table 4.3. In addition to normalising net exports by the sum of exports and imports in each sector (*NNX*), I follow the example of Baldwin and Cain (1997) in normalising net exports also by output in each sector (*NXP*). The use of alternative measures of specialisation in international trade is justified because there is no one correct measure, and the available measures may point in different directions (Ballance, Forstner and Murray, 1987). Furthermore, it turned out that the coefficients of the dummy variables (D71, . . ., D92) in (4.14) change fairly monotonically. For simplicity, they are therefore replaced by a time trend without much change in the explanatory power of the model. As in the previous section, the factor income shares relate only to direct factor use in each industry. This is acceptable under the assumption that a cost advantage reflected in positive net exports arises not from access to cheap material inputs but within the value-added chain of the particular industry (and vice versa). This will be the case, for example, when inputs are traded internationally.

Estimates of (4.14) differ substantially between Germany and the UK. The negative coefficient of $(\theta_H T)$ for both specifications of net exports indicates that West Germany has specialised *away* from industries with a high share of human capital in value added. Apart from being statistically significant, this coefficient is also of considerable magnitude. In the case of the *NNX* dependent variable, θ_H declines from approximately 6.6 in 1970 to 1.1 in 1992; in the case of *NXP*, θ_H declines from approximately 2.8 to 1.0 during the same period. Similarly, West Germany has specialised away from sectors with a high share of physical capital in value added. This finding implies that human capital per head in Germany (or, more precisely, the stock of human capital relative to the stock of unskilled

Table 4.3   Regression results for changes in net exports: West Germany and UK, 1970–92 (weighted least squares)

Explanatory variable	Germany		UK	
	NNX	NXP	NNX	NXP
constant	−3.01***	−1.31***	−0.72***	−0.17*
time trend (T)	0.03***	0.04***	−0.09***	−0.04***
θ_H	6.59***	2.83***	3.10***	1.07***
$\theta_H * T$	-0.25***	-0.08***	0.05	0.02
θ_K	2.24***	1.08***	0.18	−0.08
$\theta_K * T$	−0.12***	−0.04***	0.10***	0.05***
$\bar{R}^{2a}$	0.79***	0.81***	0.35***	0.30***
N	736	736	736	736

Notes:
***, **, * Significantly different from 0 at the $\alpha = 0.01$, $\alpha = 0.05$, $\alpha = 0.10$ level.
[a] The significance level relates to an F-test of the hypothesis that all coefficients are jointly 0.

Source: Data, see text; own calculations.

labour) has *declined* relative to the rest of the world. This result contradicts the trade impact hypothesis which implies that trade patterns reflect an increase in the global availability of unskilled labour; if this were the case, human capital per head in Germany should have *increased* relative to the rest of the world.

In the UK, there is no change in the degree of specialisation on human-capital-intensive sectors, as indicated by the insignificant coefficient of ($\theta_H T$). When dummy variables (D71, ..., D92) are included in the model to replace the time trend, the positive coefficient of ($\theta_H T$) even becomes statistically significant at the 5 per cent level for the NXP (but not for the NNX) dependent variable. Furthermore, the UK has clearly become more specialised in physical-capital-intensive sectors (significant positive coefficients of ($\theta_K T$)).

The validity of this analysis might be called into question on the grounds that the sectoral data are highly aggregated. It is conceivable that particularly German firms have specialised in relatively sophisticated (i.e. human-capital-intensive) products or product varieties in a broad range of industries. At the same time, the imports of these sectors, especially from lower-income countries, consist of much less sophisticated products. At a high level of sectoral aggregation, such trade would appear as intra-industry trade and would be 'netted out' when net exports (*NNX* or *NXP*) are calculated. Substantially, however, such trade would be of the HOS type in the sense that the human capital intensities of exports and imports differ considerably and different factor endowments of producer countries are the cause of this trade.

Streeck (1997) provides extensive circumstantial evidence that the 'West German model of capitalism' was characterised precisely by relatively high wages and 'niche production' – that is, production of sophisticated product varieties. Furthermore, in a slightly different context, Klodt and Maurer (1995) argue that Germany is more strongly specialised in human-capital-intensive, high-technology products than aggregate sectoral data suggest. Hence it is certainly possible that the decline in θ_H in the case of Germany would be less pronounced if the regressions were run on more deeply disaggregated data. However, the present findings for Germany would have to be reversed for the results to be compatible with the trade impact hypothesis, which I find unlikely.

If the present findings are accepted as essentially correct (in direction if not in degree), the different performances of Germany and the UK need to be explained. As regards changes in factor endowments abroad, competition may have increased not only in relatively labour-intensive industries due to the integration of lower-income countries into the international division of labour, but also in relatively human-capital-intensive industries because of the growing weight of Newly Industrialising Countries (NICs). This could explain why we do not find the expected shift into human-capital-intensive industries. Furthermore, depending on their specialisation in particular human-capital-intensive industries, West German firms might have felt increasing competition from newly industrialising and also from less advanced industrialised countries more keenly than UK firms. This may have been the case especially in engineering industries where relatively small German firms have traditionally held a strong position in many world market segments.

Apart from changes in factor endowments abroad, differences between Germany and the UK in the evolution of domestic factor endowments may also have affected the respective patterns of specialisation in trade. In particular, Germany experienced large-scale immigration during the 1980s that probably included a relatively large number of people with less-than-average skills. The resulting increase in the supply of 'unskilled' labour may have affected the (market-clearing) relative wage of unskilled labour – if, as is plausible, demand for German products was not infinitely price-elastic as implied by the small-country assumption. A similar effect may result from labour-saving technical progress that affects industrialised countries more strongly than developing ones and increases the productivity-adjusted stock of unskilled labour faster than the productivity-adjusted stock of human capital ($\pi_L > \pi_H$ in (4.1)). Further investigation is necessary on how such labour-saving technical progress can be measured and whether it is plausible to assume that it affects predominantly industrialised countries.

4.4   CONCLUSIONS

The regression results reported in Sections 4.2 and 4.3 fail to identify a single, main cause of the deteriorating position of unskilled labour in West Germany and in the UK. This raises the question of whether an explanation should not be sought outside the applied model. For example, growing unemployment of the (relatively) unskilled may arise when hysteresis plays a larger role in perpetuating unemployment among this group than in the case of skilled workers. Similarly, declining relative wages of the least-skilled compared with the highest-skilled group as in the UK might reflect an increasing divergence of skills in the two groups, rather than a diverging remuneration of certain given skills. However, there is little evidence that such supply-side factors in the labour market can explain the deteriorating position of relatively unskilled labour.

If an explanation is sought within the realm of the model, the preceding discussion suggests several directions for refining the analysis that may lead to less equivocal findings. First, the small-country assumption may be dropped and an attempt may be made to quantify the impact of labour-saving technical progress. Berman, Machin and Bound (1996) find pervasive skill upgrading in a wide variety of industries and countries and conclude that technical progress, rather than trade, must have been responsible for the implied decrease in demand for unskilled labour. If the Stolper–Samuelson effect related to trade had dominated, production should have become less, not more skill-intensive. A preliminary screening of the data used in the present chapter finds evidence of skill upgrading for the UK, but not for Germany. Extending this analysis to a larger number of countries would shed more light on this issue.

Second, applying the models used in Sections 4.3.2 and 4.3.3 to a larger number of countries would provide additional information on how national institutions, for example in the labour market, affect the results. Specification tests may also be undertaken to check for the sensitivity of findings to the level of sectoral aggregation, the period of observation, the use of value added rather than producer, wholesale or foreign trade prices, and the measurement of human capital.

Third, the price model used in this analysis (Section 4.3.2) may be modified to account more carefully for the outsourcing of labour-intensive processes to low-wage countries. Pioneering work in this area is undertaken by Feenstra and Hanson (1996). This approach would require the use of the value of production, rather than value added, as a measure of output. At a practical level, this would entail a change in the main data source from national accounts or industry statistics to input output tables datasets. Chapter 7 (by Anderton and Brenton) in this volume provides an analysis along these lines.

Such extensions to the present model may complement studies on the basis of computable general equilibrium CGE models such as by Cortes and Jean and Nahuis (Chapters 5 and 6) in this volume. Compared with econometric studies such as the present one, CGE models offer the possibility of explicitly accounting for general equilibrium effects such as changes in productivity-adjusted factor endowments through technical progress, and of testing for the sensitivity of findings to important underlying assumptions, such as substitution elasticities in demand as well as production. Further information may be provided by studies based on household or employee data that make it possible to link the earnings and employment experience of a large number of individuals to characteristics of the industries in which they work (cf. Aiginger, Winter-Ebner and Zweimüller, 1996).

This discussion demonstrates that the causes of the deteriorating position of the unskilled in terms of relative wages and unemployment are not only relevant from the point of view of developing policies to counter the ensuing social exclusion of significant segments of the population. The debate also raises a variety of conceptual and methodological questions about the way economists think about structural change across as well as within industries.

In this sense, the growing trade between Europe and East Asia is only a part, however important, of the larger picture of the globalisation of production and markets that presents firms, policy makers and research economists with new challenges as well as opportunities.

Notes

* This chapter reports on research funded by the Volkswagen Foundation under a project entitled 'Perspectives for the Division of Labour between Germany and Central European Transition countries'. Earlier versions have been presented at seminars in Kiel, Halle, Brussels and at the 1996 Annual Congress of the European Economic Association in Istanbul. Comments from many seminar participants as well as from Markus Diehl, Erich Gundlach, Rolf J. Langhammer, Martin Raiser, Viktor Steiner and Thomas Ziesemer are gratefully acknowledged. As usual, I am responsible for all errors.

1. For example, the ratio of the highest decile of earnings of men in the UK over the lowest decile fluctuated around 2.4 throughout the 1970s but increased markedly during the 1980s to reach 3.2 in 1992 (Central Statistical Office, *Annual Abstract of Statistics*, various issues). In West Germany, the unemployment rate for workers without formal vocational training rose from close to 0 in 1970 to 7.4 per cent in 1975 and further to around 15 per cent in the early 1990s. During the same period, the unemployment rate for workers with vocational training or tertiary education only rose to 5 per cent (Paqué, 1994).

2. A full summary of this literature until the mid-1990s is provided by Burtless (1995) and by a symposium in the *Journal of Economic Perspectives* (Freeman, 1995; Richardson, 1995; Wood, 1995). Important recent contributions include Baldwin and Cain (1997), Feenstra and Hanson (1997), Leamer (1996), Oscarsson (1996) and Sachs and Schatz (1996).

3. For the derivation, see Jones (1965, 1970); a fuller description of the model is contained in Lücke (1992). (4.1) and (4.2) reflect the Rybczinski and Stolper-Samuelson theorems, respectively.

4. Factor endowments affect factor prices only in the case of *complete* specialisation where all factors have moved into the production of one good and production of the other good has ceased. In that case, the full employment assumption requires factor prices to adjust such that all factors are employed in the one remaining industry in the proportion in which they are nationally available.

5. In a more recent paper, Leamer (1996) makes several alternative assumptions about the extent to which changes in TFP are passed through to product prices. Oscarsson (1996) uses a procedure similar to mine in her analysis of trade and relative wages in Sweden.

6. Lücke (1992) discusses the implications of this limitation in greater detail. In the case of Germany, the wide definition of manufactures that is used in the empirical analysis covers 98 per cent of German exports and 89 per cent of German imports in 1995. The labour market impact of imports from developing countries should therefore have been transmitted through the portion of trade covered in the analysis. In the case of the UK with its growing oil exports since the late 1970s, one may expect that the resulting real appreciation has affected domestic factor demand because of the induced shift of resources from the production of tradables to non-tradables. However, a strong impact of developing country imports on labour demand should still be felt in the prices of tradable goods or in the sectoral pattern of trade specialisation, independent of the level of output of tradable goods. Quite remarkably, while resources moved into (potentially unskilled-labour-intensive) services, the ratio of the highest over the lowest decile of weekly earnings among men in the UK increased from approximately 2.5 in the early 1980s to approximately 3.2 in the early 1990s.

7. Leamer (1995) presents a recent summary of such a three-factor, multiproduct framework.

8. Trefler (1995) finds that global trade patterns reflect consumer preferences in favour of domestic products (in the sense of the Armington assumption) as well as higher TFP in the advanced industrialised countries.

9. In the empirical analysis, $dv = a_{xi}^{(1)} \cdot p_x^{(1)} / p_i^{(0)}$ was initially estimated from the change in the share of gross value added (VA) in the value of production (VP):

$$dv = (VA^{(0)} / VP^{(0)} \cdot VP^{(1)} - VA^{(1)}) / VA^{(0)}$$

However, it turned out that the share of physical capital (estimated as the difference between gross value added and employee compensation) was subject to substantial cyclical fluctuations. Employee compensation was ultimately therefore used instead of gross value added.

10. (4.8) is based upon the zero-profit condition which may not hold exactly at each point in time, for reasons, such as, limited factor mobility across sectors in the short-run and measurement errors.

11. Capital stock data for the UK have kindly been provided by Mary O'Mahoney of the National Institute of Economic and Social Research, London.

12. Subindex i is suppressed from now on for simplicity.

References

Aiginger, K., Winter-Ebmer, R. and Zweimüller, J. (1996) 'Eastern European trade and the Austrian labour market', *Weltwirtschaftliches Archiv*, 123, 476–500.

94   *Trade with Low-Income Countries: West Germany & UK*

Baldwin, R. and Cain, G. (1997) 'Trade and US relative wages: preliminary results', *Working Paper*, 5934, NBER.
Ballance, R., Forstner, H. and Murray, T. (1987) 'Consistency tests of alternative measures of comparative advantage', *Review of Economics and Statistics*, 69, 157–61.
Berman, E., Machin, S. and Bound, J. (1996) 'Implications of skill-biased technological change: international evidence', Department of Economics, Boston University, mimeo.
Burtless, G. (1995) 'International trade and the rise in earnings inequality', *Journal of Economic Literature*, 33, 800–816.
Cortes, O. and Jean, S. (1996) 'Pays émergents, emploi déficient?', *Document de Travail* 96-05, CEPII.
Feenstra, R. and Hanson, G. (1996) 'The exact measurement of productivity, outsourcing and its impact on wages: estimates for the US, 1972–1990', Department of Economics, University of California, Davis/Department of Economics, University of Texas, Austin, mimeo.
Freeman, R. (1995) 'Are your wages set in Beijing?', *Journal of Economic Perspectives*, 9, 15–23.
Jones, R. (1965) 'The structure of simple general equilibrium models', *Journal of Political Economy*, 73, 557–72.
Jones, R. (1970) 'The role of technology in the theory of international trade', in Vernon, R. (ed.), *The Technology Factor in International Trade*, New York: Columbia University Press, 73–94.
Klodt, H. and Maurer, R. (1995) 'Determinants of the capacity to innovate: is Germany losing its competitiveness in high-tech industries?' in Siebert, H. (ed.), *Locational Competition in the World Economy*, Tübingen: Mohr, 137–62.
Lawrence, R. and Slaughter, M. (1993) 'International trade and American wages in the 1980s: giant sucking sound or small hiccup?', *Brookings Papers on Economic Activity: Microeconomics*, 2, 161–226.
Leamer, E. (1993) 'Wage effects of a US-Mexican free trade agreement', in Garber, P. (ed.), *The Mexico–US Free Trade Agreement*, Cambridge, MA: MIT Press, 57–125.
Leamer, E. (1994) 'Trade, wages and revolving door ideas', *Working Paper*, 4716, NBER.
Leamer, E. (1995) 'The Heckscher–Ohlin model in theory and practice', *Princeton Studies in International Finance*, 77.
Leamer, E. (1996) 'In search of Stolper–Samuelson effects on US wages', *Working Paper*, 5427, NBER.
Lücke, M. (1992) *Technischer Fortschritt und die Arbeitsteilung zwischen Industrie- und Entwicklungsländern*, Kieler Studien, 247, Tübingen Mohr.
Oscarsson, E. (1996) 'Trade and relative wages in Sweden 1968–91', Department of Economics, Stockholm University, mimeo.
Paqué, K. (1994) 'Structural unemployment and real wage rigidity in Germany', *Habilitationsschrift*, Kiel University.
Richardson, J.D. (1995) 'Income inequality and trade: how to think, what to conclude', *Journal of Economic Perspectives*, 9, 33–56.
Sachs, J. and Shatz, H. (1996) 'US trade with developing countries and wage inequality', *American Economic Review*, 86, 234–9.

Streeck, W. (1997) 'German capitalism: does it exist? Can it survive?', in Crouch, C. and Streeck, W. (eds), *Political Economy and Modern Capitalism: Mapping Convergence and Diversity* London: Sage.

Trefler, D. (1995) 'The case of the missing trade and other mysteries', *American Economic Review*, 85, 1029–46.

Wood, A. (1994) *North–South Trade, Employment and Inequality*, Oxford: Clarendon Press.

Wood, A. (1995) 'How trade hurt unskilled workers', *Journal of Economic Perspectives*, 9, 57–80.

5 Does Competition from Emerging Countries Threaten Unskilled Labour in Europe? An Applied General Equilibrium Approach

Olivier Cortes and Sébastien Jean*

5.1 INTRODUCTION

The growing role played by a number of developing countries in the world economy has greatly affected international trade in manufacturing products over the last 20 years. This phenomenon is likely to be accentuated by the rapid growth of demographic giants, such as, China and Indonesia. In this chapter we present an analysis of the future impact of this phenomenon on European labour markets using an applied general equilibrium model.

Following discussion of the background to this work, in Section 5.2, we briefly describe the model, which covers the European Community (EC), a Rest of the World (ROW) zone, and the emerging countries, in Section 5.3. These economies are broken down into 13 industries, of which 11 are manufacturing sectors. Three production factors are also used – capital, skilled labour and unskilled labour. Goods are differentiated, using various levels of substitutability. Thus, goods produced by emerging countries are perceived by consumers to be of a different nature to those produced in the developed countries. Unlike the other computable general equilibrium (CGE) models presented in this volume, we allow for imperfect competition in the manufacturing sectors, with economies of scale and oligopolistic competition *à la* Cournot. Depending on the industry, adjustment to changes in market

96

conditions occurs via the number of firms and their size.

The reference scenario considered here is based on a doubling of the relative size of the emerging countries. The results generated by the model from this shock are reported in Section 5.4. Although the structure of the model is largely based on new theories of international trade, we show that a traditional Stolper–Samuelson effect is dominant in the reference scenario. We then proceed, in Section 5.5, to provide a comprehensive assessment of the robustness of the results, a crucial element of simulation exercises such as this, and infer that the main results are unaffected by changes in assumptions regarding key parameters.

The main conclusion, presented Section, 5.6, is that the scale of the economic effects in response to the shock from the emerging countries is small. This reflects the strength of mechanisms which restrain the impact of the growth of the emerging countries, including product differentiation, sectoral entry barriers, general equilibrium constraints, and long-term trade balance constraints.

5.2 BACKGROUND

The nature of international exchange of manufactured products has overwhelmingly changed over the last 20 years. Until the beginning of the 1970s participants in international trade could be split into two separate camps: the Northern industrial countries, who exported manufacturing goods, and the Southern developing countries, who exported primary goods. Moreover, the largest part of trade occurred between the Northern countries. The emerging countries, located throughout Asia, but also in Latin America and around the Mediterranean Sea, have subsequently changed the colonial division of labour, which was previously the dominant model.

The level of wealth of these countries is still lower than that of most of the developed countries but their share in international trade has grown significantly. In 1993, 19 per cent of the exports of manufactured goods of OECD countries were destined for emerging countries, compared with 11 per cent in 1967. Over the same period, the share of OECD countries' imports of manufactured goods which came from emerging countries increased fivefold, reaching 18 per cent in 1993.

There are several reasons for the emergence of these countries. Low wages and political stability have provided for sustained export-oriented policies and enabled these areas to attract international investment. Some labour-intensive and export oriented industries, such as clothing, have been developed. These economies have also moved upstream in the production chain of products such as textiles, and have also diversified into new, more advanced product areas, as witnessed by their rapid progress in electronics.

This development is likely to spread, because of the very large number of aspiring countries. The weight of this kind of country in the world economy will increase. At the same time, there are many questions being asked about the role played by these countries in the observed shifts in the labour markets of industrialised countries.[1] Many studies assume a link between this additional supply of unskilled labour at low wages from the emerging countries and the increase in inequalities between skilled and unskilled labour in the industrialised countries. The theoretical issues of this debate are well-known, but an accurate empirical assessment of the precise effects of such a development is difficult. It is an important issue because of the fear expressed by some of the emergence of new competitors with large populations, such as China, whose share of world exports of manufactured goods remained insignificant for a long time, but increased from 0.8 per cent in 1985 to more than 3 per cent in 1993. The purpose of our study is to assess the economic impact of such a trend.

Analysis of this issue is often retrospective, within a partial equilibrium framework. In this paper we analyse the role of emerging economies using an applied general equilibrium model. This provides for an approach well suited to this problem, and is able to address key aspects of the question which the partial approach cannot tackle. Imports depend on exports and vary with trade prices. A general equilibrium model takes into account the long-term trade balance constraint, and also issues such as the impact of changes in prices on consumers' welfare, on the production decisions of firms, and on the degree of competition in markets. Lastly, both supply and demand are explicitly modelled using this tool. Nevertheless, exercises of this sort have well known limitations. Our study is not dynamic: it provides only a static comparative simulation. Moreover, some macroeconomic issues – the sustainability of growth, the allocation of savings, and the path between two equilibria – are not covered by our analysis. Indeed, our model makes a comparison between two long-term equilibria: we assume that costs of adjustment and disequilibria are just transitory.

5.3 THE MODEL[2]

5.3.1 The Shock

The shock we analyse with our model stems from the high growth of the share of emerging countries in world trade. *A priori*, three issues could be related to this development:

Trade Restrictions are Liberalised

This classical shock is not analysed in this chapter. Reducing trade tariffs would lead to an increase in OECD imports from emerging countries We believe that actual trade liberalisation is insufficient to explain the relatively large size of recent shifts.

Features to be Explained

The main features that must be explained are the very fast growth of these countries, the level of inward investment,[3] and the fact that a significant share of the active population leaves under-employment or goes from the primary sector to the manufacturing sector.[4] The accumulation of production factors is the main characteristic of growth in these countries: the capital stock increases by accumulation or by international transfer, unskilled labour increases by reduction of employment in traditional industries and skilled labour increases due to education. The hypothesis of this work is that the impact of the growth of each of these three factors of production is identical. We assume that the shares of each factor of production in total factor endowments remains unchanged in emerging countries, but the total quantity grows. This lets us maintain the specific status of emerging countries, a relative abundance of unskilled labour, while their size increases. This hypothesis provides the reference shock in our modelling exercise.

Higher Productivity Gains

Higher productivity gains for emerging countries, through technological catch-up, can also explain their increasing role in world trade. This is a dynamic phenomenon which is very hard to treat in a static comparative simulation exercise. However, productivity gains can be taken into account through growth of the endowment of production factors. The shift from unemployment to employment leads to very high growth in the average productivity of the country, even if growth in productivity remains rather low for each employed person. The size of the emerging countries may double because of a doubling of their endowment of production factors or because of a doubling of their productivity: the impact for Europe is the same in both cases. The only possible difference between the two simulations depends upon the evolution of wages in emerging countries. Indeed, a doubling of productivity leads in the long term to a doubling in the level of wealth. But both simulations provide identical prices (unit values) for goods coming from emerging countries and sold to the European consumer or the European producer. As trade is the only transmission link of the shock to Europe, the effects of both simulations are identical.

5.3.2 Supply and Demand

The traditional Heckscher–Ohlin–Samuelson (HOS) approach can be used to show the implications of a shock emanating from an increase in the stock of production factors in the South. For the South, the dominant effect is an increase in overall wealth, with all production factors benefiting. For the North, the Stolper–Samuelson theorem[5] shows that the relative prices of unskilled-labour-intensive goods decrease and that the real wage of unskilled labour falls.[6] But we believe that the assumptions underlying the HOS framework are not realistic enough, even for describing trade between Europe and the emerging countries.

Firstly, the HOS assumptions that production functions, and hence technology, are the same in both developed countries and emerging countries, and that traded goods from one area are identical to those from any other area, are not tenable.[7] Consumers have a love for variety and they differentiate goods by their origin. In addition to tariff and non-tariff barriers, distribution and after-sales networks further explain why products entering markets are differentiated by their place of origin. Finally, for some industries, the effects of size, economies of scale and market structure, which are not provided for in the standard HOS model, are very important. Our approach to modelling supply and demand attempts to take into account all of these issues.

The Armington hypothesis is a convenient way to take into account the imperfect substitutability between domestic goods and foreign goods. The elasticity of substitution determines the changes in relative demand resulting from a change in relative prices between domestic goods and imported goods. These elasticities of substitution are taken from econometric estimates, which assess shifts in market shares resulting from changes in relative prices. We distinguish two sorts of goods, those which come from developed countries and those from emerging countries.

The Armington hypothesis provides a general rule for the way consumers choose between goods but does not explain the grounds of this choice. A frequently used specification of consumer choice between different varieties of the same good is given by the Dixit–Stiglitz function. All the varieties of a given good are treated on the same level, whatever the country or the firm they are produced by. There is a constant elasticity of substitution, so that the degree of substitutability is the same for every pair of varieties: there is no good or bad substitute nor are there neighbourhood effects. The only difference comes from initial market shares according to geographical origin.

Consumer demand is modelled as a sequence of choices (see Figure 5.1). Take, for example, a European consumer. He/she allocates income between several major categories of goods, according to the hypothesis that the income shares for each type of good remain constant. For a given type of good, consumers choose between goods coming from developed countries and those coming from emerging countries, according to their relative prices. The value of the elasticity of substitution specifies this choice. Lastly, the consumer chooses between varieties of European goods or goods coming from emerging countries, according to the Dixit–Stiglitz formula.

5.3.3 Production Factors and Economies of Scale

Competition between emerging countries and developed countries may influence the wage differential between skilled and unskilled labour. Moreover, the evolution of specialisation depends upon the relative abundance of capital. Three production factors are distinguished in the model: capital, skilled labour and unskilled labour. 'Unskilled labour' covers manual workers. 'Skilled labour' groups together workshop foremen, executives and professional staff. These two bundles of workers are frequently used because they correspond to two well defined statistical categories. The production hierarchy is shown in Figure 5.2.

Figure 5.1   Consumer demand

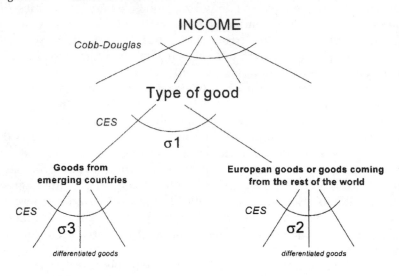

Figure 5.2   Production function

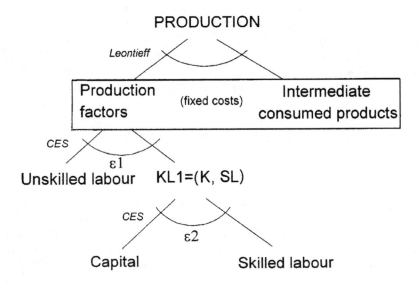

Intermediate goods and the three production factors are combined in production. In the model substitutability between intermediate goods and production factors is low and is not of direct relevance for the problems we are interested in. We assume the intermediate goods aggregate and an aggregate of the three production factors to be perfectly complementary (and therefore that they are combined using a Leontief function).

The factors of production are then split into two groups, since empirical studies generally indicate that substitutability between skilled labour and capital is lower than that between these two factors and unskilled labour.[8] This results from the key features of technical progress over the last 20 years. Automation and computerisation have tended to make capital complementary to skilled labour as production tools have become more and more complex to use. The development of information technologies should entail that this trend will continue for a considerable time. The choice of a low degree of substitutability between skilled labour and capital is thus justifiable.

So at a lower level of the production hierarchy capital and skilled labour, which have little substitutability, are grouped together. The aggregate for all the production factors is then obtained at a higher level by grouping this first bundle with unskilled labour, between which there is a higher degree of substitutability. Production factors are internationally immobile, but perfectly mobile between industries within a country. Economies of scale internal to the firm are assumed to hold in the manufacturing sector. The fixed cost, the source of such economies of scale, is defined as a fixed amount of consumption of the bundle of intermediate goods and production factors.[9]

Econometric estimates are used to provide values for the fixed costs and for the elasticities of substitution.[10] The equivalent number of firms is calibrated by the model. This is different from the approach of Gasiorek, Smith and Venables (1992) and Mercenier (1992), who use empirical estimates of the number of firms and calibrate the elasticities of substitution. Empirical estimates of the number of real competitors in each industry seem inconsistent to us. Indeed, it is fairly easy to calculate the equivalent number of firms within a given industry, for example through the Herfindahl index. It is, however, very difficult to determine the level at which competition takes place, or in other words what is the 'field' within which firms are competing.

5.3.4   Type of Competition

There is monopolistic competition *à la* Cournot between firms: the decision variable of the firm is the quantity produced.[11] The description of market structures is based on two criteria: changes in concentration and the level of differentiation between products.[12] Analysis of the dynamic of concentration is based upon a comparison of shifts in firm numbers and the evolution of sectoral turnover. An industry is defined as 'fragmented' if the number of firms grows with the level of turnover of the industry: this implies that the size of firms remains, by and large, constant. Generally such a feature characterises industries with a low level of concentration, with low economies of scale, and with low entry barriers. In the model, a fragmented industry is characterised by a variable number of firms, with free entry and exit, and the number of firms being determined by the fact that all firms in the industry make zero profits.

In contrast, an industry is defined as 'segmented' when the number of firms remains, by and large, constant: the size of firms increases with market size. These are rather concentrated industries, where entry barriers are high. It implies that the number of firms remains constant and that their profits are not necessarily zero. We distinguish four types of industries, from fragmented industries with a low differentiation of products, such as, textiles and clothing, to segmented industries with high differentiation of products, such as, pharmaceutical products (see Table 5.1).

5.4   RESULTS OF SIMULATIONS

5.4.1   The Reference Scenario

The model is used to assess the impact on the European labour market of a growth rate significantly higher in the emerging countries than in other areas. The reference shock is a doubling of the relative size of emerging countries. This implies, for example, that the growth rate would be 7 per cent higher in the emerging countries than in the other areas for 10 years, or 5 per cent higher for 15 years. The calculation is made *ceteris paribus*. We are interested only in an increase in the size of the emerging countries relative to ROW, without any hypothesis concerning the actual growth path.

Table 5.1   Sectoral classification

	Fragmented industries	Segmented industries
Low differentiation, high demand elasticity of substitution	3. Textiles–clothing 4. Wood and paper products 6. Non-metallic products	7. Iron and steel
High differentiation, low demand elasticity of substitution	8. Metal products 9. Non-electrical machinery 12. Other manufacturing	2. Food products 5. Chemicals 10. Electrical machinery 11. Transport equipment

Source: Authors' classification using works of Sutton (1991), Schmalensee (1992) and Oliveira-Martins (1993).

In a general equilibrium model, prices are the essential transmission channel of shocks. In comparison with induced trade flows, changes in relative prices between industries are rather small, because the initial shock does not discriminate between industries. There are only two reasons why these relative prices will vary. On the one hand, changes in market shares modify mark-ups, and on the other hand, shifts of production induce different price changes according to the size of fixed costs. In comparison with the initial shock, which consists of a doubling in size of the emerging countries, these two phenomena have little effect.

The general level of prices varies in order to maintain balanced trade. This balanced trade constraint induces a reduction of the price level in emerging countries with respect to those of other areas. It provides a terms of trade improvement for both other areas, that is, a welfare gain.

5.4.2   Trade Patterns

The emerging countries shock affects other areas through trade. There is an increase in the penetration rate of emerging countries' goods in the European market. In the base run, it rises from 1.6 to 3.0 per cent in manufacturing industries (see Table 5.2). In contrast, European goods take a lower market share in the emerging countries.

The evolution of trade is detailed in Table 5A2.1 in Appendix 5.2 (p. 118). The trade gains of emerging countries are generally stronger in fragmented industries than in segmented industries. In fragmented industries, growth in emerging countries leads to a wider

Table 5.2   Trade patterns

	Emerging countries		EC	
	Initial share (%)	Final share (%)	Initial share (%)	Final share (%)
Share of bilateral imports in manufacturing demand	1.9	1.6	1.6	3.0
Share of bilateral imports in final demand	1.1	0.9	0.7	1.2

Source: Database of model and authors' simulation.

Table 5.3   Terms of trade

	Emerging countries	EC	ROW
Shift of terms-of-trade	−9.5	+0.86	+2.5

Source: Database of model and authors' simulation.

Note: Terms of trade calculation is made using a weighting by the initial pattern of trade. Results are fairly similar by choosing the final pattern.

spectrum of product varieties, which enable these countries to enlarge their market share. It is analogous to horizontal differentiation of supply, which benefits countries whose growth is concentrated upon fragmented industries. In contrast, segmented industries offer better resistance to the rising penetration of the emerging countries. Entry barriers are much higher and European producers are better able to defend their positions. European producers are able to adopt a strategy akin to vertical differentiation.

Moreover, the rise in import penetration by the emerging countries is lower where the elasticity of substitution between emerging countries' goods and developed countries' goods is relatively small, in other words where goods are less similar. The fall in the relative price of emerging countries' goods has less impact on their market share for these industries. The high differentiation of products is another impediment to the market penetration of emerging countries in Europe.

In fragmented industries with high substitution elasticities, exports of emerging countries experience the strongest increase. They almost treble in textiles – clothing, and more than double in wood

– paper and non-metallic products. Then comes the iron and steel industry (segmented but with a rather high substitution elasticity) and other segmented industries. The number of firms almost doubles in fragmented industries, but increases by less than production because of economies of scale. As each firm produces its own variety, the number of varieties supplied by the emerging countries in each of these industries increases proportionally.

This close to doubling of the number of supplied varieties explains why exports from the emerging countries increase by at least 26 per cent in fragmented industries, even with a weak elasticity, while segmented industries experience an increase of nearly 17 per cent (except the steel industry: +37 per cent) and exports from both perfectly competitive industries increase by less than 10 per cent. In volume, the main increase occurs in textiles – clothing. Indeed, this industry combines a high growth rate of exports by emerging countries and a high initial penetration rate of imports in Europe. The other industries in which the increase in market share for emerging countries is significant are building materials, steel, electric materials and wood – paper.

Growth in the emerging countries creates additional demand for European products and for goods from the rest of the world. However, for the textiles – clothing, wood – paper and building materials industries, Europe and the rest of the world lose ground in nearly every market, including their own. This decline is especially marked in textiles – clothing as reflected in the 17 per cent decrease in European output in this industry. In other industries, European positions are better defended: there is a small decline in the domestic market, and exports to emerging countries increase, by between 40 and 90 per cent. Such supplementary exports are especially important in the non-electrical machinery industry, where they represent a full 4 per cent of the industry's output, and less markedly in chemicals, transport materials and electrical machinery (see Table 5A2.2 of Appendix 5.2).

European exports to ROW are subject to two contrary influences. On the one hand, the lower price of goods from the emerging countries enables those countries to gain market shares in ROW.[13] European firms therefore suffer crowding out in ROW.[14] On the other hand, the market size of ROW increases. The sum of these two effects is weakly positive for all industries, except textiles. In this industry, an especially marked crowding-out effect induces a fall of more than 17 per cent in European exports. ROW exports to Europe undergo a similar evolution in their sectoral distribution, but weaker on average, because the increase in the trade balance with emerging countries is stronger for ROW than for Europe.

Finally, three criteria account for the evolution of sectoral trade: the importance of the initial flow, the substitution elasticity and the industry's structure. The first criterion corresponds to the logic of comparative advantage and factor abundance, which sets initial trade flows. The two others underline the importance of the costs of entry into an industry, in terms of product differentiation and fixed costs. Competition from emerging countries is mainly concentrated upon low-entry cost industries, i.e. fragmented industries, with a high substitution elasticity.

5.4.3   Output and Wages

Changes in trade induce shifts in the relative output levels of industries. In emerging countries, the strongest output increases occur in the textile – clothing and building materials industries, while in Europe, these two industries see output fall by 17 and 0.8 per cent, respectively. As they are relatively unskilled intensive, this induces downward pressure on the demand for unskilled labour. Conversely machinery, chemicals, transport materials and electrical machinery industries, which are relatively skilled-intensive, experience a significant rise in their output in Europe (+4.2 per cent for machinery, +1.5 to 2 per cent for others).

In this model we assume a perfectly flexible labour market, so that these output shifts, and subsequent changes in demand for the different types of labour, induce an increase in wage disparities. The real wage of unskilled labour decreases by 0.1 per cent while the skilled wage increases by 0.7 per cent (see Table 5.4). Wage inequalities thus rise by 0.8 per cent. This is consistent with the factor proportions (HOS) theory: an increase in trade modifies European specialisation at the expense of unskilled-intensive industries and to the benefit of high-skill industries, which influences the labour market equilibrium. In contrast, in the emerging countries there is a positive effect for all production factors, but biased in favour of skilled labour, and most of all capital.

In sum, our main result is that while the penetration rate of imports from emerging countries in manufacturing almost doubles in Europe (from 1.6 per cent to 3 per cent), the real wage of unskilled workers decreases by only 0.8 per cent relative to the wage

Table 5.4   Variation of real factor rewards

	Emerging countries (%)	EC (%)
Variation in the real wage for skilled workers	+6	+0.7
Variation in the real wage for unskilled workers	+7	−0.1
Variation in the real reward of capital	+10	+0.1
Welfare variation	+115	+0.3

Source: Authors' simulations.

of skilled workers. Four important mechanisms within the model lie at the heart of this result. First, initial trade volumes, reflecting the relative factor endowments of each area and the importance of 'natural' entry barriers – such as the elasticity of substitution in demand or the level of concentration in industry – shape the sectoral evolution of trade between areas. Second, general equilibrium constraints, and especially the trade balance equilibrium, influence trade and the general price level. Third, production factor intensities by industry determine the way the effects of the trade shock are distributed between the various production factors. Fourth, other important features, such as scale elasticities or substitution elasticities between production factors, also play an important part in determining the response in Europe to growth in emerging markets. However, generally, the latter considerations modify only the magnitude of the results, and not their sign.

5.5   SENSITIVITY ANALYSIS

In numerical model exercises, such as that undertaken in this chapter, it is important to undertake analysis of the extent to which the principal results are sensitive to assumptions made regarding key parameters. We can have confidence in the final results only if they are robust, not radically altered by small changes in the assumptions that underlie the model. For a more detailed description of sensitivity analysis, see Cortes and Jean (1996). We report here the model variants presenting the most important differences with respect to the base case.

5.5.1   Armington Elasticities for all Industries

In order to preserve the scaling of elasticities between industries and the fact that each elasticity must exceed unity, we apply a simple transformation to the Armington substitution elasticities for manufacturing industries as a whole:

$$\sigma_{1,\,tested} = 1 + a(\sigma_{1,\,initial} - 1)$$

When coefficient a is high (that is, with high Armington elasticities), the evolution of real factor rewards of the various production factors hardly changes (see Figure 5.3). On the other hand, the evolution of the various rewards becomes very similar when coefficient a is small, each factor gaining between 0.4 and 1 per cent in real terms. This is accompanied by a very weak increase of the penetration rate in Europe of emerging countries' goods, which are then poorly substitutable with other goods. Such low values for elasticities, we believe, are not appropriate: they are too small compared to econometric results, and they prevent the effects of an important increase of trade with the emerging countries to be evaluated.

In conclusion, if the Armington substitution elasticities were to be set at far weaker values than in our base run, trade with the emerging countries would increase very little, which is unlikely. For higher values, the effects on European wages are scarcely modified. We therefore infer that the results are robust with regard to plausible variations in the values of the Armington elasticities.

5.5.2   Substitution Elasticities between Production Factors

Substitution between production factors takes place within two distinct levels of complementarity. We assume that capital and skilled labour are quite complementary, whilst substitution can occur more easily between the aggregate they constitute and unskilled labour. Preserving this hierarchy, we seek to test the sensitivity of the results to the values chosen for the substitution elasticities by multiplying them by a common coefficient (see Figure 5.4).

The elasticities used initially are respectively 0.4 between capital and skilled labour, and 0.5 between their aggregate and unskilled labour. With higher elasticities, the rise in inequality is smaller: the more substitutable the factors are, the more equitably the initial shock is shared out between them.

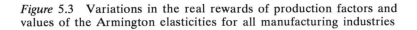

Figure 5.3   Variations in the real rewards of production factors and values of the Armington elasticities for all manufacturing industries

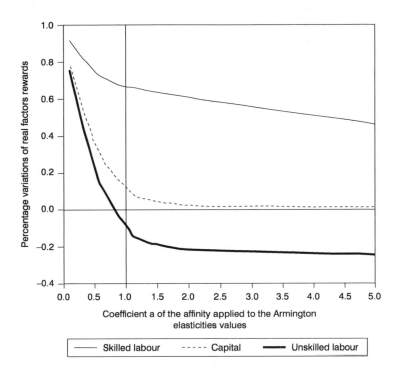

Note: When the coefficient *a* equals 1, the Armington elasticities are set to their initial values.
Source: Authors' simulations.

In contrast, when the substitutability between factors is weak, the effects on rewards is more differentiated. With substitution elasticities of 0.032 and 0.04, respectively, the unskilled real wage falls by more than 3 per cent, while the skilled wage rises by 5 per cent. However, the penetration rate of imports from emerging countries is the same as in the base run. This shows that substitutability between production factors plays a crucial role in absorbing the inequality effect of the shock, and constitutes an important explanation of the weakness of the results obtained with regards to relative factor rewards.

The values chosen here represent a low estimate of the long-term substitution elasticity between skilled and unskilled labour.

Figure 5.4   Sensitivity analysis with respect to the values of the substitution elasticities between production factors

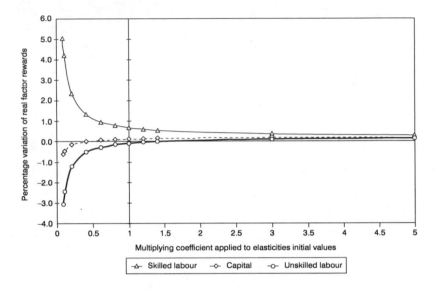

Note: When the multiplying coefficient equals one, substitution elasticities between production factors are set at their initial values; on the left-hand side of the figure (low multiplier), they are inferior to this level, on the right-hand side, they are superior.
Source: Authors' simulations.

But if we were to adopt a more detailed breakdown of skills, these values would have to be corrected downward for some categories. In particular, workers without any skills are probably not substitutable for other labour categories. The adverse effect of growth in the emerging countries for this labour category could, therefore, be much greater than the base-run results suggest. Moreover, this points to the problems linked to labour market segmentation between poorly substitutable categories. The presence of such rigidities is likely to increase considerably the inequality effect of trade with low-wage countries. This suggests that emphasis should be placed upon education and the mobility of labour within firms.

Finally, the elasticities used here are long-term ones. In the short term, the substitutability between production factors is far weaker. For the same increase in the penetration rate of imports from the emerging countries, the negative effect on unskilled labour will

Table 5.5   Sensitivity of results to the definition of fragmented industries

Industries assumed to be fragmented	Variations in real rewards within EC		
	Skilled-labour *(%)*	*Unskilled labour* *(%)*	*Capital* *(%)*
Text. – cloth., wood – paper and building mat. fragmented	+0.61	−0.17	+0.09
Text. – cloth., wood – paper, building mat., metal prod., machinery and other manuf. fragmented (base run)	+0.67	−0.08	+0.12
Base run + electrical machinery fragmented	+0.70	−0.02	+0.17
All industries fragmented	+0.80	+0.04	+0.20

Source: Authors' simulations.

therefore be more accentuated the more rapidly the rise in imports occurs.

5.5.3   Fragmentation Definition

The distinction between fragmented and segmented industries influences the conditions of market penetration by emerging countries. In order to test the sensitivity of the results to this taxonomy, we carried out a number of alternative simulations. The results, described in Table 5.5, suggest that our principal conclusions are fairly robust on this issue. The negative effect on the real wage of unskilled workers is greatest when only textile – clothing, wood – paper and building materials (the three sectors with low average labour skills) are assumed to be fragmented.

5.5.4   The Response Curves to the Magnitude of the Shock

In the long run, the problem of competition from emerging countries could be of an order of magnitude far higher than that modelled in our base run. This would be the case, for example, if the growth differential between the emerging countries and the industrial countries persists over a longer period. A further reason would be the take-off of some countries which are not yet considered as emerging countries, such as India, the former Soviet Union or the Central and Eastern European countries. Some authors draw alarming conclusions from this perspective, suggesting that it will make it even more difficult for firms in rich countries to contend with international competition. Others, on the contrary, argue that the bulk of adjustment has already been achieved in the developed economies, and the emergence of new competitors will primarily affect other emerging countries (see Wood, 1995).

To address this question, we simulated shocks of a larger magnitude than in the base run, but preserving the essential features of the base-run shock: the endowment of production factors in emerging countries is multiplied by a factor varying between one (no-shock) and eight (see Figure 5.5).

In a first stage, the response is quite proportional; inequalities rise and the real wage for unskilled workers declines. However, when the multiplying coefficient applied to the emerging countries' factors stock exceeds six, the unskilled real wage starts to rise. In this case, an increase in the shock implies an increase in the real rewards of each of the three factors.

In a manner similar to Wood (1995), we interpret these results as reflecting the fact that, after a certain threshold, trade between rich and low-wage countries would become based upon quasi-complete specialisation. Very schematically, rich countries would produce very little clothing and would almost completely specialise in machinery and services. In this case, the lowering of import prices in the textile – clothing industry would not have a large negative impact on the real wage of the unskilled in rich countries, as there is practically no production by this industry in these countries. On the contrary, this fall in price would induce gains in the real factor rewards for all production factors.

This analysis is based upon the assumption that the emerging countries do not experiment with any 'market upgrading'. Nevertheless, let us stress that such an evolution would make the emerging countries' trade more similar to the rich countries' trade. The problem then changes in kind, and such an outcome would probably be accompanied by a rise in wages in these countries. The threat to European unskilled workers' wages is then less clear, and most or all of it no longer comes specifically from trade with those countries.

5.6 CONCLUSIONS

In this chapter we have provided an analysis of the impact of deeper integration of the emerging countries into the world economy. We

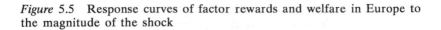

Figure 5.5   Response curves of factor rewards and welfare in Europe to the magnitude of the shock

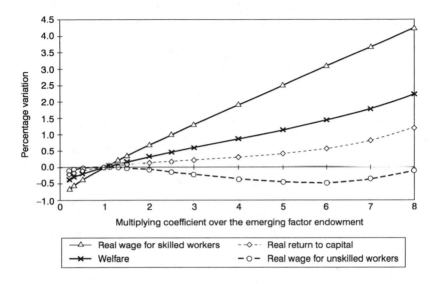

Source: Authors' simulations.

simulate what some describe as a catastrophic scenario: a large increase in scale of the tradable industries of low-wage countries. The results that our numerical model generate do not mirror the concern surrounding this perspective. In the base run, which describes a doubling in the size of the emerging countries, the penetration rate of imports from those countries in the European manufacturing market rises from 1.6 per cent to 3 per cent, while wage inequalities in Europe rise at most by 1 per cent. With a larger shock and a penetration rate reaching 8.5 per cent, wage inequalities rise by nearly 4 per cent in Europe. The unskilled workers' real wage decreases in most of the simulations, but this loss is weak, 0.5 per cent at most, and the increase in global welfare is comparatively important. Without being negligible, the consequences of this shock are of a low order of magnitude compared to the worsening of the European labour market during the last 20 years, especially in terms of increased inequalities.

There are two factors behind these results. The first has to do with the inevitable inadequacies of this type of modelling. However, we think that the model does capture some real phenomena which explain these results. Providing more detail in certain areas of our model could lead to an increase in inequalities following the trade shock from emerging countries. First, the limited breakdown of occupational categories, and of industries, is likely to induce an underestimation of the magnitude of the impact. For example, with five or six occupational categories, the increase in inequality for the extreme categories would be stronger than with two categories. Indeed, as we saw in Section 5.5.2, the more segmented the labour market is, the more important the inequality effects are. It would be interesting to distinguish segments of the labour force which have a low degree of substitutability for other segments, such as workers without any skills. Finally, this modelling work does not allow production structures to change when firms are faced with increased international competition.[15]

On the other hand, this model shows how several mechanisms can limit the impact of growth in emerging countries on European labour markets. The constraint of balanced trade in the long-run could have been relaxed, for example, by treating the trade balance, rather than the exchange rate, as endogenous. But this would not alter the general features of the results. There are natural limits to the reciprocal penetration of markets, following from demand conditions and exchange rate adjustments. In a similar way, inequalities in Europe do not rise further with growth in the emerging countries, when production specialisation is quasi-complete for some industries. Finally, barriers to entry in manufacturing industries, which are very low for clothing but much more significant for aeronautics or pharmaceutical products, also constrain the consequences of greater trade with emerging countries on the European labour market. In the most unskilled-intensive industries, a large part of the adjustment to the international integration of the emerging countries has already been achieved.

Fears are often expressed of the effects of rapid product upgrading by emerging countries. This would enable these countries to conquer substantial market shares outside of the clothing, basic electronics or wood products industries. But the problem would probably change in kind. These countries would have to penetrate markets where the advantages generated by low labour costs are far less important. Moreover, these countries would experience fairly rapid labour costs increases; the difficulty is to know how much this will hinder their market upgrading. But generally, the penetration by emerging countries of the European market for manufactured products, other than those intensive in the use of unskilled labour, will be more difficult.

Finally, the increased international integration of the emerging countries in the world economy does not appear to be the main source of problems for the European labour market. On the contrary, Europe benefits from the macroeconomic effects of this growth in emerging markets.

APPENDIX 5.1   SECTORAL DATA

	Armington elasticities	*Substitution elasticity between goods from the emerging countries and from the developed countries*	*Equivalent number of competing firms*	*Fixed cost (in % of total cost)*
1. Primary sector	1.1	1.1	1	0
2. Food products	1.5	6	23	20
3. Textiles – clothing	8	11	69	10
4. Wood – paper	4	4.5	9	30
5. Chemicals	1.5	4.3	9	30
6. Building materials	3	4.3	9	30
7. Iron and steel	3	4.3	8	30
8. Metal products	1.5	6	21	20
9. Non-electrical machinery	1.5	6	15	20
10. Electrical machinery	1.5	4.3	8	30
11. Transport material	1.5	4.3	8	30
12. Other manufacturing	1.5	6	19	20
13. Services	1.1	1.1	1	0

Note: The equivalent number of firms is calibrated.

Source: See Cortes and Jean (1996).

APPENDIX 5.2   THE RESULTS IN THE BASE RUN

Table 5A2.1   Sectoral trade variation

		Trade variation (as percentage of initial value)			Trade variation compared to output (as percentage of initial industry output)		
From		*To*			*To*		
Area	*Industry*	*Emerging countries*	*EC*	*ROW*	*Emerging countries*	*EC*	*ROW*
	1. Primary sector	99.7	8.07	10.80	92.5	0.09	0.65
	2. Food products	111.7	17.98	19.45	108.3	0.14	0.43
	3. Textiles – clothing	116.3	293.82	290.01	99.5	11.41	30.70
	4. Wood – paper	117.9	155.96	161.04	115.9	0.63	2.12
	5. Chemicals	103.3	17.50	20.80	96.9	0.25	1.00
Emerging	6. Building materials	117.6	97.35	99.21	107.1	2.14	6.68
countries	7. Iron and steel	105.5	37.54	42.07	97.4	0.62	2.55
	8. Metal products	108.5	26.24	26.81	97.0	0.47	2.37
	9. Non-electrical machinery	112.4	26.27	25.82	103.5	0.39	1.66
	10. Electrical machinery	104.3	17.65	19.53	86.5	0.58	2.69
	11. Transport material	107.0	17.86	19.47	99.7	0.17	1.15
	12. Other manufacturing	108.4	26.46	26.12	99.3	0.35	1.85
	13. Services	102.0	10.38	11.75	100.7	0.03	0.11
	1. Primary sector	84.6	−0.04	2.48	0.10	−0.04	0.04
	2. Food products	79.6	0.11	1.36	0.36	0.11	0.04
	3. Textiles – clothing	−56.5	−16.69	−17.49	−0.95	−14.30	−2.21
	4. Wood – paper	−29.5	−0.38	2.31	−0.12	−0.36	0.11
	5. Chemicals	72.8	−0.14	2.65	1.57	−0.12	0.37
EC	6. Building materials	−3.2	−1.05	1.86	−0.02	−0.92	0.14
	7. Iron and steel	49.4	−0.43	2.60	0.82	−0.37	0.32
	8. Metal products	63.1	−0.09	2.24	0.68	−0.08	0.21
	9. Non-electrical machinery	66.5	0.12	1.55	3.76	0.08	0.36
	10. Electrical machinery	73.5	−0.13	1.43	1.52	−0.11	0.22
	11. Transport material	75.8	0.08	1.44	1.52	0.06	0.29
	12. Other manufacturing	63.0	0.03	1.62	0.76	0.02	0.20
	13. Services	82.9	0.03	1.27	0.07	0.03	0.06
	1. Primary sector	84.7	−0.05				
	2. Food products	79.6	0.11				
	3. Textiles – clothing	−56.5	−16.69				
	4. Wood – paper	−29.5	−0.39				
ROW	5. Chemicals	72.8	−0.14				
	6. Building materials	−3.2	−1.06				
	7. Iron and steel	49.3	−0.45				
	8. Metal products	63.1	−0.10				
	9. Non-electrical machinery	66.5	0.11				
	10. Electrical machinery	73.5	−0.14				
	11. Transport material	75.8	0.07				
	12. Other manufacturing	63.0	0.03				
	13. Services	82.8	−0.18				

Source: Authors' simulation.

Table 5A2.2 Variation in output and in import penetration
(as a percentage of initial value)

Industry	Variation in total output		Initial share of bilateral imports in final demand		Final share of bilateral imports in final demand	
	Emerging countries	EC	Emerging countries	EC	Emerging countries	EC
1. Primary sector	93.2	0.10	0.18	0.82	0.17	0.83
2. Food products	108.9	0.50	0.38	0.90	0.36	0.94
3. Textiles – clothing	141.6	–17.46	1.04	6.35	0.25	21.95
4. Wood – paper	118.6	–0.38	0.54	0.24	0.21	0.54
5. Chemicals	98.2	1.82	2.01	1.41	1.91	1.49
6. Building materials	116.0	–0.85	0.98	1.20	0.53	2.12
7. Iron and steel	100.6	0.77	1.41	1.59	1.16	1.95
8. Metal products	99.8	0.81	2.47	0.80	2.21	0.90
9. Non-electrical machinery	105.5	4.20	8.25	0.89	7.54	1.00
10. Electrical machinery	89.8	1.64	2.12	2.87	1.95	3.14
11. Transport material	101.0	1.87	2.79	0.65	2.66	0.68
12. Other manufacturing	101.5	0.98	2.64	0.56	2.37	0.63
13. Services	100.9	0.16	0.23	0.11	0.23	0.11

Source: Authors' simulation

Table 5A2.3 Price variation, by industry (as percentage of initial value)

Industry	Variation in the prices of European goods on the markets of:			Variation in the prices of the emerging countries' goods on the markets of:		
	Emerging countries	EC	ROW	Emerging countries	EC	ROW
1. Primary sector	–0.10	–0.10	–0.10	–6.94	–6.94	–6.94
2. Food products	–0.13	–0.13	–0.13	–10.48	–10.48	–10.48
3. Textiles – clothing	–0.13	–0.11	–0.12	–10.82	–10.22	–10.23
4. Wood – paper	–0.14	–0.09	–0.11	–14.34	–10.25	–10.11
5. Chemicals	–0.11	–0.11	–0.11	–10.37	–10.38	–10.38
6. Building materials	–0.15	–0.08	–0.11	–13.88	–10.33	–9.75
7. Iron and steel	–0.39	–0.15	–0.14	–10.01	–10.40	–10.41
8. Metal products	–0.11	–0.13	–0.10	–11.86	–11.17	–10.04
9. Non-electrical machinery	–0.14	–0.25	–0.08	–11.76	–11.17	–9.95
10. Electrical machinery	–0.06	–0.06	–0.05	–10.38	–10.41	–10.41
11. Transport material	–0.11	–0.10	–0.10	–10.41	–10.43	–10.43
12. Other manufacturing	–0.10	–0.12	–0.09	–11.83	–11.16	–10.04
13. Services	0.00	0.00	0.00	–8.56	–8.56	–8.56

Source: Authors' simulation.

Notes

* The authors are especially grateful to Joaquim Oliveira-Martins and Dominique van der Mensbrugghe for very helpful advice and comments.
1. See Cortes and Jean (1995 a and b).
2. The technical aspects of the model are discussed in detail in Cortes and Jean (1996).
3. See Rodrik (1995).
4. See Pack (1988).
5. Assuming that specialisation remains incomplete, i.e. that each country continues to produce all goods.
6. See, for example, Lancaster (1957) and Bhagwati (1959).
7. For example, Bonnaz *et al.* (1994) show that the average ratio between the prices of imported goods from the South and French goods is about 2.
8. See for example Hammermesh (1986).
9. The size of fixed costs is presented in Appendix 5.1 (p. 117).
10. These choices are justified in Cortes and Jean (1996).
11. Firms are assumed to determine their level of output by taking as fixed the production of other firms. Each firm assumes that any change in its output does not induce a reaction from the part of its competitors (zero conjectural variations).
12. See Sutton (1991) and Schmalensee (1992). On the other hand, Oliveira-Martins (1993) highlights the influence of market structure in the analysis of the link between trade and wages.
13. This is also true in their own market and is why the penetration rate of European goods in the emerging countries market decreases.
14. See for example Mathieu and Sterdinyak (1994) for an attempt at calculating the magnitude of this effect in a different framework.
15. See Cortes and Jean (1997).

References

Bhagwati, J. (1959) 'Protection, real rewards and real income', *Economic Journal*, 69.
Bismut, C. and Oliveira-Martins, J. (1986) 'Le rôle des prix dans la compétition internationale', in Fouquin, M. (ed.), *Industrie Mondiale: La Compétitivité à Tout Prix*, Paris: Economica.
Bonnaz, H., Courtot, N. and Nivat, D. (1995) 'La balance en emplois des échanges de la France avec les pays en développement', *Economie et Statistique*, 279–280, 13–34.
Cortes, O. and Jean, S. (1995a) 'Comment mesurer l'impact du commerce international sur l'emploi? Une note méthodologique', *Economie et Statistique*, 279–80, 3–12.
Cortes, O. and Jean, S. (1995b) 'Echange international et marché du travail: une revue critique des méthodes d'analyse', *Revue d'Economie Politique*, 105, 359–407.

Cortes, O. and Jean, S. (1996) 'Pays émergents, emploi déficient?', *Document de Travail*, 96–05, CEPII.

Cortes, O. and Jean, S. (1997) 'Quel est l'impact du commerce extérieur sur l'emploi? Une analyse comparée des cas de la France, de l'Allemagne et des Etats-Unis', Document de Travail 97–08, CEPII; *Document d'études*, 13, DARES.

Cortes, O., Jean, S. and Pisani-Ferry, J. (1996) 'Trade and the labour markets: the French case', *Document de Travail*, 96–04, CEPII.

Gasiorek, M., Smith, A. and Venables, A. (1992) '1992 trade and welfare: a general equilibrium model', in Winters, L.A. (ed.), *Trade Flows and Trade Policy after '1992'*, Cambridge: Cambridge University Press.

Hammermesh, D.S. (1986) 'The demand for labour in the long-run', in Ashenfelter, O.C. and Layard, R (eds), *Handbook of Labour Economics*, vol. 1, Amsterdam: North-Holland, 429–71.

Lancaster, M. (1957) 'Protection and real wages: a restatement', *Economic Journal*, 67.

Mathieu, C. and Sterdyniak, H. (1994) 'L'émergence de l'Asie en développement menace-t-elle l'emploi en France?', *Observations et Diagnostiques Économiques*, 48, 1–52.

Mercenier, J. (1992) 'Can '1992' reduce unemployment in Europe? On welfare and employment effects of Europe's move to a single market', *Discussion Paper*, 2292, CRDE, Montréal University.

Oliveira-Martins, J. (1993) 'Market structure, international trade and relative wages', *Working Paper*, 134, OECD.

Pack, H. (1988) 'Industrialisation and trade', in Chenery, H. and Srinivasan, T.N. (eds), *Handbook of Development Economics*, vol. 1, Amsterdam: North-Holland.

Pratten, C. (1988) 'A survey of the economies of scale', in *Research on the 'Cost of Non-Europe'*, vol. 2, Brussels: Commission of the European Communities.

Rodrik, D. (1995) 'Trade strategy, investment and exports: another look at East Asia', *Working Paper*, 5339, NBER.

Schmalensee, R. (1992) 'Sunk costs and market structure: a review article', *The Journal of Industrial Economics*, 51, 125–34.

Smith, A. and Venables, A. (1988) 'Completing the internal market in the European Community: some industry simulations', *European Economic Review*, 32, 1501–25.

Sutton, J. (1991) *Sunk Costs and Market Structure*, Cambridge, MA: MIT Press.

Szpiro, D. and Cette, G. (1994) 'Returns to scale in the French manufacturing industry, *European Economic Review*, 38, 1493–1504.

Wood, A. (1995) 'How trade hurt unskilled workers', *Journal of Economic Perspectives*, 9, 57–80.

Data sources

Chelem (1995) harmonised international trade data, CD-ROM, CEPII.

Eurostat (1994) *Input–Output Table of the European Union in 1991*.

Hambley, J. (1990) *Annual Input–Output Table for China for 1987*, ONU.

INSEE (1991) *Structure des emplois 1990.*

Institute of Developing Economies (1991) *International Input–Output Tables Indonesia–Japan 1985.*

Institute of Developing Economies (1991) *International Input–Output Tables Thailand–Japan 1985.*

Institute of Developing Economies (1992) *International Input–Output Tables Malaysia–Japan 1985.*

Institute of Developing Economies (1992) *International Input–Output Tables Philippines–Japan 1985.*

State Statistical Bureau of the People's Republic of China (1990) *China Statistical Yearbook 1989.*

UNIDO (1990) *Industry and Development Global Report.*

6 Global Integration and Wages in a General Equilibrium World Model: Contributions of WorldScan*

Richard Nahuis

6.1 INTRODUCTION

A decline in real wages of 11 per cent in the USA in the 1980s! Are we living in an age of diminished prosperity? This decline in real wages was not just experienced by a small fraction of all workers. Less-skilled workers have actually been facing declining wages for a long period. Somewhat counterintuitively, this decline in the relative wage of less-skilled workers has been paralleled by an increase in the relative skill level in the work force.

Before 1973, average real hourly earnings rose on average by 1.9 per cent per year: the American dream. After 1973 this dream grew pale; by 1992 earnings were actually lower than in 1973! After correcting for the employers' contribution to social security and medical and retirement insurance there was a modest increase of 5 per cent over the whole period. This, together with the fact that inequality rose dramatically, resulted in a real earnings decline of more than 10 per cent for workers at the lower end of the earnings distribution.[1] Thus, at the heart of the problem we are considering is the distribution of income. In the populist press, the rise in inequality in the 1980s has been connected immediately to trade with low-wage countries. As obvious explanations are not always correct explanations, academic economists have sought to provide a reasoned analysis. By doing so, they have initiated a lively debate on the causes of the observed trend in inequality.

The widening of the gap (in the USA and elsewhere) between

123

the wages of the unskilled and the wages of the skilled[2] has evoked an intense effort by economists to identify the cause. Three main explanations have been put forward; education, technology and international trade. As the review in Chapter 2 has made clear, empirical analysis is required to identify the precise role played by each of these factors in the rise in inequality. This chapter seeks to provide numerical estimates of the extent of the increase in inequality that can be explained by trade. The chapter continues in Section 6.2 by presenting and discussing the key labour market trends which have stimulated the debate. Thereafter, in Sections 6.3 and 6.4, a discussion of key elements in the 'trade versus technology' debate followed by analysis of methodological issues sets the stage for our contribution to this debate. The Computable General Equilibrium (CGE) model, WorldScan, that we use to generate the numerical results is presented in Section 6.5. Section 6.6 explains the experiment that we undertake to assess the relevance of trade to widening wage inequality and discusses the results. Section 6.7 provides an evaluation and some conclusions.

6.2 THE FACTS

This section documents the facts that have given rise to the question we address in this chapter. A few prominent trends characterise the US labour market in the 1970s and 1980s. The first is the stagnant development of average real wages. Until 1973 real wages rose rapidly. In the period from 1963 to 1973 this amounted to an increase of 25 per cent! In the period from 1973 to 1989, real wages remained roughly constant (Murphy and Welch, 1992). The second feature is that, in clear contrast with the 1970s, the earnings differential between groups with high and low levels of education increased (see Table 6.1). The third trend is that average educational attainment rose over the 1980s (see Table 6.2). Combining the second and third trend we could, reasonably, formulate a fourth trend: overall inequality increased tremendously.

For later reference it is convenient to discuss the numbers regarding the second trend, the increased earnings differential, in some detail. As can be seen in Table 6.1, for all the OECD countries (with the exception of Japan) the education premium rose remarkably in the 1980s. Table 6.1 is constructed using the ratio of payment to workers having finished college to those who finished only

Table 6.1   Change in education wage premium, 1970s and 1980s

	1970s	1980s
USA	−0.08	0.09
Australia	−0.17	0.03
Canada	−0.13	0.03
Germany		0.10
Japan	−0.04	0.00
Sweden	−0.09	0.03
UK	−0.06	0.08

Note: Five-year average absolute change in the ratio of earnings of college level workers to high school level workers.

Source: OECD (1993); Davis (1992).

Table 6.2   Relative supply of college-educated workers,[ab] 1970–89

	1970	1980	1989
USA	10.8	16.6	21.5
Germany	6.0	7.4	9.4
Japan	12.0	17.9	22.5
France	5.3	8.3	11.8
UK	8.0	12.0	18.3

Notes:
[a] Percentages of the population.
[b] For details, see OECD (1993).

high school. For the US, this ratio increased from 1.37 in 1979 to 1.52 in 1987. For the UK, the ratio increased from 1.53 to 1.65 in eight years (1980–88). For a more extended overview of labour market trends in the 1980s, see Kosters (1994).

6.3   THE TECHNOLOGY–TRADE DEBATE AND EMPIRICAL ISSUES

The Introduction identified three main suspects for the widening wage gap between skilled and unskilled workers. The first was education – or, more precisely, the change in the relative supply of unskilled workers. The other two were international trade and technology – or, stated differently, a shift respectively along and of the relative demand curve for skill. The literature on this debate is surveyed elsewhere in this volume (see Chapter 2 by Paul Brenton). Here, we narrow our focus on the trade–technology debate, without wanting to deny a (minor) role for changes in relative supply of workers, institutional changes, migration and so on.

A large number of studies find little or no role for trade in the explanation of the increased education premium (see, for example, Krugman and Lawrence, 1993; Katz and Murphy, 1992; Berman, Bound and Griliches, 1994; Lawrence and Slaughter, 1993). In Section 6.5 we will argue, using a numerical general equilibrium model,[3] that this judgement that the role of trade is negligible might be based upon a mis-trial (hence supporting Leamer's, 1996a view). To support this assertion we first point to some key flaws in earlier work. The remainder of this section discusses briefly two imperfections of the Heckscher-Ohlin-Samuelson (HOS) based studies, that we are able to overcome in our work (for a more extensive discussion of these issues, see Nahuis, 1997).

The first key problem of previous studies is somewhat difficult to label suitably. In an effort to be original it will be labelled 'diagonal product differentiation within industries'.[4] The assumption that we criticise is that goods produced within an industry are homogeneous. The hypothesis postulated here is that it is possible to distinguish more activities within a single industry. Before formulating the argument, some intuition might help clarify the issue. Industries (even at detailed levels of disaggregation) consist of different goods with different input requirements. For example, in the telecom equipment industry, high-tech/high-skill products might be found together with standard technology products (e.g. telephones), assembled by unskilled workers (horizontal product differentiation). A single production process for an industry's good – for example, a television set – may consist of high-tech/high-skill parts but also of low-skill assembly of parts (vertical product differentiation).

To simplify matters, think about how indigenous firms respond to increased competition from LDC firms, probably by shedding their labour-intensive parts (by outsourcing) and, in the face of fierce competition, an industry will necessarily upgrade its products, via firms at the low-tech end leaving the sector. These two processes can be summarised as 'diagonal product differentiation within industries'.[5] More formally: an industry, as usually defined by product group-oriented data categories, does not correspond to the analytical concept of an industry necessary to apply factor proportions theory, as factor-use ratios differ more among varieties of a product and among separable stages of a production line than between different industries.[6]

The fact that the ratio of skilled to unskilled workers has increased in most sectors appears to be inconsistent with trade being the cause of rising inequality. Cheaper unskilled labour should be substituted for the now relatively dearer skilled labour in all sectors. The 'wrong' changes in factor use ratios within industries that have been observed have led authors such as Krugman and Lawrence (1993) to reject the trade explanation.

The arguments above suggest that once one allows for activities with different factor intensities within industries then rising skill intensities are consistent with trade being the source of increasing wage inequality. This approach can also explain why the evidence on the decline in the relative price of unskilled-labour-intensive goods prices, necessary to support the Stolper–Samuelson theorem, is mixed (Lawrence and Slaughter, 1993; Sachs and Shatz, 1994).[7] Finally, evidence suggesting complementarities between skill and technology (for example, the regressions of the type by Berman, Bound and Griliches, 1994) also fits with this story. The non-R&D-intensive parts (unskilled labour-intensive parts) of production are relocated to low-wage countries, so skill upgrading in the developed countries and R&D activity go hand in hand.

The second key problem is that the logic of the Stolper–Samuelson prediction holds only in the case of unchanged endowments in the $2 \times 2 \times 2$ (2-country, 2-factor, 2-product) version of the model. Three influences changing endowments are apparent. First, the fact that the overall size of the manufacturing sector has shrunk The decrease in the size of the manufacturing sector is an important issue its own right (Krugman, 1995c), but one that makes it difficult to evaluate the relevance of trade in the textbook version of the HOS model. Second, the relative supply of high-skilled workers continued to increase during the 1980s. Hall (1993)[8] has raised the point that this continuing increase in the supply of skill might complicate the picture. The Rybczynski theorem tells us that factor intensities are unaffected by changes in factor endowments. Unfortunately, the Rybczynski theorem strictly holds only for small countries (those who cannot influence the world prices of traded goods) and hence does not resolve the problem. Third, changes in unemployment may also confuse the analysis. This issue, raised by Sachs and Shatz (1994), has not been widely discussed in the literature.

We can summarise our arguments on the unreliability of the tests of the Stolper–Samuelson theorem as follows: first, the typical treatment of industries that are classified for statistical purposes by type of goods as homogenous entities with a single factor input requirement obfuscates the analysis; second, as the Stolper–Samuelson theorem is formulated with unchanged endowments it is necessary to keep in mind the fact that endowments have not been unchanged.

6.4   ON METHODOLOGY

In this section we discuss the different methods that have been used to assess the role of trade in influencing wage inequality. This allows us to highlight the fact that the principal contribution of this chapter is the application of an alternative approach. The appropriate methodology to assess the question of the relevance of trade in the widening of the wage gap has generated a heated debate in itself, and is therefore worth discussing in its own right.

Leamer condemns work based on the factor content of trade (FCT) as 'incompetent, immaterial and irrelevant', whereas Krugman (1995b, p. 38) calls FCT 'a procedure that turns out to be entirely reasonable'. Leamer's (1994b, 1996a, 1996b) critical argument runs as follows: the Stolper–Samuelson theorem connects factor rewards with goods prices via zero-profit conditions, without the volume of trade entering the formulation of the theorem. Suppose a country faces increased competition in unskilled-labour-intensive goods, but that it succeeds in keeping a constant share of the home market by lowering (primarily) the wages of low-skilled employees. When we examine whether trade can be blamed for the lower wages, we will not see any change in the FCT, so the answer will be no. This is obviously the wrong conclusion. *Ex post* trade volumes are thus an unreliable indicator of the *ex ante* threat.[9] To restate the argument as briefly as possible: factor prices are set on the margin.

In a clarifying paper, Deardorff and Staiger (1988) show that the translation from FCT to domestic factor prices is indeed not as obvious as it seems.[10] An intuitive explanation of the problem with FCT calculations is that factors embodied in trade are determined simultaneously by tastes, technologies, factor supplies, external goods markets and the deficit or surplus on the trade balance.[11] Leamer (1996b), Bhagwati and Dehejia (1994), Sachs and Shatz (1994) and

Lawrence and Slaughter (1993) conclude that it is the development of relative goods prices that should be analysed.

Krugman (1995b), however, calls the FCT calculations an 'entirely reasonable' exercise, with the restriction that trade deficits should be handled with care. How is this radically different view possible? The fundamental difference[12] is Krugman's rejection of the argument that prices can be treated as exogenous. This is the key to the debate. The proponents of the price approach see a country as price taker, the others see relative world market prices as being determined endogenously. Krugman's (1995b) argument runs as follows. First, he asserts that for the USA, let alone the whole OECD, goods prices will alter if technology or factor supplies change. The price approach is thus incapable of disentangling domestic and foreign causes of changes in relative prices. Since we want to know what the impact of low-wage countries has been, the volume of trade is a crucial piece of evidence.

So we are left with two compelling arguments favouring two different approaches. The verdict on the appropriate methodology (and with it the use of FCT) depends on whether we believe that prices can be taken to be exogenous or need to be treated as endogenous. Krugman (1995b, p. 22) suggests that the relevant question is:

> is it possible to imagine an alternative history in which the OECD countries have acquired the technology and resources of the mid-1990s, but in which trade with newly industrialising countries remains negligible (either because these countries did not develop, or because protectionist barriers have blocked off the potential trade)?

But there still remains the matter of deciding between the endogeneity of prices[13] against the fact that prices are set on the margin and that therefore small volume changes can cause large factor price effects. For the remainder of the chapter, we adopt the approach that the endogeneity of prices cannot be ignored.

Krugman argues (1995b, p. 27) that:

> many economists studying the impact of trade on wages have been reluctant to commit themselves to a specific Computable General Equilibrium (CGE) model. Instead, they have tried to use a shortcut, by estimating the 'factor content of trade' [and] this shortcut has been almost universally rejected by trade theorists – myself included – as an invalid procedure.[14]

In the next section we take up Krugman's (1995c, p. 22) challenge:

> At the very least, I would challenge those economists who main-
> tain that trade has in fact had large impacts on wages to pro-
> duce an illustrative CGE model, with plausible parameters, that
> is consistent with that view. I claim that it cannot be done.

Here a fully specified CGE model will be used to analyse the impact of an 'alternative history' and to answer the question of what
relative wages would have been but for the possibility of trading
with the non-OECD countries.[15]

6.5 WORLDSCAN, A DESCRIPTION OF THE MODEL[16]

In 1992 the CPB (Netherlands Bureau for Economic Policy Analysis)
published a long-term scenario study of the world economy, containing a comparative strength analysis of major world regions, which
were confronted with a number of emerging trends providing a set
of major policy challenges for each region. The study contained a
number of possible future scenarios which were distinguished by
the way in which regions might react to these policy challenges.
Stated loosely, regions could react by choosing a free market approach, a co-operative approach, or an equilibrium approach. The
WorldScan model was developed with these possibilities in mind.[17]
It was therefore constructed as a flexible model, with a long-term
focus, but with the central aim to construct medium-to-long-term
scenarios and perform stylised policy simulations. Figure 6.1 summarises the major features of the model.

In order to analyse long-run developments in the world economy,
while being interested mainly in a transition process of 25–30 years,
the core of the model was set up with more than one analytical
time phase in mind. The long-run outcomes are analysed with the
standard textbook trade model, namely the HOS model of trade
combined with the neoclassical (Solow) model of economic growth.
The assumption of uniform technologies across regions is relaxed
in WorldScan – that is, differences in production technology between countries can exist. Technological change is modelled as a
catching-up process by less advanced countries to the levels in advanced countries. In the short to medium run, an Armington approach is used to allow for two-way trade between countries and

Figure 6.1   Overview of the WorldScan model

The Core Model

WorldScan is a multi-sector, multi-region, dynamic computable general equilibrium model (CGE) for the world economy. It has been designed to support economic scenario studies on a time frame of 25–35 years. The model contains a neo-classical core model for long-term development, based on a Solow growth model and a Heckscher-Ohlin trade model, the dimensions of which are presented below:

Regions	Sectors	Production factors
Western Europe	Agriculture and food	Low-skilled labour
Japan	Raw materials and energy	High-skilled labour
Other OECD and South Africa	Intermediate goods	Capital
Latin America	Consumption goods	(fixed factor)
China Economic Area	Capital goods	
Dynamic Asian Economies	Non-tradables	*Intermediate inputs*
India and other South Asia	International transport	Raw materials and
Sub-Saharan Africa		energy
Middle East and Northern Africa		Intermediate goods
Eastern Europe/FSU		

Extensions to the Core Model

Extensions are made to add realism to scenarios and in so doing bridge the gap between academic and policy discussions. These include

- A disequilibrium closure is introduced to illustrate medium-term dynamics of shocks
- Catching-up of productivity levels to a specified technological frontier, depending upon a number of endogenous factors
- A capital-vintage approach is used to reflect short- to medium-term rigidities in changing production capacity
- An Armington trade specification, allowing market power to determine medium-term trade patterns, while allowing Heckscher-Ohlin mechanisms in the long run
- Imperfect financial capital mobility with a portfolio model, with a specification allowing penetration in financial markets without continuously increasing interest rates
- A consumption demand system depending upon *per capita* income, and developing towards a universal pattern
- A Lewis-type informal sector in developing regions, which provides a surplus of labour resource to the formal economy, enabling growth due to low wages during a longer period.

The model is calibrated on a 1990 database containing consistent bilateral trade flows and input–output information, with no Rest of the World (ROW) region. Elasticities are 'guesstimates' – i.e. no attempt has been made to estimate them using econometric methods.

The version used here aggregates all non-OECD regions into one aggregate region – 'non-OECD'.
Source: Geurts *et al.* (1995).

the role of national market power in determining trade patterns.[18]

The labour market is separated into two types of labour, high and low-skilled and is able to generate unemployment, unemployment being caused by a combination of efficiency considerations and search activity (affected by social security measures) on the labour market. Appendix 6.1 (p. 139) shows data on skill endowments across regions.

The model has a rather stylised input–output table in which one intermediate goods sector delivers to all other sectors. This sector is the only one to use raw materials as a direct input. Figure 6.2 shows the structure.

The model meets the key limitations of the literature that were stressed in Section 6.3. The first was labelled 'diagonal product differentiation within industries'. This limitation is related to the fact that factor-use ratios differ substantially between (in principle separable) activities within a single industry. To apply factor proportions theory appropriately it is necessary to reaggregate the most detailed industrial data available according to the nature of the production process, that is to the factor use ratios. Within certain bounds, WorldScan's data set is reaggregated to achieve this goal.[19] Although the sector names may suggest otherwise, the nature of production has been decisive in the classification. Appendix 6.2 characterises the sectors by the production elasticities in the Cobb–Douglas production functions. The Capital Goods sector and the Sheltered sector are relatively skill-intensive whereas the Agricultural Products and the Consumer Goods are relatively unskilled-labour-intensive.

Richardson (1995, p. 35) summarises the second basic problem common to the existing literature that was stressed in Section 6.3:

> international economists usually work with models that ignore any natural rate of unemployment (or hold it exogenous); that neglect the way education and training can change the endowments of human capital and pure labour; and that pay little attention to transitional dynamics, including intersectoral and interregional immobility of labour and how subtle and chronic ... the frictions can be.

WorldScan meets these omissions, although space constraints prevent a full discussion here (for a detailed discussion, see Geurts *et al.*, 1995).

Figure 6.2   The WorldScan input–output natrix

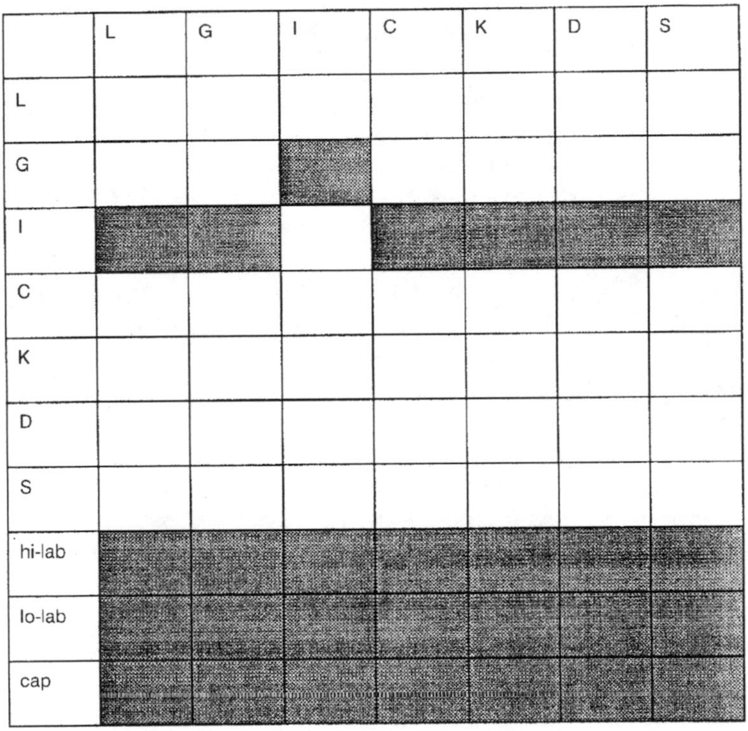

	L	G	I	C	K	D	S
L							
G			▓				
I	▓	▓		▓	▓	▓	▓
C							
K							
D							
S							
hi-lab	▓	▓	▓	▓	▓	▓	▓
lo-lab	▓	▓	▓	▓	▓	▓	▓
cap	▓	▓	▓	▓	▓	▓	▓

L = agriculture and food
G = raw materials and energy
I = intermediate goods
C = consumption goods
K = capital goods

D = international services (cif-fob margin)
S = sheltered
hi-lab = high-skilled labour
lo-lab = low-skilled labour
cap = capital

6.6   THE EXPERIMENT, THE NON-OECD IN ISOLATION

6.6.1   Introduction

Most economists will agree that the further integration of developing countries into the world economy is a plausible scenario. What could be the effect of the recent and future integration? This section describes an experiment designed to answer this question. For this experiment, WorldScan is used under two scenarios, a common sense baseline scenario and an alternative scenario in which non-OECD countries are delinked from world markets as a result of protectionist barriers in those countries.

The baseline simulation, aimed at mimicking the actual developments in the world economy since 1990, is used as a reference path. The model is calibrated such that it reproduces a 1990 dataset. In the extrapolation from the base year onwards, a certain arbitrariness is unavoidable, as we have to infer how average growth in a diverse group of non-OECD countries will develop. The extrapolation is necessary as the world economy, mimicked in WorldScan, is characterised by rigidities and hence needs time to adjust to the drastic measures we inflict upon on it in the experiment.

The baseline data on the labour market, as is to be expected, show unemployment in Europe exceeding that in the USA, which in turn exceeds that in Japan. In these three regions unemployment primarily afflicts low-skilled workers. The growth of real wages in the baseline is moderate in these three regions and slightly unfavourable to low-skilled workers. There are high unemployment rates in the non-OECD region in the baseline reflecting the dual character of the economy. No social safety net is available, and therefore workers not employed in the primary sector of the economy have to work in the secondary sector at subsistence level. There is strong growth of real wages in this region in the baseline due to technological catch-up.

The baseline trade patterns show that the OECD regions are net importers of the low-skilled-intensive consumer goods and exporters of the high-skilled-intensive capital goods. Europe and Japan are particularly strong in intermediate products. Japan (as well as Europe) is a huge importer of raw materials. The USA exports raw materials. The non-OECD is mostly dependent on the exports of primary products to finance the imports of high-skilled-intensive capital goods (the baseline data are presented in Nahuis, 1996).

6.6.2　The Alternative Scenario

The design of the alternative scenario is as follows. The non-OECD region raises drastic trade barriers with the aim of becoming isolated from the OECD region. On all (potential) trade flows, import and export taxes are levied in order to squeeze the actual trade flows as quickly and as far as possible. Technology and preferences, endogenous in Worldscan, are kept at the baseline level in this exercise in order to separate out the pure Heckscher-Ohlin

Table 6.3 Tax levels in the non-OECD region, 1995

	Import tax	*Export tax*
Intermediary goods	240.0	95.0
Consumer goods	240.0	95.0
Capital goods	240.0	95.0
Agriculture	1175.0	1175.0
Raw materials	1175.0	1175.0

trade effect.[20] Tax revenues are returned in a non-distortionary manner to a representative consumer – that is, the propensity to consume out of government income is not different from other types of income. In Table 6.3 the actual implemented tax levels are reported. The different rates are those necessary to eliminate actual trade flows, given the limitations of obtaining a numerical solution.[21]

6.6.3 The Results

This section discusses the results of our experiment in the following manner. Three questions need to be answered. First, as the experiment relies on indirect measures (trade taxes) to achieve the aim of removing all trade with non-OECD countries, we need to check whether these measures succeeded in their aim. Second, what is the sign and magnitude of the results? The third question is: Can we explain the results? The experiment's design was aimed at answering the 'but for' question of how factor rewards change when the possibility of trade with LDCs is removed. Simply, legally restricting trade would be the most direct measure, but this is not feasible in this modelling exercise. Hence we first check whether the indirect measures are effective in eliminating trade between the rich and poor regions.

Table 6.4 shows the fraction of output that is exported and the fraction of non-OECD absorption that is imported in the alternative scenario. A small fraction (less than a half per cent) of consumer goods is still exported and a similar fraction of capital goods is still imported. As consumer goods and capital goods are differentiated (and imperfect substitutes) across the world, irrespective of the price, a small volume is always demanded.[22] The small import shares for the homogeneous goods (Agriculture and Raw materials) exist for technical reasons (see n. 21).

Table 6.4   Trade dependence indicators

	Export[a]	Import[b]
Agriculture	0.000	0.018
Raw materials	0.000	0.016
Intermediary prod.	0.000	0.000
Consumption goods	0.005	0.000
Capital goods	0.000	0.003

Notes:
[a] Export share in output in reference year.
[b] Import share in absorption in reference year.

Source: Own simulation results.

The somewhat less than complete cut-off of the non-OECD from the world economy in principal hampers the interpretation, at least using FCT methods (see Leamer, 1996b). However, this is not troublesome here. Leamer's argument hinges on the assumption of the law of one price on world markets. In our alternative scenario, the relative prices of OECD products differ significantly from the relative prices of non-OECD products. Hence, prices and factor rewards are determined by OECD endowments and are virtually independent of conditions outside the OECD.

We now turn to look at the effects of the trade contraction. Table 6.5 shows the impact on the labour market in the four regions. The labour market adjusts in, what might be called a 'Stolper–Samuelson manner'. The terms of trade worsen considerably, the price of the (low-skilled-intensive) imports rises relative to the price of (high-skilled-intensive) exports.[23] The logic of the Stolper–Samuelson theorem is that to maintain zero profits the relative wage of the unskilled should increase when trade with low-wage economies ceases. All OECD regions show a considerable decrease in the skill premium from approximately 1.65 in the baseline to around 1.50 in the alternative simulation. This means that, compared to the baseline, the skill premium cumulatively declines by 15 percentage points. The effect on relative wages is slightly less in Europe than in the USA and Japan. At the same time, Europe shows some decline in the unemployment rate of low-skilled workers, while this decline is negligible in the other two OECD regions.

Hence, the retreat of non-OECD countries from the world markets improves the relative position of low-skilled workers in the OECD. In other words, according to this simulation, a perceptible

Table 6.5 Differences between the baseline and the experiment in 2010 for the labour market

	USA	Europe	Japan	Non-OECD
Wage low skilled as % high skilled	5.8	5.0	5.7	–3.0
Unemployment low as % of supply	–0.3	–1.1	–0.1	4.6
Skill premium baseline (2010)	1.66	1.60	1.65	3.05
Skill premium experiment (2010)	1.51	1.48	1.51	3.37
Change in skill premium	–0.15	–0.12	–0.14	0.32

Source: Own simulation results.

part of the actual and further expected worsening of the relative position of low-skilled workers may be attributed to the integration of non-OECD into the world economy. The model shows that in Europe, low-skilled jobs are more likely to disappear as a result of non-OECD competition, while in the rest of the OECD a further adjustment in relative wages prevents the loss in low-skilled jobs, although the differences are modest.

In the non-OECD countries, the opposite happens. As a consequence of sheltering its industries from world markets, the wage disparity within the non-OECD countries increases. High-skilled workers become even more scarce, because the import of relatively high-skilled products almost stops. At the same time there is a significant increase in unemployment – that is, in the number of people in the secondary or informal sector. Lack in export possibilities hampers the development in the formal sector and the slower rate in wage increase in the formal sector diminishes the flow out of the informal sector.

All these changes in the labour markets are the result of changes in trade patterns and sectoral structures. The most significant change in the OECD countries is the increased production of low-skill-intensive consumption goods at the expense of the production of high-skill intensive capital goods. The capacity for production of consumption goods in the OECD expands for two reasons. First, the demand for OECD products increases because non-OECD products become too expensive. Second, OECD producers of consumption goods require lower risk premiums because growing non-OECD prices increase the probability of higher future profits. Capacity reduction in the capital goods sector is mainly the result of the fall in non-OECD import demand. Outside the manufacturing sectors, similar shifts occur.

Delinking of the non-OECD countries with respect to world goods markets could have grave consequences for the international capital markets. It could easily lead to a debt crisis because, without exports, countries with a net debt cannot pay the interest payments. If existing debt is not remitted, and if international capital markets remain linked, then such debt problems may have severe domestic consequences, particularly if countries are not able to adopt monetary policies to stabilise the domestic economy after the huge tax increases that would be necessary. The model experiment shows that these financial instabilities could ultimately lead to an enormous fall in income. But even without financial instabilities, the fall in income in the non-OECD region would still be huge from delinking from the world markets. The main reason is the diminishing flow of workers out of the informal sector. Because productivity levels and wage levels in the informal sector are only a fraction of those in the formal sector, this shift results in a severe loss of welfare.

To summarise, the model experiment shows that integration of non-OECD countries with large reserves of low-skilled labour may lead to rapid welfare gains in those countries and to problems for low-skilled workers in OECD labour markets. These latter effects are more significant than most partial equilibrium empirical studies show. The model experiment suggests that the small effects of trade on inequality in existing studies may be the result of the different methodology used.

6.7 EVALUATION AND CONCLUSIONS

Comparing the numbers in Table 6.5 and Table 6.1 shows that a substantial part of the increased skill premium might be attributed to trade. Take the example of the USA where the skill premium rose approximately 18 percentage points (2 × 0.09) in the 1980s (Table 6.1). Our numerical analysis suggests that trade can explain up to 15 percentage points. A few remarks are necessary to temper this result. First, in the baseline the skill premium exceeds the one reported by Davis (1992) and OECD (1993) somewhat. Secondly (and related to the first remark), the skill classification in WorldScan and in other studies is different (see Appendix 6.1). Our qualitative judgement is that trade is responsible for half of the rise in inequality for unskilled workers, a judgement similar to that of Minford, Riley and Nowell (1996), also derived from a numerical general equilibrium model.[24]

The increase in the relative wage of skilled workers in the 1980s in the USA is the basic observation we have sought to explain. This change is hard to explain by movements in the relative supply of skilled and unskilled workers. We argue that the rejection of a role for trade in most of the existing literature (and with it, by default, the identification of biased technological change as the main source of increasing inequality) is premature.

We show, in an exercise with a numerical general equilibrium model, that neglecting a potential role for trade in explaining the widening wage gap is indeed hasty. The exercise, a complete cut off of the non-OECD region from the world economy, yielded a decline of the wage premium of up to 15 percentage points in OECD regions: far too much to neglect!

APPENDIX 6.1 SKILL REPRESENTATION AND POPULATION IN WORLDSCAN

Skill Endowments in WorldScan

	Share world population (%)	*Ratio skilled/unskilled*
North America	6.2	1
Western Europe	8.4	1
Japan	2.3	1
Non-OECD	83.1	0.15

In the skill representation in the literature several approaches are followed. To give a flavour of the possibilities and with it the problems, a few approaches are summed up in the following. Wood (1994, Appendix 1 and 2), deals with this more extensively.

Production and non-production workers – i.e. *the actual occupations* – are used by Lawrence and Slaughter (1993). Leamer (1994b) describes and criticises this division. A problem is that the division line is drawn above the line-supervision level. Therefore, for example, workers doing product development (supervised) are classified as production workers, and highway truck drivers (not supervised) are classified as non-production workers. The division of the dataset is thus not optimal. Baldwin (1995, p. 24) is far less sceptical:

Their main data source is the US Annual Survey of Manufactures, which provides information about the use of production and non-production workers in four-digit SIC industries. This classification of workers closely mirrors the distinction between blue-collar and white-collar occupations, as well as between those who do not have a high school education and who do.

Murphy and Welch (1992) as well as Bound and Johnson (1992) apply a labour market framework with in principle separated markets for workers with different *education* (and age and experience). Another approach is to analyse *the wage structure* like Juhn, Murphy and Pierce (1993) and assume that the lower percentiles accord to the low-skilled workers and the higher percentiles to high-skilled workers.

APPENDIX 6.2   SECTORS AND SKILL INTENSITY IN WORLDSCAN

Production Elasticities in Four-region Version of WorldScan

	High skilled	Low skilled	Capital goods	Intermediary goods	Raw materials
Capital goods	0.45	0.15	0.30	0.10	0.00
Sheltered	0.40	0.20	0.30	0.10	0.00
Transport (int. serv.)	0.40	0.20	0.30	0.10	0.00
Raw materials	0.35	0.35	0.20	0.10	0.00
Agriculture	0.15	0.45	0.15	0.25	0.00
Intermediate goods	0.15	0.15	0.20	0.00	0.50
Consumer goods	0.15	0.50	0.20	0.15	0.00
Informal sector	0.00	0.80	0.10	0.10	0.00

To obtain an indication of the actual skill intensity of sectors it is necessary to take intermediary inputs into account. These calculations have not actually been performed as the difference in production elasticity with respect to the intermediate input hardly differs between the sectors, with the exception of the Agricultural sector.

APPENDIX 6.3   THE STOLPER–SAMUELSON THEORY AND DIAGONAL PRODUCT DIFFERENTIATION

The Initial Situation

Two industries, where the left square represents the skilled-intensive one, the right square the unskilled-intensive industry. The number of skilled workers is represented by the light coloured surface, the number of unskilled is denoted by the dark coloured surface.

Initial situation

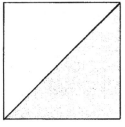

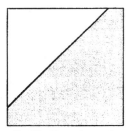

Skilled-intensive sector   Unskilled-intensive sector

Stolper–Samuelson Mechanism

To help get acquainted with the use of this type of graphs, the Stolper–
Samuelson mechanism is depicted for the case of a decrease in the relative price of the unskilled-intensive industry's product. Employment shifts
to the skilled-intensive industry and both industries become less skilled-
intensive.

Stolper–Samuelson

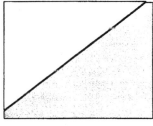

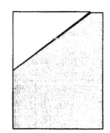

Skilled-intensive sector   Unskilled-intensive sector

Diagonal Product Differentiation within Industries

The case with 'diagonal product differentiation within industries' is depicted in the next graph. When foreign trade causes outsourcing of the
most unskilled intensive slices of an industry or bankruptcy of the most
unskilled intensive varieties of the domestic industry, the aggregate skill
intensity within both industries increases and the sum of both industries
employment decreases. The shrinking manufacturing sector causes an outflow
of mostly unskilled workers to the service sector.[25]

Outsourcing/heterogenous production function hypothesis

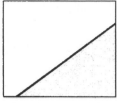

Skilled-intensive sector

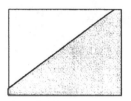

Unskilled-intensive sector

Notes

* Valuable comments and suggestions, by Ben Geurts, Henri de Groot, Theo van de Klundert, Paul Tang and Hans Timmer are gratefully acknowledged.
1. Numbers in the introduction are taken from Lawrence and Slaughter (1993).
2. The labelling of workers as 'skilled' and 'unskilled' is a short cut that is necessary for analysing the issue at stake in the framework that we adopt. Though the aggregation of workers into such groups is of course necessary, it is not without problems; see Appendix 6.1 (p. 139).
3. The Ricardian characteristics, the total factor productivity (TPF) levels, are equal in both runs of the model.
4. Wood (1994) talks of non-competing imports in specific industries. Finger (1975) refers to trade overlap, which differs from the concept of intra-industry trade. Feenstra and Hanson (1995) stress the importance of outsourcing.
5. See Appendix 6.3 (p. 140) for a graphical exposition of the difference between the Stolper–Samuelson theorem and the 'diagonal product differentiation' approach. The choice of 'diagonal' will also become clear.
6. Nahuis (1997) is more elaborate on the rationale for this hypothesis. Finger (1975) is an early contribution stressing this problem. Leamer (1994a) clearly shows that reaggregation of goods categories according to the nature of the production process is necessary to use factor proportions theory.
7. For the story to fit the facts, one should remember the declining size of the manufacturing sector. It is necessary or at least plausible that the trends in this story are accompanied by an on average shrinking manufacturing sector. Besides that, the increased skill intensity in manufacturing has to be met with a response somewhere else in the economy, as it is not solely supply-driven. Somewhere the low-skilled should be absorbed. Either the composition of the group of unemployed should become more unskilled, or the sheltered sector should show an opposite skill intensity development. The minimum requirement for this story not to be rejected is that the skill intensity of the sheltered sector is increasing less than the one in the exposed part of the

economy, as the relative supply increase of skilled workers has to be taken into account.

8. In his comment on Lawrence and Slaughter (1993). A solution to this problem is offered: consider the development of skill intensity within sectors compared to the national average (this should fall if the Stolper–Samuelson effect has been dominant).

9. See also Bhagwati and Dehejia (1994).

10. By constructing an equivalent autarky equilibrium – for example, by adjusting domestic resources for the amount of resources that are contained in trade – they are able to exclude the counter intuitive result, that is factor prices moving along with endowments, only under fairly restrictive assumptions (unitary substitution elasticity on the demand and production side). Leamer (1996b) reiterates and extends the analysis by Deardorff and Staiger and adds to their conclusions that only the repercussions for earnings shares (not levels) of a complete elimination of trade can be established under these highly restrictive assumptions.

11. The issue, raised also by Bhagwati and Dehejia (1994) – that it is highly problematic to calculate the FCT where there is a serious trade imbalance – certainly makes it troublesome to use the FCT approach for the 1980s.

12. Krugman is also eager to accept the restrictions following from the Deardorff and Staiger analysis as being not too far from realistic.

13. As Leamer (1996, p. 22) says:

> Even if the US has market power, internal prices of tradables can be affected by tariffs and or nontariff barriers. Thus we are getting an answer to the policy question, whether or not the shock is internal or external.

14. In the remainder of his paper Krugman (1995b) is considerably less harsh on FCT calculations.

15. Deardorff and Hakura (1994) is an excellent reference on the formulation of the right questions.

16. Arjan Gielen is gratefully acknowledged for his contribution to the model description.

17. This means that an unequivocal representation of one economic paradigm – as is present in many CGE models – is not found in WorldScan. The model can be run with a focus on the equilibrium perspective, hence neoclassical theory is the core of the model. Alternatively a coordination perspective might be used more or less dominantly: a Keynesian model. A free market perspective reflects the class of theories that reflects neo-Austrian and Schumpeterian thought. More elaboration on the perspectives can be found in CPB (1992), more on theory and the model in Geurts et al (1995).

18. The Armington (1969) approach implies that goods are not perfect substitutes, as they are differentiated by country of production. In this respect there is strong resemblance to the monopolistic competition approach by Dixit and Stiglitz (1977). In other respects the approaches

differ, especially that every entity (region, country) has no specified
number of producers. Hence the supply within a single entity is depicted by a representative firm. To illustrate (for countries) you might
think of French cheese as an imperfect substitute for Dutch and Dan-
ish cheese.

19. As can be seen in Figure 6.2, the I–O matrix of the model is very
empty. This implies that the dataset has to be adapted. In this process care has been taken that sectors with similar input intensities are
rearranged such that they end up in a WorldScan sector with appropriate production elasticities.

20. Trade-induced technological change would potentially build a
bridge between opponents and proponents of the view that trade is
relevant.

21. To smooth the numerical exercise, the tariff rate, reported in Table
6.3, is valid only when net trade reaches a sufficient proportion of
domestic absorption, thus the tariffs are brought into effect with an s-
curve related to net trade. The tariff rate that operates if trade is
only a very small fraction of domestic use is much more moderate.
Here, a choice is made in the trade-off between obtaining a numerical solution and squeezing trade sufficiently.

22. In WorldScan, slowly vanishing brand loyalty is introduced, such that
changes in relative prices of differentiated varieties are translated gradu-
ally into changing market shares. In the end, markets can be lost completely (if a price difference is persistent).

23. A different way to understand the tendency for the relative wage to
move in a direction beneficial for those with less skills is to see the
world as a (single) closed economy. After tax walls have been raised,
the relative endowment of the closed world economy consisting of
Europe, Japan and the USA, are such that unskilled workers are much
more scarce (the numbers in Appendix 6.1 reveal that a negligible
role for trade is very hard to imagine).

24. Lawrence and Evans (1996) use a very simple model to perform an
exercise that tries to capture the maximum impact of trade with LDCs.
In the most comparable simulation a relative wage change of almost
8 per cent is the final result (keep in mind that their shock is bigger
– we eliminate existing trade, they maximise possible trade). To mention two important differences: their consumption share of the non-
tradable sector exceeds ours and the sectoral disaggregation used by
Lawrence and Evans is too limited to grasp the full impact of the
emergence of low-wage countries.

25. For the picture to fit the facts, one should remind oneself of the declining manufacturing sector size. It is necessary, or at least plausible
that driving forces in this approach (i.e. outsourcing) are accompanied
by an on average shrinking manufacturing sector. Besides that, the
increased skill intensity in manufacturing has to be met with a response
somewhere else in the economy. Either the composition of the group
of unemployed should become more unskilled, or the sheltered sector
should show an opposite skill-intensity development. The minimum
requirement for this story not to be rejected is that the skill intensity

of the sheltered sector is increasing less than the one in the exposed part of the economy, as the relative supply increase of skilled workers has to be taken into account.

References

Armington, P.S. (1969) 'A theory of demand for products distinguished by place of production,' *IMF Staff Papers*, 16, 159–178.

Baldwin, R.E. (1995) 'The effect of trade and foreign direct investment on employment and relative wages,' *Working Paper*, 5037, NBER.

Berman, E., Bound, J. and Griliches, Z. (1994) 'Changes in the demand for skilled labor within US manufacturing: evidence from the annual survey of manufacturers,' *Quarterly Journal of Economics*, 109, 367–97.

Bhagwati, J. and Dehejia, V. (1994) 'Freer trade and wages of the unskilled – is Marx striking again?', in Bhagwati, J. and Kosters, M.H. (eds), *Trade and Wages. Levelling Wages Down?*, Washington, DC: AEI Press, 36–75.

Bound, J. and Johnson, G. (1992) 'Changes in the structure of wages in the 1980s: an evaluation of alternative explanations,' *American Economic Review*, 82, 371–92.

CPB (1992) *Scanning the Future, A Long-term Scenario Study of the World Economy 1990–2015*, The Hague: SDU Publishers.

Davis, S.J. (1992) 'Cross-country patterns of change in relative wages', in Blanchard, O. and Fischer, S. (eds), *NBER Macroeconomics Annual 1992*, 239–300.

Deardorff, A.V. and Hakura, D.S. (1994) 'Trade and wages – what are the questions?', in Bhagwati, J. and Kosters, M.H. (eds), *Trade and Wages. Levelling Wages Down?*, Washington, DC: AEI Press, 76–107.

Deardorff, A.V. and Staiger, R.W. (1988) 'An interpretation of the factor content of trade', *Journal of International Economics*, 24, 93–107.

Dixit, A.K. and Stiglitz, J.E. (1977) 'Monopolistic competition and optimum product diversity,' *American Economic Review*, 67, 293–7.

Feenstra, R.C. and Hanson, G.R. (1995) 'Foreign investment, outsourcing and relative wages', *Working Paper*, 5121, NBER.

Finger, J.M. (1975) 'Trade overlap and intra-industry trade,' *Economic Inquiry*, 13, 581–9.

Geurts, B., Gielen, A., Nahuis, R., Tang, P. and Timmer, H. (1995) 'WorldScan: An economic worldmodel for scenario analysis,' paper prepared for the review meeting of WorldScan, 9–10 November 1995.

Hall, R.E. (1993) 'Comments and Discussion: Comment by Robert E. Hall' in Laurene, R.Z. and Slaughter, M.A.

Katz, L.F. and Murphy, K.M. (1992) 'Changes in relative wages, 1963–1987: supply and demand factors', *Quarterly Journal of Economics*, 107, 35–78.

Kosters, M.H. (1994) 'An overview of changing wage patterns in the labor market', in Bhagwati, J. and Kosters, M.H. (eds), *Trade and Wages. Levelling Wages Down?*, Washington, DC: AEI Press, 1–35.

Krugman, P.R. (1995a) 'Growing world trade: causes and consequences,' *Brookings Papers on Economic Activity*, 1, 327–62.

Krugman, P.R. (1995b) 'Technology, trade, and factor prices,' *Working Paper*, 5355, NBER.

Krugman, P.R. (1995c) 'Trade and wages', paper presented at the Econometric Society meeting, Tokyo.

Krugman, P.R. and Lawrence, R.Z. (1993) 'Trade, jobs and wages,' *Working Paper*, 4478, NBER.

Juhn, C., Murphy, K.M. and Pierce, B. (1993) 'Wage inequality and the rise in returns to skill,' *Journal of Political Economy*, 101, 410–42.

Lawrence, R.Z. and Evans, C.L. (1996) 'Trade and wages: insights from the crystal ball', *Working Paper*, 5633, NBER.

Lawrence, R.Z. and Slaughter, M.A. (1993) 'International trade and American wages in the 1980s: giant sucking sound or small hiccup?,' *Brookings Papers: Microeconomics*, 2, 161–226.

Leamer, E.E. (1994a) 'Wage effects of a US–Mexican free trade agreement', *Working Paper*, 3991, NBER.

Leamer, E.E. (1994b) 'Trade, wages and revolving door ideas', *Working Paper*, 4716, NBER.

Leamer, E.E. (1996a) 'In search of Stolper–Samuelson effects on US wages', *Working Paper*, 5427, NBER.

Leamer, E.E. (1996b) 'What is the use of factor contents?', *Working Paper*, 5448, NBER.

Minford, P., Riley, J. and Nowell, E. (1996) 'The elixir of development: trade, technology and western labour markets,' unpublished manuscript.

Murphy, K.M. and Welch, F. (1992) 'The structure of wages', *Quarterly Journal of Economics*, 107, 285–326.

Nahuis, R. (1996) 'Global Integration and Wages in a General Equilibrium World Model: Contributions of WorldScan' unpublished working paper, Tilburg University.

Nahuis, R. (1997) 'On globalisation, trade and wages', Tilburg University, FEW Research Memorandum, 747.

OECD (1993) *OECD Employment Outlook 1993*, Paris: OECD.

Richardson, J.D. (1995) 'Income inequality and trade: how to think, what to conclude,' *Journal of Economic Perspectives*, 9, 33–55.

Sachs, J.D. and Shatz, H.J. (1994) 'Trade and jobs in US manufacturing', *Brookings Papers on Economic Activity*, 1, 1–84.

Wood, A. (1994) *North–South Trade, Employment and Inequality*, Oxford: Clarendon Press.

7 Did Outsourcing to Low-wage Countries Hurt Less-skilled Workers in the UK?

Bob Anderton and Paul Brenton*

7.1 INTRODUCTION

Over much of the past two decades the relative wages and employment of the low skilled have fallen dramatically in the UK. Between 1980 and 1992, for example, the real earnings of the top tenth of male earners in the UK rose by 51 per cent, whereas the earnings of the bottom tenth only increased by 11 per cent.[1] Nickell (1996) shows that the unemployment rate of less-skilled males in the UK rose from 6.4 per cent in the mid-1970s to 18.2 per cent in the mid-1980s, whereas over the same period the unemployment rate of skilled males rose only from 2.0 per cent to 4.7 per cent.

The rise in UK wage inequality has also been in many directions. Although the most significant widening of relative wages has occurred between manual and non-manual workers, there has also been a large increase in the dispersion of wages *within* the categories of both manual and non-manual workers (see Gregg and Machin, 1994).

Most research into the causes of this deterioration in the economic fortunes of the less skilled in the UK finds that increased trade has had very little impact on either the employment or relative wages of low-skilled workers (see, for example, Machin, Ryan and van Reenen (1996) and Haskel, (1996a, 1996b)).[2] However, recent econometric research on the USA, based on the notion of outsourcing, where firms respond to competition from low-wage countries by moving low-skill-intensive production activities abroad, does find a significant impact of trade on the relative employment and wages of unskilled workers (see Feenstra and Hanson, 1995, 1996).[3]

147

According to many measures, the deterioration in the economic circumstances of the low skilled has not grown at a steady rate in the UK, with much of the rise in wage inequality and the increase in the relative employment of skilled workers occurring in the early 1980s. The timing of these changes is suggestive of a relationship between outsourcing and the exchange rate (sterling appreciated strongly at the start of the 1980s).[4]

The objective of this chapter is to examine the impact of outsourcing on the relative wages and employment of the less skilled in the UK and to evaluate whether the large appreciation of sterling during 1979–81 encouraged a disproportionate increase in outsourcing. Did the appreciation make imports from the Newly-Industrialising Countries (NICs) so cheap that the higher profits made possible by outsourcing outweighed the risks and costs of switching to a new and untried supplier? Our analysis, by using proxies for outsourcing based solely on imports from low-wage countries, differs from previous studies which have proxied outsourcing by total sectoral imports from *all* countries, including advanced industrial countries.

7.2 FRAMEWORK AND METHODOLOGY

Part of the explanation for the decline in the economic fortunes of the less skilled seems to be a shift in demand towards higher-skilled workers. Two explanations are frequently offered for such a demand shift: first, that labour-saving technical progress has reduced the relative demand for unskilled workers; secondly, that increased international trade with the NICs, nations with an abundant supply of low-skill and low-wage labour, has decreased the demand for low-skilled workers in the advanced industrialised countries.

There are various mechanisms by which technical progress may reduce the relative wage of the less skilled. Technical progress which is biased towards reducing the use of unskilled labour will tend to increase the share of skilled, relative to unskilled, labour in production. This fall in demand for unskilled workers will tend to push down their wages and employment relative to the skilled in all industries. The increasing use of computers in the production process is often held up as a reason for the fall in demand for unskilled workers, and for the increase in the relative demand for skilled workers who are required to operate such machines.

Traditional trade theories primarily explain movements in relative wages across industries, whereas what needs to be explained is the dramatic fall in the relative wages and employment of unskilled workers *within* sectors. In this chapter we use the idea of outsourcing as the framework for analysing how trade with low-wage countries may push down the relative wages and employment of unskilled workers within industries. Outsourcing is where firms take advantage of both the low-wage costs of the NICs and modern production techniques, where the process of manufacturing a product can be broken down into numerous discrete activities, by moving the low-skill-intensive parts of production abroad to the NICs, but continuing to carry out the high-skill-intensive activities themselves in the high-wage industrialised countries.[5]

Once the low-skill activities have been performed, the goods are then imported back from the NICs and either used as intermediate inputs or sold as finished goods. Hence, trade with the NICs via this route will shift employment away from less-skilled towards skilled workers in countries such as the UK, and put downward pressure on the relative wages and employment of low-skilled workers within industries.

Several researchers have been puzzled by the 'lumpiness' of changes in the economic fortunes of the less skilled. Particularly large changes in the economic circumstances of the less skilled seem to have occurred in the early 1980s in the UK and USA (see Haskel, 1996a, Machin, 1996; Anderton and Brenton, 1996, for the UK, and Feenstra and Hanson, 1996, for the USA).[6] These periods roughly correspond with *large* appreciations of the currencies of the UK and USA which, in effect, decreased the cost of imports to UK and US purchasers. In the case of the UK, this period was certainly characterised by both a large increase in imports and a decline in the size of the manufacturing sector. During the period 1979–84, UK import penetration by all overseas countries rose by around 27 per cent and at the same time there was an increase of more than 120 per cent in the value of UK imports from the NICs; this coincided with a 25 per cent fall in manufacturing employment (resulting in a net loss of 1.8 million jobs).[7]

One explanation for a possible link between exchange rate movements and outsourcing can be derived from Orcutt (1950), who argues that the costs of switching from domestic to foreign suppliers may cause the price elasticity of imports to be bigger for large price changes than for small changes. A similar argument can be made for disproportionately large increases in outsourcing. When considering whether or not to outsource, UK producers have to take into the account the costs incurred when switching from in-house (or other domestic) supplies to foreign suppliers. For instance, when switching to foreign suppliers UK producers may have to modify production techniques to be compatible with the newly imported product and spend time ensuring that the new supplier is both reliable and produces a product of the required specifications and quality (as there is always some degree of uncertainty regarding the characteristics of previously untried imported goods and suppliers). Small changes in the price of foreign goods will consequently not be acted upon as the change in price differential will not cover switching costs.

In contrast, a large appreciation of sterling will result in a substantial differential between the costs of producing in-house (or domestic) goods and imports, which may be at least sufficient to cover the costs of switching. In summary, *switching costs* may cause a *disproportionate* increase in outsourcing during *large* exchange rate appreciations, which may partially explain the 'lumpiness' of changes in the economic circumstances of the less skilled. The increase in outsourcing will be difficult to reverse, even if the large appreciation of sterling is fully reversed, as UK producers will now have a greater understanding of the benefits of outsourcing since they are now familiar with the quality of goods not previously imported. In effect, the large temporary appreciation of sterling in the early 1980s may have acted as an introductory discount on import prices which encouraged UK producers to sample the quality of previously untried imported goods. Indeed, Anderton (1996a, 1996b) finds that the substantial temporary appreciation of sterling encouraged UK purchasers to permanently switch from domestic to foreign goods (which is consistent with a disproportionate increase in outsourcing at a time when the economic fortunes of the less skilled deteriorated very rapidly).[8]

Feenstra and Hanson (1995) use industry import shares (imports as a share of consumption in each industry) as a proxy for outsourcing and estimate that the growth of imports over the period 1979–87 explains 15–33 per cent of the increase in the share of wages of non-production labour in the US. In a later paper (Feenstra and Hanson, 1996), a measure of imports of intermediate inputs is used which generates a higher estimate of the impact of outsourcing: between 30 and 50 per cent of the increase in the wage share of skilled workers.

However, in both of these papers outsourcing is proxied using total imports from all countries, which implicitly captures outsourcing of US production to advanced industrialised countries as well as the NICs. There is no reason why firms would outsource low-skill-intensive activities, which is a key mechanism by which outsourcing affects the less skilled, to advanced industrialised countries which are high-skill-abundant. In contrast, in this chapter we disaggregate UK imports according to individual supplier countries and thereby construct an import share term for each industry based on imports solely from low-wage countries, thereby more accurately proxying outsourcing to them. In addition, by using dummy variables we will test whether the high level of sterling during the early 1980s had a disproportionate impact on outsourcing.

7.3 DATA AND ECONOMETRIC ANALYSIS

In this chapter we define non-manual workers as skilled and manual workers as less skilled using data published in the UK Census of Production (full details of all data used are given in Appendix 7.1, p. 161). Technology is proxied by R&D expenditure as a proportion of GDP.[9] The capital stock data are from O'Mahony, Wagner and Paulsen (1994). Imports and domestic production data were obtained from the bilateral dataset derived by Brenton and Winters (1992). The majority of the above data are disaggregated to the 4-digit level of the International Standard Industrial Classification (ISIC), covering about 80 manufacturing sectors. However, we concentrate here on two broad industries, textiles and non-electrical machinery production, and pool the data across 4-digit ISIC sectors within each of these industries in order to provide sufficient data for 'panel estimation'. We use annual data for the sample period 1970–87. Figures 3.6 and 3.7 of Chapter 3 (pp. 62–3) show movements in the wage bill and employment shares of non-production workers in the aggregate textiles and non-electrical machinery sectors. These data clearly suggest a substantial deterioration in the economic fortunes of the less skilled during the high level of sterling in the early 1980s.

The equations that we estimate are based upon the specifications for the relative wage and employment equations used by Machin, Ryan and van Reenen (1996). We begin with a simple restricted variable translog cost function for industry (i), as shown in (A) below, from which we derive the wage bill (*WB*) share equation in first differences, as shown in (B) below, and in which we proxy technology by R&D expenditure:[10]

$$C[\log W_{it}^{ls}, \log W_{it}^{hs}, \log K_{it}, \log Y_{it}, TECH_{it}] \qquad (A)$$

$$\Delta SW_{it} = \alpha_1 \Delta \log K_{it} + \alpha_2 \Delta \log Y_{it} + \alpha_3 (R\&D/Y)_{it} + \eta_{it} D_{it} + u_{it} \qquad (B)$$

where:

W_{it}^{ls}	= wage rate of low-skilled (manual workers) in industry i
W_{it}^{hs}	= wage rate of higher-skilled (non-manuals) in industry i
K_{it}	= capital stock in industry i
Y_{it}	= output in industry i
$TECH_{it}$	= proxy for technology in industry i
SW_{it}	= high-skilled wage bill share (i.e. $WB_{it}^{hs}/(WB_{it}^{ls} + WB_{it}^{hs})$)
WB	= wage bill
$R\&D_{it}$	= R&D expenditure in industry i
D_{it}	= set of time dummies
u	= error term

We then supplement (B) by adding our disaggregated measures of outsourcing, as in (C) below:

$$\Delta SW_{it} = \alpha_1 \Delta \log K_{it} + \alpha_2 \Delta \log Y_{it} + \alpha_3 (R\&D/Y)_{it} + \eta_{it} D_{it}$$
$$+ \alpha_4 \Delta \log MS_{it} + u_{it} \qquad (C)$$

where:

MS_{it} = UK imports of good i expressed as a share of total UK demand for good i (expressed in *value* terms)

We experiment with three different versions of the import variable, *MS*:

1. *MSN* = UK imports of good i from the NICs (that is, Singapore, South Korea, Taiwan and Hong Kong)
2. *MSV* = UK imports from the NICs plus the very-low-wage countries, such as the former COMECON countries plus a Rest of the World (ROW) category which includes China and other Asian economies, Latin American countries and African countries, but excludes the advanced industrialised countries[11]
3. *MSI* = UK imports from the advanced industrialised countries

We also estimate similarly specified relative employment share equations for the skilled as in (D) below:[12]

$$\Delta SE_{it} = \alpha_1 \Delta \log K_{it} + \alpha_2 \Delta \log Y_{it} + \alpha_3 (R\&D/Y)_{it} + \eta_{it} D_{it}$$
$$+ \alpha_4 \Delta \log MS_{it} + \alpha_5 \Delta \log RW_{it} + u_{it} \qquad \text{(D)}$$

where:

ΔSE_{it} = High-skill employment share in sector i (i.e., $E_{hsi}/(E_{hsi} + E_{lsi})$)

E_{lsi} = Employment of low-skilled workers (i.e. manuals) in sector i

E_{hsi} = Employment of higher-skilled workers (i.e., non-manuals) in sector i

$RW_{i,t}$ = Wage rates of high-skilled relative to low-skilled (i.e., W_{it}^{hs}/W_{it}^{ls})

Further, we test whether increasing imports by the UK affects the economic fortunes of the less skilled via changes in relative price competitiveness by estimating (E) below using the wage bill share as an example (again we experiment with three versions of the relative price term, according to the source of imports, in a similar fashion to the import penetration term).

$$\Delta SW_{it} = \alpha_1 \Delta \log K_{it} + \alpha_2 \Delta \log Y_{it} + \alpha_3 (R\&D/Y)_{it} + \eta_{it} D_{it}$$
$$+ \alpha_4 \Delta \log RP_{it} + u_{it} \qquad \text{(E)}$$

where RP = UK import price for good i divided by UK domestic price for good i. The RP term in (E) can be interpreted as representing price incentives to outsource. We expect the coefficient on RPV – the relative price of imports from low-wage countries – to have a negative sign, as a decline in RPV should encourage outsourcing and so decrease the demand for less-skilled workers.

Finally, we test whether large exchange rate movements have a disproportionate impact on the low-skilled by dummying our various relative price measures as shown in (F) below (again using the wage bill share as an example):

$$\Delta SW_{it} = \alpha_1 \Delta \log K_{it} + \alpha_2 \Delta \log Y_{it} + \alpha_3 (R\&D/Y)_{i,t} + \eta_{it} D_{it} +$$
$$\alpha_4 \Delta \log RP_{i,t} + \sum_{k=1}^{n} \alpha_4' \Delta \log RP_{it} + u_{it} \qquad \text{(F)}$$

The $\sum_{k=1}^{n} \alpha_4' \Delta \log RP_{it}$ terms in (F) are n annual dummies representing each year from 1978 onwards (that is, n dummies which have a value of 1 for a specific year and zero otherwise multiplied by the relative price term). The n individual α'_4 parameters there-fore give us a time profile of the elasticity of the relative price term and tell us whether the size of the elasticity varies in line with large movements in the exchange rate.

7.4 EMPIRICAL RESULTS

Our major empirical result is that outsourcing to low-wage coun-tries does appear to have had a significant impact upon the rela-tive fortunes of unskilled workers in the UK. We began our econometric analysis by experimenting with our three different measures of import penetration. We estimated our basic equations (C) and (D) above including the different import penetration meas-ures separately both with and without the technology, R&D, term. We consistently found that only the import penetration term which includes the very low-wage countries (MSV) was positively signed and statistically significant.[13]

(1) and (2) of Tables 7.1 and 7.2 show the results for the wage share and employment share specifications, respectively, using the import penetration MSV term.[14] In general, the equations perform fairly well with an R^2 usually exceeding those reported in Machin, Ryan and van Reenen (1996). (2) in each table adds the R&D term to the previous equation, but we exclude the capital stock term as the inclusion of both terms tends to decrease the 't'-stat-istic of both variables (possibly due to multicollinearity).[15] It can be seen that the R&D term always has a positive sign in both the wage and employment share specifications but is not statistically significant (although the t-statistic is usually above 1). However, the import penetration term is strongly significant and positively signed regardless of whether or not the R&D term is included.

The wage share equation (1) shows that the change in output is negatively signed and the change in the capital stock is positively signed, but both variables are not statistically significant. The signs for these two variables conform with our priors as we expect complementarities between capital and skill and a short-run de-cline in output tends to hurt the wages and employment of the less skilled relative to the skilled.[16] The employment share equation (1) shows that an increase in the relative wages of skilled workers does indeed decrease the relative demand for skilled workers. Both equations show that an increase in import penetration from lower-

Table 7.1   Wage bill share equations (ΔSW_{it})

Equation	(1)	(2)	(3)	(4)	(5)	(6)
C	0.32[1]	0.12[2]	0.33[1]	0.11[1]	0.35[1]	−0.14[1]
	(0.75)	(0.03)	(0.77)	(0.23)	(0.84)	(0.31)
$\Delta logY_{it}$	−0.63[1]	−0.81[1]	−0.98[1]	−0.012	−0.91[1]	−0.011
	(1.03)	(1.28)	(1.60)	(1.86)	(1.51)	(1.78)
$\Delta logK_{it}$	0.089	–	0.112	–	0.128	–
	(1.04)		(1.25)		(1.46)	
$(R\&D/Y)_{it-1}$	–	0.143	–	0.198	–	0.214
		(1.06)		(1.41)		(1.56)
$\Delta logMSV_{it}$	0.014	0.015	–	–	–	–
	(3.23)	(3.25)				
$\Delta logRPV_{it}$	–	–	0.38[1]	0.47[1]	0.44[1]	0.55[1]
			(0.80)	(0.85)	(0.98)	(1.04)
$\Delta logRPV80_{it}$	–	–	−0.034	−0.033	–	–
			(1.74)	(1.70)		
$\Delta logRPV80_{tx,t}$	–	–	–	–	−0.074	−0.074
					(2.97)	(2.87)
N	176	143	176	143	176	143
R^2	0.3374	0.3309	0.3075	0.2922	0.3318	0.3205
SEE	.01296	.01325	.01329	.01368	.01306	.01340

Notes:
[1,2,3] Values are actual parameters multiplied by 10^2, 10^3 and 10^4 respectively; (i) OLS estimation (full set of time dummies included); (ii) '*t*'-statistics are in parentheses; (iii) C = intercept; (ΔSW_{it}) = change in the non-manual wage bill in sector i; $\Delta logY_{it}$ – change in the log of real output in sector i; $\Delta logK_{it}$ = change in the log of capital stock for sector i; $(R\&D/Y)_{it-1}$ = R&D expenditure divided by nominal GDP for sector i; $\Delta logMSV_{it}$ = change in the log of value of UK imports from low-wage countries divided by UK domestic sales *plus* total imports for sector i; $\Delta logRPV_{it}$, etc. = price of UK imports from very low-wage countries divided by price of UK domestic sales for sector i; $\Delta logRPV80_{it}$ = $\Delta logRPV_{it}$ multiplied by a dummy variable taking a value of 1 for 1980 and 0 otherwise; $\Delta logRPV80_{tx,t}$ = $\Delta logRPV80_{it}$ multiplied by a value of 1 for textiles sectors and zero otherwise.

wage countries pushes down the relative wage and employment shares of the less skilled. We re-estimated (1) using a non-logged version of the import penetration term (that is, we replaced $\Delta log\ MSV_{it}$ with ΔMSV_{it}). The non-logged import penetration terms remained strongly significant with parameters (*t*-statistics) of 0.4368 (2.28) and 0.4446 (3.18) for the wage bill and employment share equations respectively. The parameters and *t*-statistics of the other variables remained virtually unchanged.

Table 7.2 Employment share equations (ΔSE_{it})

Equation	(1)	(2)	(3)	(4)	(5)	(6)
C	0.41[1]	0.14[2]	0.42[1]	0.65[2]	0.44[1]	0.39[2]
	(1.36)	(0.41)	(1.31)	(0.19)	(1.44)	(0.12)
$\Delta logY_{it}$	0.28[2]	−0.11[1]	−0.31[1]	−0.44[1]	−0.23[1]	−0.38[1]
	(0.06)	(0.22)	(0.67)	(0.90)	(0.52)	(0.77)
$\Delta logK_{it}$	0.067	–	0.079	–	0.097	–
	(1.07)		(1.18)		(1.51)	
$\Delta logRW_{i,t}$	−0.037	−0.049	−0.040	−0.051	−0.036	−0.047
	(2.13)	(2.38)	(2.21)	(2.36)	(2.07)	(2.22)
$(R\&D/Y)_{it-1}$	–	0.119	–	0.158	–	0.176
		(1.19)		(1.48)		(1.70)
$\Delta logMSV_{it}$	0.013	0.013	–	–	–	–
	(4.06)	(3.83)				
$\Delta logRPV_{it}$	–	–	0.21[1]	0.17[1]	0.31[1]	0.28[1]
			(0.61)	(0.38)	(0.93)	(0.69)
$\Delta logRPV80_{it}$	–	–	−0.022	−0.021	–	–
			(1.53)	(1.38)		
$\Delta logRPV80_{tx,t}$	–	–	–	–	−0.063	−0.061
					(3.40)	(3.11)
N	176	143	176	143	176	143
R²	0.3247	0.3099	0.2647	0.2412	0.3054	0.2851
SEE	.00942	.00991	.00986	.01044	.00959	.01013

Notes:
As for Table 7.1 except: (ΔSE_{it}) = change in the employment share of non-manual workers in sector i; $\Delta logRW_{i,t}$ = change in the log of wage rate of non-manual workers relative to manual workers in sector i;

We then replaced the import penetration term (*MSV*) with the disaggregated *relative price* term (*RP*) – that is, the price of UK imports relative to the UK domestic price for the same product broken down into the same three categories as the import penetration terms, and estimated equation (E). None of the relative price terms were found to be statistically significant, which ostensibly suggests that the impact of low-wage countries on the less skilled seems to be primarily via the trade *quantities* route rather than the trade *prices* mechanism of the Stolper–Samuelson theorem.

Our next step was to add the relative price annual dummies

$$\left(\sum_{k=1}^{n}\alpha_4'\log RPV_{it}\right)$$

and estimate (F) to see if there is any evidence that there was a disproportionate response to the decline in *RPV* during the large appreciation of sterling in the early 1980s. We began by adding the annual dummies from 1978 onwards and the results tended to show negative parameters and relatively higher t-statistics for the dummies during the large temporary appreciation of sterling in the early 1980s, particularly the 1980 dummy. However, none of the year dummies were individually significant. (3) and (4) in Tables 7.1 and 7.2 show our estimates of specification (F) including only the 1980 relative price dummy ($\Delta logRPV80_{it}$). Although the individual relative price dummies in (3) and (4) are not quite significant, they do provide some support for the idea that switching costs may play a role in explaining the degree of outsourcing.

Our earlier tests showed that it is acceptable to impose a common slope parameter across all of the different sectors, but this is a joint test of *all* of the slope parameters and it may be the case that some of the parameters differ between the textiles and non-electrical machinery production industries. Therefore, we re-estimated (3) and (4) and added a 1980 relative price dummy for the textiles industry alone ($\Delta log\ RPV_{it}$ multiplied by a dummy variable with a value of 1 for the textile sectors in 1980 and 0 otherwise). The results of this experiment are shown in (5) and (6) of Tables 7.1 and 7.2 and the statistical significance of the $\Delta logRPV80_{tx,t}$ term suggests that only the textile industry was disproportionately hit by outsourcing due to the large deterioration in relative price competitiveness in the early 1980s.[17]

Returning to our import penetration term (MSV), we also tested whether non-electrical machinery production is less prone to outsourcing relative to the textile industry (which is possible because the former industry employs a higher proportion of skilled employees). We re-estimated (1) and (2) but added a dummy variable for import penetration in non-electrical machinery production ($\Delta logMSV_{it}$ multiplied by a dummy variable with a value of 1 for non-electrical machinery production sectors and 0 otherwise). In both the wage bill and employment share equations the parameter on this term was negative, which suggests that non-electrical machinery production may be less prone to outsourcing relative to textiles (the parameter was roughly half the magnitude of the aggregate MSV parameter), although it should be noted that it was not statistically significant.[18]

We also estimated specifications including the import penetration term (MSV) together with the relative price dummy for textiles in 1980 ($\Delta logRPV80_{tx,t}$). Both terms were found to be strongly statistically significant in both the wage bill and employment share equations. It might be thought that, if the relative price term reflects some element of outsourcing, it would become statistically insignificant when the import share term was added to the equation, since the latter would capture any rise in outsourcing due to the improved price competitiveness of very-low-wage countries relative to the UK in the early 1980s. However, the continued significance of the relative price parameter suggests that this term also captures other effects in addition to the increase in import penetration that may be due to outsourcing, for example:[19]

1. The $\Delta \log RPV80_{tx,t}$ term may capture the extra downward wage pressure on unskilled workers wages in non-outsourcing firms resulting from the additional price competitive pressures due to outsourcing to low-wage countries by other firms of similar products (in response to the combination of switching costs and the high level of sterling). Similarly other firms, in an attempt to avoid losing their customers to low-wage countries, may have responded to the high level of sterling by making the same product more efficiently, or increasing the quality of their product, by increasing the share of skilled workers in their production process.
2. If a significant proportion of UK *exporters* are engaged in the manufacture of relatively low-quality products they may primarily be competing against low-wage countries. Hence, a large deterioration in UK export price competitiveness may cause buyers of UK exports to switch to low-wage suppliers (i.e., foreign importers who previously outsourced to UK exporters may now prefer to outsource to low-wage countries). If the UK import relative price term broadly mimics movements in the UK export price relative to the exports of low-wage countries then the $\Delta \log RPV80_{tx,t}$ term may also be capturing the impact of outsourcing in UK export markets on the economic fortunes of the less skilled in the UK.

7.5 COMPARISONS WITH PREVIOUS WORK

As mentioned earlier, the various calculations of Feenstra and Hanson (1995, 1996) imply that outsourcing may explain a large proportion of the increase in the wage bill share of skilled workers in the USA. One obvious question to ask is whether our estimates of outsourcing lead to similar conclusions for the UK. In the following calculations we concentrate on the period 1970–83 as Figures 3.6 and 3.7 of Chapter 3 show that most of the change in the wage share and employment of the unskilled occurred during these years.

In order to make our calculations more straightforward we use the non-logged import penetration parameters and concentrate upon the textiles sector. Using sectoral weights based on the import values of the 4-digit sectors, we calculate that UK import penetration in the 'aggregate' textiles sector virtually doubled from just over 4 per cent to almost 8 per cent between 1970 and 1983.[20] At the same time, the wage bill share of skilled workers rose by just over 4 percentage points and their employment share increased by almost 5 percentage points. Consequently, for the period 1970–83, we estimate that outsourcing may account for as much as 40 per cent of the rise in the wage bill share of skilled workers and approximately one-third of the increase in their employment share in the UK textiles sector.[21]

In contrast to the above results, neither Haskel (1996a, 1996b) or Machin, Ryan and van Reenen (1996) find a significant impact of trade on the relative wages and employment of the less skilled in the UK. However, unlike our analysis, both of the aforementioned studies do not use trade data which separately identifies imports from the low-wage countries (for example, UK import penetration variables used in these studies correspond to UK imports from *all* countries and are therefore dominated by imports from the advanced industrialised countries).[22] Haskel (1996a, 1996b) and Machin, Ryan and van Reenen (1996) find that technology and changes in labour market institutions explain the bulk of the declines in the economic fortunes of the less skilled in the UK. The UK labour market reforms since 1979, for example, aimed at reducing the power of trade unions, which have also been associated with a substantial decline in trade union density, may have enabled or caused wage differentials to widen and made it easier for firms to fire unwanted (unskilled) workers.

Both Haskel and Machin, Ryan and van Reenen empirically find that declines in union density (associated with UK labour market reforms) are correlated with the fall in the relative employment and wages of less-skilled workers. However, one might argue that the bulk of the decline in the relative employment of the less-skilled occurred too early in the 1980s to be caused by a decline in union power proxied by the fall in union density. Indeed it seems more plausible that the decline in trade union density was the *outcome* of the relative employment decline of production workers, which begs the question as to what caused the job losses of the less skilled in the UK in the early 1980s. However, Anderton (1997) does find that UK labour market reforms, such as the curtailing of trade union power and measures which made it more difficult for the unemployed to avoid taking low-paid jobs, did depress the wages of unskilled workers, but that these measures did not have an impact until 1986 onwards.

This chapter suggests that 'outsourcing' to low-wage countries, switching costs and the high value of sterling in the early 1980s also provides part of the answer. Interestingly, the 'lumpiness' of the decline in the economic fortunes of the less skilled in the USA also seems to be associated with a period of prolonged and substantial appreciation of the dollar. It may also be no coincidence that the economic fortunes of the less skilled have also deteriorated across the rest of Europe during a period when the ERM members experienced higher exchange rates than they otherwise would have done. In contrast, one ERM member which probably has *not* experienced a higher exchange rate relative to what it otherwise would have done – namely, Germany – has avoided any substantial deterioration in the relative employment and wages of its less-skilled workers.

7.6 CONCLUSIONS

Although it should be noted that this study only looks at a small part of UK manufacturing, we do find some evidence that outsourcing to low-wage economies may have damaged the economic fortunes of the less skilled in the UK. In addition, as expected we find that low-skill sectors such as textiles are more likely to be influenced by outsourcing than higher-skill sectors.

Using our parameter estimates, we calculate that outsourcing to low-wage countries may explain around 40 per cent of the rise in the wage bill share and perhaps one-third of the increase in the employment share of skilled workers in the UK textiles sector. Furthermore, we provide some tentative support for the notion that the high value of sterling in the early 1980s may have also contributed to the decline in the relative employment and wages of the less skilled.

APPENDIX 7.1　DEFINITIONS AND DATA SOURCES

Non-manual employment and wages correspond to the UK Census of Production category *Administrative, technical and clerical employees*: This is defined as including managing and other directors in receipt of a definite wage, salary or commission; managers, superintendents and work foremen; research experimental, development, technical and design employees; draughtsmen and tracers; editorial staff, staff reporters, canvassers, competition and advertising staff; and office (including works office) employees (4-digit ISIC disaggregation).

Manual employment and wages correspond to the UK Census of Production category *Operatives*, which includes all manual wage earners. This includes all those employed in and about factory works; operatives employed in power houses and transport work; stores, warehouses, shops and canteens; inspectors, viewers and similar workers; maintenance workers; cleaners; operatives engaged in outside work of erecting, fitting, etc. (4-digit ISIC disaggregation).

Sectoral research and development expenditure: *Source*: OECD ANBERD Database (3-digit ISIC disaggregation).

Capital stock data: *Source*: O'Mahony (1994), 3-digit disaggregation.

Bilateral trade and production database: The highly disaggregated data for the value and volume of UK imports and domestic sales are the same data as in Brenton and Winters (1992). These are annual data disaggregated to the 4-digit level for the sample period 1970–87. The original trade and production data were supplied by the OECD and, where necessary, first converted to a consistent SITC REV (Standard International Trade Classification) and then into ISIC categories (International Standard Industrial Classification).

4-digit Sectors

We pool the data across eleven ISIC sectors (six in the textiles industry and five in the non-electrical machinery production industry) over an annual sample period from 1970–86. Given that we lose one observation because we estimate a first difference model, our estimation period 1971–86 therefore provides us with 176 observations (i.e. 16*11). Estimates including the R&D term are based on 143 observations over the sample period 1974–86 (as the R&D data only begin in 1973). The 4-digit ISIC sectors used in the estimation are as follows:

ISIC3211　Spinning, weaving and finishing textiles
ISIC3212　Manufacture of made-up textile goods, except wearing apparel
ISIC3213　Knitting mills
ISIC3214　Manufacture of carpet and rugs
ISIC3215　Cordage, rope and twine industries
ISIC3219　Manufacture of textiles not elsewhere classified
ISIC3821　Manufacture of engines and turbines
ISIC3822　Manufacture of agricultural machinery and equipment
ISIC3823　Manufacture of metal and woodworking machinery

ISIC3824   Manufacture of special industrial machinery and equipment except metal and wood working machinery

ISIC3829   Machinery and equipment except electrical not elsewhere classified

UK data from the Census of Production are first classified to a common UK SIC as the data are defined in terms of the 1968 UK SIC (i.e. Minimum List Headings: MLH) for the first part of the sample period but defined in terms of the 1980 UK SIC (Activity Headings: AH) in the latter part of the sample period. Therefore, the first task is to compile consistent industry series for the whole sample period by linking the MLH and AH series. This was achieved by following the CSO's *Standard Industrial Classification Revised 1980: Reconciliation with Standard Industrial Classification 1968* (CSO, 1980) which gives the correspondence between the AH and MLH series. In cases where only a proportion of the MLH should be allocated to the appropriate AH we calculate the relevant proportion by using the 1979 Census of Production data which was published on the basis of both SIC 1968 and SIC 1980 (hence we have an overlapping observation for the SIC 1968 and 1980 classifications). The second step was to 'map' the consistent UK SIC series to the above ISIC classifications (using a similar methodology to that in Anderton, 1996b).

Notes

* We are extremely grateful to Mary O'Mahony for supplying us with Census of Production and capital stock data. Anderton would also like the thank the British Academy for financing part of his research in this paper.
  1. OECD (1993), Table 5.3, pp. 157–84.
  2. Wood (1994), on the other hand, suggests that trade has had a large impact on European labour markets.
  3. Others find that multinational outsourcing contributed very little to the increase in wage inequality in the USA (see Slaughter, 1995). Differences in definitions of outsourcing partly explain why the results of Feenstra and Hanson differ from those of Slaughter. The former study includes outsourcing to independent foreign suppliers and captures operations, typified by companies such as Nike, where foreign companies are contracted to manufacture a product designed and distributed in OECD countries. Slaughter measures outsourcing only as the purchase of inputs from foreign subsidiaries.
  4. In addition, unemployment figures disaggregated by skill are also consistent with a link between the early 1980s' sterling appreciation and the deterioration of the economic circumstances of the less skilled. Nickell (1996) shows that the unemployment rate of the unskilled relative to the high-skilled rose substantially between 1983 and 1986, but that this ratio returned to its original level in the early 1990s, when sterling depreciated markedly following the departure of the UK from the Exchange Rate Mechanism (ERM) in 1992.

5. More direct evidence suggests that outsourcing can play a significant role in modern production. For example, Nike only employs 2500 persons in the USA for marketing and other headquarters services, whereas about 75 000 persons are employed in Asia producing shoes that are sold to Nike, whilst General Electric currently imports all of the microwaves marketed under its brand name from Samsung in Korea (Magaziner and Patinkin, 1989). Outsourcing is also claimed to be an important activity in industries such as footwear (Yoffie and Gomes-Casseres, 1994, case 7), textiles (Waldinger, 1986; Gereffi, 1993), and electronics (Alic and Harris, 1992). Many of these examples – such as the General Electric case – also illustrate that outsourcing applies to finished goods as well as intermediate inputs.

6. Feenstra and Hanson (1996) note that the decline in the relative employment of the less skilled in the USA during 1979–87 mostly occurred during the 1979–81 period, and was abnormally large in comparison with preceding and succeeding recessions.

7. Note that Gregg and Machin (1994) argue that UK income inequality continued to rise rapidly during the second half of the 1980s, but Anderton and Brenton (1996) show that the UK textiles industry, an industry likely to be prone to outsourcing, shows a large rise in wage inequality only in the first half of the 1980s.

8. Switching costs may not be the only mechanism which explains the 'lumpiness' of changes in the economic circumstances of the unskilled. Keane and Prasad (1996), for example, argue that the oil price shock of the early 1980s increased the relative wages and employment of skilled workers in the USA because energy price increases encouraged a shift in production towards using less energy and more capital and skilled labour. In addition, in the case of the UK, trade union density also fell substantially at the start of the 1980s.

9. OECD ANBERD database.

10. We assume that the cost function has a translog functional form because it is then easy to derive the equation for the share of non-manual wage costs in total wage costs, etc.

11. Unfortunately, the ROW category also includes Australia and New Zealand. Since we concentrate on trade in *manufactures* the inclusion of these latter two countries should not have an important impact on our results.

12. In a similar fashion to Berman, Bound and Griliches (1994), we drop the relative wage rate term from the wage bill share equation because of endogeneity problems, but include the relative wage term in the employment equation.

13. Although import penetration from the NICs (*MSN*) was positively signed it was not significant, whereas import penetration from the industrialised countries was always negatively signed and not significant.

14. *F*-tests on our basic specifications show that we can restrict both the intercept and slope parameters to be equal across all of the sectors.

15. Consequently our procedure throughout this chapter is to show the results including the capital stock and R&D terms separately but not together. This procedure has the added advantage that whenever we

exclude the R&D terms we also benefit from a longer sample period.
16. Kraft (1996) argues that the ratio of skilled to unskilled workers will vary countercyclically because skilled workers will be retained by a firm during a recession because they are costly to train. Hence, primarily unskilled workers will be laid off during a recession.
17. A similar term for the non-electrical machinery sectors was not statistically significant. In addition, replacing the whole sample period *RPV* term with a whole sample period textiles' relative price term did not change the statistical significance of the relative price term (hence we report the results using the whole sample period RPV term for *all* of the sectors).
18. If we replace the non-electrical machinery dummy with a textiles dummy we obtain the expected *positive* sign.
19. Indeed, the $\Delta logRPV80_{tx,t}$ parameter declines in magnitude when the *MSV* term is also included which indicates that some proportion of the import penetration is one of the factors captured by the relative price term.
20. Although the import penetration of low-wage countries in the UK textiles sector seems small at 8 per cent, it should be noted that this implies that low-wage countries actually account for about one-fifth of total import penetration in this sector (since import penetration by all countries in UK textiles in 1984 was about 44 per cent – see Anderton, 1996a)
21. These calculations simply take the change in the non-logged *MSV* term between 1970 and 1983, multiply this by the appropriate parameter (0.4368 and 0.4446 for the wage bill and employment share equations, respectively) and express this as a proportion of the change in the wage bill and employment shares of non-production workers in the textiles sector during the same period.
22. However, it should be noted that the Haskel and Machin, Ryan and van Reenen studies may give different results for other reasons (i.e. both studies use different sample periods; Haskel uses the *New Earnings Survey* Panel Dataset and Machin, Ryan and van Reenen uses UN data to construct relative employment and earnings series).

References

Alic, J.A. and Harris, M.C. (1992) 'Appendix: the NBER immigration, trade and labour markets data files', in Borjas, G. and Freeman, R., (eds), *Immigration and the Workforce: Economic Consequences for the United States and Source Areas*, Chicago: University of Chicago Press, 407–20.

Anderton, R. (1996a) 'UK trade performance and the role of product quality, innovation and hysteresis: some preliminary results', *Discussion Paper*, 102, National Institute of Economic and Social Research.

Anderton, R. (1996b) 'Trade performance and the role of R&D, patents, investment and hysteresis: an analysis of disaggregated import volumes for the UK, Germany and Italy', *Discussion Paper*, 101, National Institute of Economic and Social Research.

Anderton, R. (1997) 'UK labour market reforms and sectoral wage formation', *Discussion Paper*, 121, National Institute of Economic and Social Research.

Anderton, R. and Brenton, P. (1996) 'What has been contribution of trade with the NICs to adverse relative wage movements for the unskilled in Europe?', paper presented at the conference 'Europe and Asia: The Impact of Trade With Low-Wage Economies on Employment and Relative Wages in the European Union', Brussels: EIAS (December).

Anderton, R. and Soteri, S. (1996) 'Wage determination and active labour market programmes', *Discussion Paper*, 96, National Institute of Economic and Social Research.

Berman, E., Bound, S. and Griliches, Z. (1994) 'Changes in the demand for skilled labour within US manufacturing industries', *Quarterly Journal of Economics*, 109, 367–98.

Brenton, P. and Winters, L.A. (1992) 'Estimates of bilateral trade elasticities and their implications for the modelling of 1992', *Discussion Paper 717*, Centre for Economic Policy Research.

Feenstra, R.C. and Hanson, G.H. (1995) 'Foreign investment, outsourcing and relative wages', *Working Paper*, 5121, NBER.

Feenstra, R.C. and Hanson, G.H. (1996) 'Globalization, outsourcing and wage inequality', *American Economic Review, Papers and Proceedings*, 86, 240–5.

Freeman, R. and Katz, L. (1995) 'Rising wage inequality: the United States versus other advanced countries', in Freeman, R. and Katz, L. (eds), *Differences and Changes in Wage Structures*, Chicago: University of Chicago Press.

Gereffi, G. (1993) 'The role of big buyers in global commodity chains: how US retail networks affect overseas production patterns', in Gereffi, G. and Korzeniewicz, M. (eds), *Commodity Chains and Global Capitalism*, Westport, CT: Praeger, 95–122.

Gregg, P. and Machin, S. (1994) 'Is the rise in UK inequality different?', in Barrell, R. (ed.), *The UK Labour Market*, London: Sage.

Haskel, J. (1996a) 'The decline in unskilled employment in UK manufacturing', *Discussion Paper*, 1356, Centre for Economic Policy Research.

Haskel, J. (1996b) 'Small firms, contracting-out, computers and wage inequality: evidence from UK manufacturing', *Discussion Paper*, 1490, Centre for Economic Policy Research.

Keane, M. and Prasad, E. (1996) 'The employment and wage effects of oil price changes: a sectoral analysis', *Review of Economics and Statistics*, 78, 389–399.

Kraft, K. (1996) 'Wage differentials between skilled and unskilled workers', *Weltwirtschaftliches Archiv*, 132.

Machin, S. (1996) 'Wage inequality in the UK', *Oxford Review of Economic Policy*, 12, 1, 47–64.

Machin, S., Ryan, A. and van Reenen, J. (1996) 'Technology and changes in skill structure: evidence from a panel an international industries', *Discussion Paper*, 1434, Centre for Economic Policy Research.

Magaziner, K. and Patinkin, M. (1989) 'Fast heat: how Korea won the microwave war', *Harvard Business Review*, January–February, 83–92.
Nickell, S. (1996) 'Unemployment and wages in Europe and North America', *The Labour Market Consequences of Technical and Structural Change*, *Discussion Paper Series*, 6 (sponsored by the Leverhulme Trust).
OECD (1993) *Employment Outlook* (July), Paris: OECD.
O'Mahony, M., Wagner, K. and Paulsen, M. (1994) 'Changing fortunes: an industry study of British and German productivity growth over three decades', *National Institute Report Series*, 7.
Orcutt, G. (1950) 'Measurement of price elasticities in international trade', *Review of Economics and Statistics*, 51, 320–33.
Slaughter, M. (1995) 'Multinational corporations, outsourcing, and American wage divergence', *Working Paper*, 5253, NBER.
Waldinger, R.D. (1986) *Through the Eye of the Needle*, New York: New York University Press.
Wood, A. (1994) *North–South Trade, Employment and Inequality: Changing Fortunes in a Skill-Driven World*, Oxford: Clarendon Press.
Yoffie, D.B. and Gomes-Casseres, B. (1994) *International Trade and Competition*, New York: McGraw-Hill.

8 Europe and Asia: An Assessment of 20 More Years of Growth

Dominique van der Mensbrugghe*

8.1 INTRODUCTION

Many countries in Asia have seen remarkable growth in the last 25 years, starting with Japan in the 1950s and 1960s, followed by the first wave of Asian tigers – South Korea, Chinese Taipei, Hong Kong and Singapore – and then the second wave – Thailand, Malaysia, the Philippines and Indonesia. Perhaps more stunningly has been the evolution and success of China which has transformed its economy from almost virtual autarky and a highly regulated economy to an increasingly open and very dynamic economy. The success of the so-called 'Asian model' is catching on in the rest of Asia – notably in India and Bangladesh – accompanied by the introduction of outward-looking policies, deregulation, privatisation and financial market reforms.

The rapid growth in Asia over the last 25 years has already raised the living standards in several countries close to OECD levels, and if current trends continue, the Asian region as a whole will converge significantly towards OECD income levels. Further, given the absolute size of the Asian economy, its weight in the world economy and its share in world trade, will inevitably increase and shift perceptibly the centre of global economic activity.

High aggregate growth is likely to affect political relations both within the Asian region as well as between Asia and the rest of the world. The economic impact of rapid aggregate growth is not necessarily easily discernible. However, detailed economic analysis provides a richer picture of how economic relations could potentially evolve, including answering some of the following questions:

- What will be the evolution in the structure of production and demand, and hence the impact on trade relations?
- What are the impacts of changes in labour supply and labour productivity on the composition of production?
- How do wages evolve with respect to these factors?

This chapter attempts to provide some food for thought on these and related questions. The underlying analysis relies on a global applied general equilibrium model known as LINKAGE.[1] Appendices 8.1–8.3 provide a brief description of the main features of the LINKAGE model including a description of the regional and sectoral coverage. The model is used to project the world economy forward to the year 2020, incorporating dynamic elements such as population and labour growth, capital accumulation (through saving and investment), and productivity improvements. These basic trends, coupled with changes in (trade and fiscal) policies and the underlying natural resources, provide a consistent and plausible picture of the structure of world economic activity including changes in terms of trade, wages, and real exchange rates.

Section 8.2 provides the aggregate view – that is, changes in real GDP, aggregate trade, and relative weights of the regional economies. Section 8.3 derives conclusions concerning structural changes, particularly in terms of the composition of output and trade. Section 8.4 develops some of the results concerning labour markets, notably the impact of productivity and changes in the composition of production on wages. Concluding comments are provided in the section 8.5.

8.2   AGGREGATE RESULTS

This section paints the overall picture of a potential scenario of the evolution of the world economy through the year 2020. The scenario is not a projection. The principle assumption underlying the scenario is one of high growth in all regions of the world: that is, it is a scenario where all goes right – best-practice economic reforms are implemented in all regions, there are no systemic failures, major conflicts or natural catastrophes with global implications, and each region is able to expand to its maximum potential its production possibility frontier.[2] While the likelihood that either one or more regions fail to maximise their potential is high, this scenario provides a useful benchmark for assessing the benefits and costs from rapid global growth and further globalisation of the economy. The first part of this section sets out the underlying assumption behind the so-called 'high-growth scenario', and the second part describes the aggregate implications of these assumptions.

8.2.1　The Underlying Assumptions

Exogenous trends

Attaining the growth rates underlying the high-growth scenario requires a set of (exogenous) trends in productivity, factor availability, and a few other variables. The aggregate GDP growth rates are provided in Table 8.1. Under this scenario global world growth will grow at an annual average rate of 3.7 per cent between 1995 and 2020, with the OECD region growing at a rate of 2.7 per cent, and the non-OECD region growing at a rate of 6.5 per cent.[3] Europe would grow at a slightly lower rate than the OECD average, though on a *per capita* basis would have a slightly higher growth rate (2.5) than the OECD average. The (five) Asian regions grow at an even faster rate than the aggregate non-OECD region, at a rate of 7.2 per cent.

The population and labour growth rates are derived from the most recent UN population projections using the Medium Variant. The population growth rates are projected to decline (in all regions), though with significant regional variations.[4] The OECD growth rate will be cut in half by 2010, with a more modest reduction in the non-OECD region (see Table 8.2). Europe's population is projected to be roughly the same as today in the year 2020, albeit with a different age profile. The latter notably implies a declining supply of labour. Asia overall will see a more rapid drop in the population growth rate than the non-Asian region as a whole. The growth rate of labour supply is more rapid than the population growth rates in all non-OECD regions, reflecting a combination of changing demographics and labour force participation rates (see Table 8.3).

The dynamic scenario is calibrated along a so-called balanced-growth path. Under this assumption, labour supply in efficiency terms (i.e. incorporating both the absolute increase in the labour supply, as well as the increase in labour productivity), grows at the same rate as GDP. In essence, this is almost equivalent to assuming that

Table 8.1   Average annual growth rate of real GDP, 1992–2020 (per cent)

	1992 1995	1995 2000	2000 2005	2005 2010	2010 2015	2015 2020	1995 2020
ANZ	4.0	4.3	4.7	4.7	4.3	4.3	4.5
CHN	11.8	9.3	8.2	8.2	7.2	7.2	8.0
DAE	7.0	7.7	7.0	7.0	6.4	6.4	6.9
ECE	1.7	5.5	5.5	5.5	4.0	4.0	4.9
EUR	1.8	2.4	2.8	2.8	2.3	2.3	2.5
IDN	6.9	7.5	7.0	7.0	6.7	6.7	7.0
IND	4.5	6.5	7.2	7.2	6.6	6.6	6.8
JPN	1.3	3.3	2.9	2.9	2.3	2.3	2.7
LAT	3.8	4.3	5.9	5.9	5.1	5.1	5.3
MNA	2.8	5.0	7.1	7.1	6.9	6.9	6.6
NFT	2.6	2.2	2.7	2.7	2.6	2.6	2.6
NIS	–3.8	3.5	6.0	6.0	6.9	6.9	5.9
RAS	6.0	6.5	6.6	6.6	6.5	6.5	6.5
ROW	6.0	6.5	6.6	6.6	6.5	6.5	6.5
SSA	1.8	4.6	5.0	5.0	5.5	6.0	5.2
Total	**2.5**	**3.3**	**3.7**	**3.9**	**3.6**	**3.8**	**3.7**
OECD	2.0	2.6	2.9	2.9	2.5	2.5	2.7
Non-OECD	4.4	6.1	6.7	6.8	6.4	6.4	6.5
Asia	7.8	7.9	7.4	7.4	6.7	6.7	7.2
Non-Asia	2.0	2.8	3.3	3.4	3.1	3.2	3.2

Notes: (1) OECD includes ANZ, ECE, EUR, JPN, and NFT, but does not include Korea. (Due to data limitations, Turkey is included in the region ROW.)
(2) Asia includes CHN, DAE, IDN, IND, and RAS. (Due to data limitations, Vietnam is included in the region ROW.)
(3) Aggregate averages are weighted at 1992 market exchange rates.
(4) Country and commodity acronyms are defined in Appendices 8.2 and 8.3.

Source: Linkage model results.

labour productivity is the difference between GDP growth and labour supply growth. Table 8.4 provides the labour productivity growth rate assumptions. The world average over the period 1995–2020 is 2.3 per cent. The balanced-growth assumption implies that the labour:capital ratio (in efficiency units) is constant. Given the exogenous set of GDP growth rates for each region of the model, capital productivity is calibrated to the GDP targets and constrained by the balanced-growth assumption.

Table 8.2 Average annual population growth rate, 1992–2020
(per cent)

	1992 1995	1995 2000	2000 2005	2005 2010	2010 2015	2015 2020	1995 2020
ANZ	1.1	1.1	1.1	1.0	1.0	1.0	1.0
CHN	1.1	0.9	0.7	0.6	0.6	0.6	0.7
DAE	1.5	1.4	1.2	1.1	0.9	0.8	1.1
ECE	–0.1	–0.1	–0.1	–0.1	–0.1	–0.1	–0.1
EUR	0.4	0.2	0.1	0.0	–0.1	–0.1	0.0
IDN	1.6	1.5	1.3	1.1	1.0	0.9	1.2
IND	1.8	1.6	1.5	1.3	1.0	1.0	1.3
JPN	0.2	0.2	0.1	0.0	–0.2	–0.3	0.0
LAT	1.7	1.5	1.4	1.3	1.2	1.1	1.3
MNA	2.6	2.4	2.4	2.2	2.0	1.8	2.1
NFT	1.2	1.0	0.9	0.9	0.9	0.8	0.9
NIS	0.3	0.0	0.0	0.1	0.1	0.0	0.1
RAS	2.1	2.2	2.2	2.1	1.9	1.6	2.0
ROW	1.9	2.0	1.5	1.3	1.2	1.2	1.4
SSA	2.8	2.8	2.7	2.6	2.5	2.4	2.6
Total	**1.5**	**1.4**	**1.3**	**1.2**	**1.1**	**1.0**	**1.2**
OECD	0.6	0.5	0.4	0.4	0.3	0.3	0.4
Non-OECD	1.7	1.6	1.5	1.4	1.3	1.2	1.4
Asia	1.5	1.4	1.2	1.1	1.0	0.9	1.1
Non-Asia	1.5	1.4	1.4	1.3	1.3	1.2	1.3

Source: UN Medium Variant population projections and Linkage model results.

Several sectors are given special treatment. First, it is assumed that total factor productivity (TFP) in agriculture is given, and in the high-growth scenario, it has been fixed at 1.5 per cent per annum in all regions. Second, the (autonomous) energy efficiency improvement factor (also called AEEI factor) is given. Due to the existing higher levels of efficiency in the OECD countries, the AEEI factor is assumed to grow by 1 per cent per annum in the OECD regions, and to grow by 2 per cent per annum in the non-OECD regions. Third, trade and transport margins are assumed to decline, thereby reinforcing further globalisation. Under the high-growth scenario, the trade and transport margins decline by 1 per cent per annum (uniformly across regions and sectors).

The world oil market has a prominent role in the Linkage model. Supply of crude oil and natural gas is determined by resource depletion submodels. Each region has an existing pool of proven

Table 8.3   Average annual growth rate of labour supply, 1992–2020
(per cent)

	1992 1995	1995 2000	2000 2005	2005 2010	2010 2015	2015 2020	1995 2020
ANZ	1.1	1.2	1.2	1.0	0.6	0.5	0.9
CHN	1.3	1.1	1.4	1.0	0.5	0.0	0.8
DAE	2.0	1.8	1.5	1.4	1.1	0.8	1.3
ECE	0.4	0.3	0.3	0.0	–0.5	–0.6	–0.1
EUR	0.4	0.2	0.1	–0.1	–0.4	–0.5	–0.1
IDN	2.3	2.1	1.7	1.5	1.4	1.1	1.6
IND	2.2	2.2	2.1	1.8	1.5	1.3	1.8
JPN	0.2	–0.2	–0.4	–0.7	–1.0	–0.7	–0.6
LAT	2.3	2.2	1.9	1.6	1.3	1.1	1.6
MNA	3.1	3.0	3.1	2.8	2.5	2.2	2.7
NFT	1.3	1.3	1.3	1.1	0.6	0.4	0.9
NIS	0.2	0.6	0.4	0.5	0.0	–0.3	0.2
RAS	2.7	3.2	3.0	2.4	2.3	2.1	2.6
ROW	2.4	2.4	1.9	1.9	1.8	1.4	1.9
SSA	3.0	3.0	3.1	3.1	3.1	2.9	3.0
Total	**1.7**	**1.7**	**1.7**	**1.4**	**1.2**	**0.9**	**1.4**
OECD	0.7	0.6	0.5	0.3	0.0	–0.1	0.3
Non-OECD	1.9	1.9	1.9	1.7	1.4	1.1	1.6
Asia	1.7	1.7	1.7	1.4	1.1	0.7	1.3
Non-Asia	1.6	1.6	1.6	1.5	1.3	1.2	1.5

Notes: Labour supply projections are based on overall population projections, projections of the working age population, and projections of labour
force participation rates.

Source: UN Medium Variant population projections and LINKAGE model
results.

resources, and a finite limit of unproven (or uneconomical resources).
Regions which produce more oil (or natural gas), than they dis-
cover, will inevitably run out of fuel. This by and large determines
trade patterns of oil and gas. Oil is treated somewhat differently
from natural gas. The Middle East/North African region (MNA),
is assumed to have some degree of market power over the crude
oil market. In concrete terms, the price of oil (with respect to a
basket of OECD export goods) is fixed in the model, and the MNA
region is the supplier of last resort. Under the high-growth scenario, the world price of oil is assumed to increase by 2 per cent
per annum in real terms through the year 2010, and then to increase

Table 8.4   Average annual growth rate of labour productivity, 1992–2020 (per cent)

	1992 1995	1995 2000	2000 2005	2005 2010	2010 2015	2015 2020	1995 2020
ANZ	2.9	3.1	3.5	3.7	3.6	3.7	3.5
CHN	10.4	8.1	6.7	7.2	6.6	7.2	7.2
DAE	4.9	5.8	5.4	5.5	5.2	5.5	5.5
ECE	1.4	5.2	5.2	5.5	4.5	4.7	5.0
EUR	1.4	2.2	2.7	2.9	2.7	2.8	2.7
IDN	4.5	5.3	5.2	5.4	5.2	5.5	5.3
IND	2.3	4.2	5.0	5.3	5.0	5.3	4.9
JPN	1.0	3.5	3.4	3.7	3.4	3.0	3.4
LAT	1.5	2.1	3.9	4.2	3.7	3.9	3.6
MNA	–0.3	1.9	3.9	4.2	4.3	4.6	3.8
NFT	1.3	0.9	1.4	1.6	2.0	2.2	1.6
NIS	–4.1	2.9	5.6	5.5	6.9	7.2	5.6
RAS	3.2	3.1	3.5	4.1	4.1	4.3	3.8
ROW	3.5	4.0	4.6	4.6	4.7	5.0	4.6
SSA	–1.1	1.6	1.9	1.8	2.4	3.0	2.1

Note: The balanced growth assumption implies that labour productivity growth essentially equals the rate of growth of real GDP *less* the rate of growth of labour supply.

Source: LINKAGE model results.

by only 1 per cent per annum afterwards. (The drop in the increase in the price of oil after 2010 is the outcome of two assumptions. The first is that exploration and production costs will drop, increasing potential supply after 2010. The second assumption is that alternative sources of oil will become competitive after 2010, lessening the market power of the large oil suppliers).

Policy Assumptions

The key policy assumption in the high-growth scenario is the elimination of all import tariffs and export subsidies/taxes by the year 2020. Reaching this target will require tremendous political will, but it has been a stated goal in several fora, including APEC, ASEAN, the free trade in the Americas initiative, and in a new trans-Atlantic partnership. These four regions encompass a major share of both world income and trade.

The model assumes that governments target their public sector borrowing requirements (PSBR). This is achieved in the model by having a shifting direct tax curve on household income. The PSBR is assumed to decline to zero in all regions by the year 2020. Coupled with the removal of tariffs, this could lead to rather significant increases in household taxation. However, economic growth can enhance government revenues from other sources. Government (real) expenditures grow at the same rate as GDP.

Model closure assumes that foreign investment flows are exogenous (implying the trade balance is fixed). They are allowed to vary across time, constrained to sum to zero across regions. Given the difficulties in endogenising foreign investment flows and the constraints of achieving sustainable economic growth, foreign investment flows are fixed at their base year levels. (Any assumption which has the foreign flows declining with respect to national income would meet the sustainability requirement. The crucial assumption is the exogeneity of foreign investment flows. Changes in trade relations are reflected by changes in the real exchange rate.)

8.2.2   Aggregate Implications

This section will briefly describe the aggregate implications of the high-growth scenario. It is a relatively trivial exercise to calculate the relative shift in economic weight across the regions. The rapid growth of the non-OECD member economies leads to a shift in the distribution of income away from the OECD economies. At an aggregate level, the OECD region's share drops from around 80 per cent in 1995 (at market exchange rates), to 62 per cent by the year 2020 (see Figure 8.1). The Asian region's weight increases from 8.5 per cent to 19.5 per cent. This significant shift is even more impressive taking into account purchasing power parity (PPP) estimates of income.

While growth in aggregate income in the non-OECD regions is impressive, and the population growth rates are declining, there will continue to be a significant gap in income levels. Using PPP exchange rates, the OECD: non-OECD income differential in 1995 is 6: 1. In the year 2020, the gap falls to 3: 1, i.e. a halving of the average income gap in 25 years. Convergence of the Asian regions is even more impressive. The gap between the OECD and Asia is 7: 1, and this ratio drops to less than 3: 1 in 2020. Figure 8.2 shows the relevant figures for each of the individual regions. Under the high-growth assumptions, the DAE region not only surpasses the 1995 level of OECD income, but there is an absolute convergence

Figure 8.1   Regional distribution of GDP, based on 1992 USD official exchange figures, 1995 and 2020 (per cent)

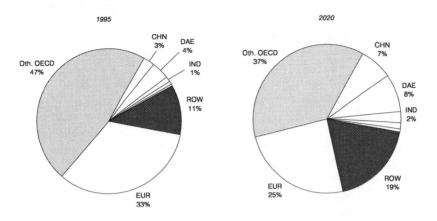

Source: LINKAGE model results.

Figure 8.2   *Per capita* income, 1995 and 2020 (1992 $US, using PPP exchange rates)

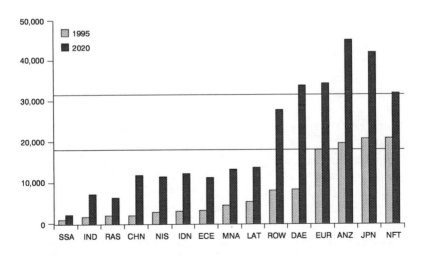

Note: The two lines represent the average level of OECD per capita income in 1995 (the lower line), and 2020.

Source: LINKAGE model results.

beyond the 2020 level of OECD income. The only other non-OECD region which converges beyond the current level of OECD income is the rather heterogeneous ROW (Rest of the World) region. Given the recent growth experience of many developing regions, one could anticipate significant reductions in the absolute level of poverty if these growth assumptions were to hold.

The removal of trade barriers, the reduction in trade and transport costs, and the high growth rates, generate a boom in world trade. Exports from the Asian region may increase by a factor of 6.5, significantly more than exports from the non-Asian region on aggregate, which will grow by a factor of 3.3. Trade barriers are higher in the non-OECD countries, which partly explains the higher growth in trade to be expected in these countries. The regional patterns of trade also evolve. The growth in trade between the developing regions is more significant than either intra-OECD trade, or trade between the OECD and the non-OECD region. In 1995, intra-OECD trade represents 45 per cent of total world trade, by 2020, this share drops to 27 per cent.[5] Europe significantly diversifies its export partners (see Figure 8.3).[6] Overall European exports will increase by a factor of 2.5, but with Asia, the factor jumps to 4.2. Intra-Asian trade, and Asian trade with other non-OECD regions would increase dramatically, by a factor of almost 9, whereas Asia's exports to Europe would increase by a factor of 5.1 under this scenario.

8.3   STRUCTURAL RESULTS

This section starts with a brief presentation of the trade and tariff structure of the OECD and Asian regions (see Table 8.5). By and large, the destination of the OECD exports are the other OECD regions, respectively 63 per cent for ANZ, 66 per cent for EUR, 56 per cent for JPN, and 75 per cent for NFT.[7] Japan is significantly different from the other OECD regions, since roughly one-third of its trade is with the Asian countries, though ANZ is not far behind. The NFT region has roughly balanced trade between Asia and ROW. Europe exports roughly twice as much to ROW as it does to the Asian countries.[8]

The export trade shares for the Asian regions are not so different. CHN, DAE, IDN, IND, and RAS export shares to the OECD are respectively 61, 61, 65, 64, and 71 per cent. To other Asian

Figure 8.3   Intra-regional trade, 1992 and 2020 (per cent)

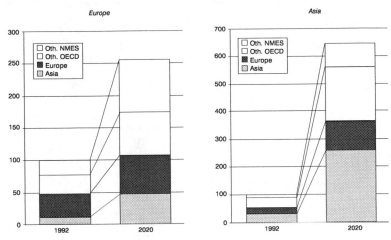

Source: LINKAGE model results.

countries the shares are respectively 28, 30, 28, 18, and 16 per cent. India is the only Asian country with export shares to ROW approaching 20 per cent.

OECD exporters typically face higher tariffs than they apply, and the tariffs they face in non-OECD countries are higher than in OECD countries. For example, Europe faces an average tariff of 8 per cent, but the average tariff on its exports to OECD countries is only 4 per cent, whereas it faces a tariff of 16 per cent on average on its exports to non-OECD countries. On the other hand, the average import tariff in Europe is 6 per cent. The story is roughly similar for the NFT region. However, for exporters from ANZ and JPN the tariff structure is more uniform across trading partners. ANZ is a large exporter of agricultural and food products and faces high tariffs in all regions, particularly in the OECD regions. Japan, on the other hand, exports a significant volume of capital goods (including transportation equipment), and the tariffs faced by Japanese exporters of these goods are high and relatively uniform across all regions.

A quick glance at the tariff structure clearly indicates that the most distorted markets are agriculture and food, consumer goods (particularly textiles and apparel), and to a lesser extent capital goods, particularly in the non-OECD countries. Due to grossly

Table 8.5　Tariff and trade structure, 1992 (per cent)

	Tariffs faced by exporters				Export structure				Import tariffs	Import structure
	OECD	Asia	Other	Total	OECD	Asia	Other	Total	Average	Average
ANZ										
LA	58.3	49.9	25.2	51.8	57.3	30.9	11.7	31.8	3.7	4.7
RE	0.7	4.0	20.4	2.2	69.5	27.5	3.0	22.4	0.2	3.8
CO	2.4	13.4	33.7	7.5	66.0	27.3	6.7	8.6	16.0	17.9
IM	1.0	7.2	10.8	4.7	45.9	46.5	7.7	10.9	6.3	6.9
KA	2.2	15.6	22.8	8.0	62.8	25.4	11.8	10.7	13.1	44.4
SH	0.0	0.0	0.0	0.0	77.3	16.2	6.5	15.6	0.0	22.1
Total	17.5	21.8	20.4	19.0	63.3	28.6	8.1		9.3	
EUR										
LA	30.6	40.5	23.1	28.8	55.8	8.8	35.4	6.1	31.7	8.0
RE	0.1	2.9	23.2	2.9	79.6	9.5	10.9	3.7	0.1	10.1
CO	5.0	19.9	24.3	10.8	67.7	10.1	22.2	16.8	8.6	16.0
IM	1.8	16.0	16.2	5.6	73.6	8.5	17.9	9.0	1.2	8.6
KA	3.9	20.0	20.6	9.8	64.4	11.7	23.9	39.5	5.1	35.7
SH	0.0	0.0	0.0	0.0	64.1	11.7	24.2	24.9	0.0	21.6
Total	4.2	14.8	15.9	8.1	65.7	10.9	23.4		5.8	
JPN										
LA	9.9	24.9	33.7	21.1	31.6	57.3	11.1	0.7	78.6	16.1
RE	0.4	6.1	5.2	3.0	52.5	39.9	7.6	0.3	2.1	18.0
CO	21.4	23.1	31.2	23.2	37.9	53.0	9.1	9.3	7.7	12.7
IM	7.4	12.2	15.6	11.4	23.2	66.0	10.8	5.7	1.4	6.5
KA	18.7	18.6	24.2	19.3	60.6	28.4	11.1	74.5	1.7	20.4
SH	0.0	0.0	0.0	0.0	55.5	30.8	13.8	9.5	0.0	26.4
Total	16.7	16.9	21.4	17.3	55.6	33.3	11.1		14.4	
NFT										
LA	49.3	67.9	16.5	46.3	66.3	15.6	18.1	10.0	15.9	6.1
RE	0.3	5.2	9.4	1.2	87.2	6.2	6.6	4.3	0.5	7.4
CO	7.7	16.5	18.8	10.7	69.8	15.2	15.0	11.5	11.5	15.4
IM	1.6	6.8	9.4	3.0	77.8	12.8	9.4	7.8	3.4	7.1
KA	3.7	13.0	18.5	6.6	75.9	12.6	11.5	46.1	9.4	50.5
SH	0.0	0.0	0.0	0.0	75.5	10.5	14.0	20.3	0.0	13.5
Total	7.1	17.4	13.4	9.2	74.8	12.5	12.7		7.8	
CHN										
LA	41.2	68.0	21.6	48.2	46.1	37.8	16.1	8.6	7.4	8.4
RE	2.5	2.6	22.5	4.3	68.7	22.8	8.5	3.1	1.7	3.3
CO	16.1	18.3	27.2	17.8	66.8	22.3	10.9	38.1	27.1	26.7
IM	3.1	9.1	16.3	7.9	31.0	60.2	8.8	3.4	9.5	10.9
KA	6.1	14.7	22.6	10.9	53.4	37.1	9.5	29.5	22.1	41.8
SH	0.0	0.2	0.0	0.0	73.5	15.4	11.1	17.3	0.1	8.9
Total	11.1	19.9	20.0	14.6	61.1	28.1	10.8		18.2	

continued on page 179

Table 8.5   continued

	Tariffs faced by exporters				Export structure				Import tariffs	Import structure
	OECD	Asia	Other	Total	OECD	Asia	Other	Total	Average	Average
DAE										
LA	39.2	23.6	25.4	33.3	60.9	28.9	10.2	9.2	69.7	8.2
RE	0.8	9.2	18.3	5.4	48.4	49.1	2.5	2.3	4.3	8.0
CO	13.1	30.0	33.7	21.3	53.5	36.8	9.7	21.9	14.5	13.9
IM	3.5	6.4	9.2	5.8	29.9	61.1	9.1	6.6	6.7	10.7
KA	7.0	13.7	24.0	10.2	65.4	26.2	8.4	48.1	12.8	44.5
SH	0.0	0.0	0.0	0.0	77.9	13.8	8.3	11.9	0.0	14.6
Total	9.8	17.1	22.7	13.1	61.1	30.1	8.7		14.5	
IDN										
LA	21.5	25.3	37.7	23.2	68.2	27.5	4.3	13.8	27.3	7.4
RE	1.3	4.5	5.2	2.2	72.3	27.1	0.6	29.0	1.0	4.5
CO	12.3	11.0	39.9	15.7	59.9	26.5	13.6	25.7	13.2	17.6
IM	1.8	6.8	25.6	6.1	41.2	51.5	7.3	4.5	5.6	11.4
KA	7.5	13.1	24.0	10.7	57.9	34.7	7.4	20.8	16.8	42.3
SH	0.0	0.0	0.0	0.0	87.3	6.5	6.2	6.1	0.0	16.7
Total	7.9	11.2	32.0	10.4	65.1	28.4	6.5		12.2	
IND										
LA	23.5	34.2	21.1	24.9	50.2	20.0	29.8	15.9	19.5	6.4
RE	0.4	3.1	18.9	1.7	76.2	19.5	4.3	16.4	3.5	27.7
CO	12.3	23.6	20.4	14.9	72.1	11.7	16.3	37.0	68.5	15.6
IM	4.6	7.2	17.2	7.0	49.3	39.9	10.8	5.1	45.4	12.0
KA	6.0	14.0	22.3	12.8	48.4	19.7	31.9	12.0	58.4	22.3
SH	0.0	0.0	0.0	0.0	59.3	20.4	20.3	13.5	0.0	16.0
Total	8.9	15.0	17.8	11.7	63.5	17.9	18.6		31.4	
RAS										
LA	26.4	31.5	18.6	25.9	39.7	32.3	27.9	16.7	14.6	15.8
RE	0.1	3.9	21.6	2.2	64.1	31.9	4.0	1.6	34.5	7.7
CO	13.7	19.2	31.9	16.7	73.3	14.5	12.1	54.7	31.9	24.4
IM	0.9	10.3	14.4	7.9	33.9	47.8	18.4	0.5	9.7	10.7
KA	6.5	18.9	21.7	9.7	76.9	11.3	11.8	4.3	15.1	32.1
SH	0.0	0.0	0.0	0.0	87.8	6.9	5.3	22.3	0.0	9.3
Total	10.5	20.8	23.8	13.9	70.8	16.1	13.1		18.6	

Notes:
1. The OECD aggregate region includes ANZ, ECE, EUR, JPN, and NFT. The Asia aggregate region includes CHN, DAE, IDN, IND, and RAS. The Other aggregate region includes the remaining five regions: LAT, MNA, NIS, ROW, and SSA.
2. The definition of the aggregate sectors is given in the Appendix 8.3 in the sectoral concordance table. They are respectively: agriculture and food (LA), energy and mining (RE), consumer goods (CO), intermediate goods (IM), capital goods (KA) and non-tradable goods (SH).

Source: Hertel, 1997.

deficient data, trade barriers in the service sectors are missing entirely. Clearly, these sectors will play a prominent role in the future, particularly for OECD countries. There has already been significant progress over the last few years in reducing barriers in the telecommunications and information technology sectors, and to a lesser extent financial and transportation services.

Changes in the patterns of output and trade in the dynamic scenario will be the result of several factors: income growth, changing demand patterns, tariff elimination and changing comparative advantage. The demand structure has been calibrated so that as countries raise their income levels, the share of the budget allocated to basic necessities declines, and there is a rise in the consumption of luxury goods and services.

Under such a scenario there will be some significant shifts in the structure of output in all of the regions. On aggregate, the OECD regions will witness a larger concentration of economic output in the service sectors, where the sheltered sector (construction *plus* services) share in total output could increase from 61.5 per cent to 66 per cent (see Figure 8.4 and Table 8.6). This is probably an understatement since implicitly the scenario assumes no change in trade barriers in the service sectors. There will also be a shift towards the capital goods sector, though not as pronounced. Growth will be slowest in agriculture and food and the consumer goods sector. This reflects both stagnant demand and changes in tariff structure. There is some variation across the OECD countries. Growth in food production will be brisk for ANZ, ECE, and NFT, reflecting their comparative advantage in producing competitively priced agricultural produce. Food production could actually decline in Japan if it were to completely remove all trade restrictions, and would grow only very modestly in EUR.

The production structure in the Asia region will change quite substantially. Growth in all sectors will be high, reflecting the high GDP growth rate. Growth will be the highest in intermediate goods, capital goods, and services (over 8 per cent per annum). It will average only 3.6 per cent per annum in agriculture and food, therefore, this sector's share in total output will decline from 22 per cent to 8 per cent, converging towards the OECD average. The sheltered sector share will increase from 40 per cent to 48 per cent, in part because of the high income demand elasticity for services, but also because of the rapid pace of construction generated by high saving and infrastructure requirements.

Figure 8.4   Production structures, 1992 and 2020 (index 1992 = 100)

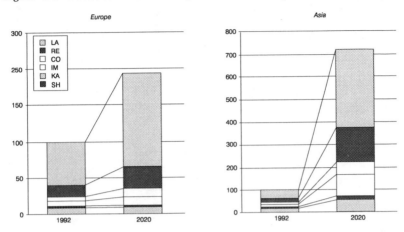

Notes:
1. The OECD aggregate region includes ANZ, ECE, EUR, JPN, and NFT. The Asia aggregate region includes CHN, DAE, IDN, IND, and RAS.
2. The definition of the aggregate sectors is given in the Annex in the sectoral concordance table. They are respectively: agriculture and food (LA), energy and mining (RE), consumer goods (CO), intermediate goods (IM), capital goods (KA), and non-tradable goods (SH).

Source: LINKAGE model results.

Table 8.6   Output and trade structure, 1992 and 2020 (index: total = 100)

	Exports		Imports		Output	
	1992	*2020*	*1992*	*2020*	*1992*	*2020*
ANZ						
LA	31.8	28.3	4.7	4.2	11.4	7.7
RE	22.4	22.1	3.8	9.2	4.0	3.3
CO	8.6	7.7	17.9	16.9	5.0	3.7
IM	10.9	15.9	6.9	7.0	6.2	6.4
KA	10.7	12.0	44.4	42.8	8.8	8.4
SH	15.6	13.9	22.1	19.9	64.6	70.5
Total	100.0	100.0	100.0	100.0	100.0	100.0
		4.5		4.5		4.3
ECE						
LA	11.6	11.6	10.0	11.4	21.0	12.0
RE	3.9	5.1	10.6	13.3	4.5	3.7
CO	21.7	18.0	20.5	17.2	11.1	10.6

Table 8.6   continued

	Exports		Imports		Output	
	1992	2020	1992	2020	1992	2020
IM	13.2	17.1	7.5	8.4	7.0	8.4
KA	28.4	31.3	36.0	36.5	13.2	16.8
SH	21.2	17.0	15.4	13.2	43.2	48.5
Total	100.0	100.0	100.0	100.0	100.0	100.0
		4.8		4.5		4.5
EUR						
LA	6.1	5.2	8.0	10.0	9.6	5.2
RE	3.7	2.8	10.1	9.8	1.4	1.1
CO	16.8	14.6	16.0	15.5	7.5	5.8
IM	9.0	10.9	8.6	7.7	6.3	6.1
KA	39.5	45.1	35.7	36.7	14.6	15.5
SH	24.9	21.4	21.6	20.2	60.5	66.2
Total	100.0	100.0	100.0	100.0	100.0	100.0
		3.4		3.5		2.4
JPN						
LA	0.7	0.7	16.1	16.5	8.7	3.8
RE	0.3	0.2	18.0	12.6	0.3	0.2
CO	9.3	8.5	12.7	13.8	7.8	6.5
IM	5.7	6.2	6.5	8.5	6.3	6.2
KA	74.5	78.3	20.4	24.1	19.9	23.1
SH	9.5	6.2	26.4	24.4	57.0	60.2
Total	100.0	100.0	100.0	100.0	100.0	100.0
		4.0		4.7		2.5
NFT						
LA	10.0	21.2	6.1	5.7	7.5	7.3
RE	4.3	2.2	7.4	5.2	2.0	1.2
CO	11.5	8.4	15.4	17.0	6.0	4.4
IM	7.8	6.6	7.1	8.4	5.5	4.6
KA	46.1	44.8	50.5	51.8	14.2	14.0
SH	20.3	16.7	13.5	12.1	64.8	68.6
Total	100.0	100.0	100.0	100.0	100.0	100.0
		3.5		3.5		2.5

Notes:
1. The definition of the aggregate sectors is given in the Appendix 8.3 in
   the sectoral concordance table. They are respectively: agriculture and
   food (LA), energy and mining (RE), consumer goods (CO), intermediate goods (IM), capital goods (KA) and non-tradable goods (SH).
2. The aggregate (average per annum) growth rate in per cent is provided below the Total line.

Source: Hertel, 1997 for 1992, and Linkage model results for 2020.

The diversity of the Asian region is reflected in more disaggregated results. China, for example, sees a relatively more rapid growth in the sheltered sector than Asia in general. Beyond the infrastructure needed for rapid growth, the integration of Hong Kong with the mainland Chinese economy provides a boost to the service industry, particularly in finance, media and tourism. Agricultural and food output declines rapidly as a share of total output, from 24 per cent to 6 per cent. The DAE region benefits from rapid growth in the intermediate and capital goods sectors. The regions of South Asia (IND and RAS) also witness a large drop in the share of food and agriculture, but nonetheless, these sectors continue to be relatively important, particularly in RAS.

In an alternative simulation, where all growth parameters (except for total GDP) are held fixed, but tariffs are not removed, there is no dramatic change in the structure of production patterns between the OECD and the Asian region, with the most significant changes occurring in agriculture and food and the consumer goods sector. (The subregional differences are of course more important.) This would suggest that dynamic factors are a more important element in explaining the evolution of production and trade patterns than trade policies *per se*.

For the OECD as a region, the major trade expansion occurs in agriculture and food, and intermediate and capital goods (see Figure 8.5 and Table 8.6).[9] While trade increases in all sectors, there is a relative decline in the share of trade in resources, consumer goods and the sheltered sector. Again there are significant regional variations reflecting different endowments and policy changes. Though food exports increase in Europe, their share in total exports decline, particularly for raw agricultural commodities. Europe maintains a relative comparative advantage in processed foods, which could even be enhanced with the decline in agricultural trade barriers. Exports in Asia expand at almost twice the rate as in the OECD. The largest expansion is in the intermediate goods sector, followed by the capital goods sector. Exports of food grow rapidly, particularly from India and RAS.

8.4   LABOUR MARKETS

The composition of the labour force in OECD countries is already heavily skewed towards the service (and construction) sectors where close to 70 per cent of the labour force is employed (see Figure 8.6). Agriculture employs about 11 per cent, with manufacturing (and resource extraction) taking up the remaining 19 per cent, mostly concentrated in the so-called capital goods sector. The overall growth rate of labour supply is a modest 0.3 per cent on average through 2020, with the highest growth in the services sector. Agriculture, resource extraction and consumer goods would shed labour on aggregate in the OECD. This story is somewhat different for Europe. For example, both ECE and EUR would see a decline in the labour force over the next 25 years (in the ECE perhaps 1 million out of a base of 50 million, and in EUR around 4 million out of a base of 176 million). There will be a small shift towards services in EUR, from 71 per cent of the total labour to 74 per cent in 2020. The largest drop in employment would occur in agriculture and food, perhaps as much as 50 per cent conditional on total free trade in agricultural commodities. The consumer goods sector could also witness a significant drop, as much as 25 per cent, though from an already low base. The largest positive shifts would occur in the capital goods sector and the sheltered sectors.

The labour structure in Asia is quite different in the base year. Agricultural (and food) employment represents roughly 61 per cent of total employment, with employment in the sheltered sectors at about 29 per cent. Even in the rapidly emerging economies in DAE, agricultural and food employment is 45 per cent in the base year, with a 42 per cent share in the sheltered sector. Overall labour growth is assumed to be 1.4 per cent per annum on average, considerably higher than the OECD (0.3 per cent per annum), though declining towards the end of the period. Coupled with high productivity, the growth of labour in efficiency units is very rapid. China (and Hong Kong) account for about 55 per cent of the total labour force in the Asian region, with India representing an additional 26 per cent. By the year 2020, China's share will drop to 47 per cent, and India's will rise to 30 per cent.

The most rapid growth in employment will occur in the manufacturing sectors, particularly in intermediate and capital goods. Agriculture and food's share declines, from 61 per cent to 53 per cent, but perhaps less rapidly than one would anticipate from the high growth in this region. First, there are significant differences in development across the region. South Asia (India and RAS), and China have very sizeable rural populations, many living at best at subsistence levels. Second, in the basic scenario, agricultural growth

Figure 8.5- Export structure, 1992 and 2020 (index 1992 = 100)

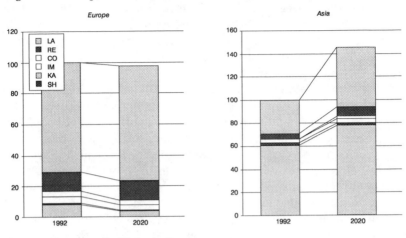

Source: LINKAGE model results.

Figure 8.6 Labour structure, 1992 and 2020 (index 1992 = 100)

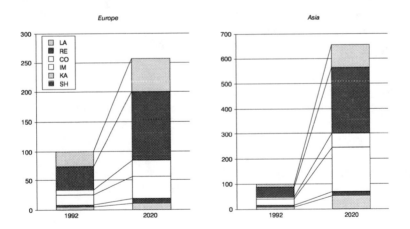

Source: LINKAGE model results.

occurs from a uniform growth in the production curve – that is,
there is no bias in production towards mechanisation and/or chemicals. Changes in the composition of inputs are generated by relative
price differences, not technology. Labour productivity in the non-
agricultural sectors is much higher than in agriculture, hence it is
possible to have higher growth in non-agricultural production using

relatively less labour. Third, the basic scenario assumes perfect labour mobility between rural and non-rural activities. An alternative specification would be to implement some labour market segmentation and have an explicit rural – urban labour migration function, thereby most likely increasing the relative supply of labour for manufacturing and services.

Is the scenario realistic? In the case of China, significant reform, particularly in the domain of property rights, will be needed to achieve significant modifications in the structure of production. It is also readily apparent that manufacturing productivity has ample scope for rapid increases. State-owned enterprises, which represent a considerable share of total manufacturing potential, are widely believed to be heavily overstaffed. There is significant concern about a large labour surplus in the cities, but it is not obvious that rapid growth in manufacturing and services will be able to absorb this surplus easily. India's situation is somewhat different, though manufacturing has been hiding behind closed borders for many years. One would expect that elimination of tariffs could have a dramatic impact on the productivity of manufacturing and could also lead to (relative) labour shedding, somewhat in a similar vein privatisation could do this in China. In both of these large countries, government expenditures on agricultural research has been declining, and investment in agricultural infrastructure lagging. Under these circumstances, it is hard to conceive of continued growth in agriculture without an increase in labour input.

Real wages increase significantly in all regions, ranging from a low of 1.2 per cent per annum to 4.8 per cent per annum. There are a variety of factors which influence real wage growth: tightness of the labour market, terms of trade effects and labour productivity. The OECD countries benefit from the first two. Labour supply growth is low – if not negative in some regions – creating tight labour market conditions. The combination of high embodied productivity and increased competition leads to a drop in the price of imports into the OECD, hence an improvement in the terms of trade. Real wages in the OECD therefore increase from 1.7 to 4.2 per cent on average per annum, with the lower rate observed in NFT, which has a higher labour supply growth and lower base tariffs. Real wage growth tends to be higher in the non-OECD countries, reflecting the overall catch-up momentum towards OECD income levels.

8.5 CONCLUSION

The world economy could be at the beginning of an age of global prosperity. The resolution of major regional conflicts, the determined opening up of many previously closed economies, and productivity growth engendered by a panoply of pro-competition policies could put many economies on a virtuous cycle of growth. The recent past and the best-informed guesses of many economists suggest that non-OECD economies, particularly those in Asia, are likely to grow at rates significantly higher than those likely to be feasible in the OECD economies, and better than historical rates.

The first impact of these high and different growth rates will be to shift the centre of economic weight away from the OECD countries. Depending on the choice of weighting schemes, the non-OECD countries' share of total world income could range from 36 per cent (at market exchange rates) to 67 per cent (at PPP exchange rates) if these growth rates are obtained. Second, there will be a significant convergence in income levels, with the average non-OECD income rising to 30 per cent of the average OECD income from a level of only 15 per cent today (at PPP exchange rates). By the year 2020, many non-OECD countries could achieve a level of income of the lower-income OECD countries, and some could even rank with the richest countries in the world. These aggregate growth numbers will be more than surpassed by the growth in trade, both within non-OECD countries as well as between the OECD and the non-OECD.

Income growth, changing patterns of consumption, evolving comparative advantage and changes in the policy environment will inevitably lead to changes in the structure of production, labour force and trade. To a significant extent, these changes have largely occurred already in the OECD economies, and we are simply likely to see a small reinforcement of the service sectors. Changes in trade policies will force some rationalisation in agriculture, and textiles and apparel. High growth in the non-OECD countries will provide significant opportunities for the OECD countries, particularly in intermediate and capital goods and services. Labour income in the OECD will rise significantly, and assuming the OECD successfully resolves its employment and skill problems, will provide a basis for equitable growth.

There will be significantly more structural adjustment in the non-OECD countries. Demand for higher quality manufactured goods and services, as well as derived demand for construction and capital goods, will lead to a significant shift in production and trade shares. Labour demand growth could continue to be significant – though slower than overall labour growth – in agriculture and food processing, particularly in the poorer and larger countries. Land reform combined with increased investment in agricultural research and infrastructure could lead to an increased shedding of agricultural workers.

Achieving these high levels of growth simultaneously in all regions will not be easy. Significant policy reforms need to be undertaken in all regions to tackle current and future bottlenecks. All regions need to provide adequate educational resources to ensure growth in a high-quality labour force. In non-OECD countries, further progress must be made to liberalise trade in goods and services, as well improving the efficiency of financial systems. OECD countries need to implement policies to deal with the looming pension and medical needs of a rapidly ageing population. Further regulatory reforms in the OECD would also promote growth-enhancing competition, particularly in Europe and Japan. Internationally, significant progress needs to be achieved to lower remaining trade barriers and to provide a better environment for foreign investment flows.

While high growth is not guaranteed, there is a relatively broad consensus among policy analysts of the best-practice policies which can improve the chances of success. If the right recipes are implemented, global prosperity will provide the opportunity to deal with some pressing and acute problems, such as marginalisation of the poorest countries and environmental degradation.

APPENDIX 8.1 MODEL FEATURES

Summary Description of Linkage Model

The Linkage Model is an applied dynamic general equilibrium model. The regional and sectoral model definitions are provided in the following appendices, including their correspondence with the GTAP data set.[10] The base year of the data is 1992, and the model is solved forward for the years 1995, 2000, 2005, 2010, 2015 and 2020. The dynamic structure is recursive dynamic, hence the model is solved in sequential steps, greatly reducing the dimensionality of finding a solution.

The broad features of the model resemble fairly standard AGE models. Constant returns to scale is assumed in production in all sectors. Producers choose an optimal mix of intermediate goods, capital and labour to produce goods, subject to exogenous substitution elasticities. Production in the model differs in three ways from the standard model:

• The production structure is differentiated by crops, livestock, and the remaining sectors. Land, chemicals (in crops), and feed (in livestock) are distinguished in the agricultural sectors.
• Energy plays a prominent role in the production structure in all sectors. It is possible to substitute energy for the other factors of production (for example labour), as well as to choose the optimal mix of fuels (as a function of relative fuel prices and existing technology).
• A distinction is made between old (or installed) capital, and new capital (i.e. a vintage capital model is assumed, also called a putty/semi-putty technology). Typically, the substitution possibilities with older capital are smaller than with new capital. Economies with higher rates of investment will have more flexibility since on average they will have a larger share of new capital.

There is a single representative household to which all factor income accrues. Households purchase an optimal bundle of goods, under a modified Stone–Geary demand system, known as the Extended Linear Expenditure System. The level of savings is directly integrated into the decision making of households.

Government receives tax revenues from households, and an assortment of indirect taxes (production, consumption, import tariffs, and export taxes/subsidies). Aggregate government expenditures are fixed as a proportion of GDP, and a fixed coefficient expenditure function is used to determine sectoral purchases. One of the closure rules is that the government deficit to GDP ratio is fixed. The household direct tax schedule is endogenous in order to achieve the given target.

Investment is savings-driven – i.e. aggregate investment is equated to national savings (private and public) *plus* foreign inflows (or outflows). A fixed coefficient expenditure function is used to determine the allocation of investment expenditures on goods and services.

Trade in goods and services assumes that goods are differentiated by region of origin (this is the so-called Armington assumption). Typically, the more homogeneous the definition of a good, the higher will be the substitution elasticity between domestic and imported goods, though a low degree of substitution can also reflect high or prohibitive transportation costs (e.g. natural gas). The one exception to the Armington assumption is crude oil. It is both a relatively homogeneous commodity, as well as having low transportation costs relative to its value. Equilibrium on the oil market is achieved by equating world demand with world supply. All regions are assumed to be on their oil resource depletion profile, except for the Middle East/North Africa (MNA) region. Assuming the MNA region targets a given price for crude oil, it becomes the supplier of last resort (i.e. its extraction rate is endogenous, see below).

The model distinguishes four different trading prices: pre-fob (i.e. at producer prices), fob (at border price), cif (inclusive of international trade and transport margins), and post-cif (i.e. inclusive of import tariffs). All price wedges are distinguished both by region of origin and destination. Unlike most standard models, there is no distinction between domestic output sold on domestic markets and exported – in other words, there is a single price for domestic production.

The final closure rule concerns the trade balance (or equivalently the capital balance). In each time period, and for each region, the trade balance is fixed. Equilibrium on the current account is achieved through an endogenous real exchange rate. For example, a reduction in tariffs typically leads to a real exchange rate depreciation as an increase in imports needs to be matched by an increase in exports.

Labour is assumed to be perfectly mobile across sectors, and the wage level is fully flexible and determined by the labour equilibrium condition. New capital is similarly perfectly mobile across sectors, and is allocated such that the rate of return is uniform across the economy. Sectors in decline – i.e. whose demand for capital is less than the initially installed capital – release capital according to a supply schedule. The released capital is added to the pool of new capital – i.e. released capital is assumed to be equivalent to new capital. The rate of return on old capital in declining sectors will be determined by equating the sectoral capital demand with the (remaining) sectoral capital supply.

The Linkage Model is recursive dynamic. It is solved as a series of sequential equilibria. Each time period is linked to past time periods by updating of factor stocks and changes in productivity factors. Population and labour growth are exogenous, based on the latest UN population projections. The capital stock in each period is equated to the previous period's depreciated stock plus new investment. Overall land supply is assumed to be available in fixed quantity, though actual demand may be less than the maximum available supply. (A logistic supply curve is implemented.) The other factors include energy resources: coal, oil and gas reserves and non-fossil fuel-generated electricity. Coal and the non-fossil fuel electric factor are assumed to follow a constant elasticity supply curve. Oil and gas resources are determined using a resource depletion module. Oil and gas reserves are split into two components – proven and unproven reserves. Production comes from proven reserves at a given extraction rate (except for the MNA region). Unproven reserves are converted to proven reserves according to a price sensitive discovery rate.

Productivity is calibrated in a reference scenario in order to achieve a given GDP growth rate. The basic assumption is that of balanced growth – i.e. the labour: capital ratio (in efficiency units) remains constant. Labour productivity is assigned exogenously so that labour in efficiency units grows at the same rate as GDP. Capital productivity is determined residually, consistent with GDP and labour projections. Energy efficiency improvement is exogenous. Finally, productivity in the agricultural sectors is also set exogenously.

APPENDIX 8.2   REGIONAL CONCORDANCE FOR THE
LINKAGE MODEL[11]

1	ANZ	Australia and New Zealand *Australia (AUS), New Zealand (NZL)*
2	CHN	China including Hong Kong *The People's Republic of China (CHN), Hong Kong (HKG)*
3	DAE	Dynamic Asian Economies *Republic of Korea (KOR), Malaysia (MYS), Philippines (PHL), Singapore (SGP), Thailand (THA), Chinese Taipei (TWN)*
4	ECE	Eastern and Central Europe *Bulgaria, Czech Republic, Hungary, Poland, Romania, Slovakia, Slovenia (CEA)*
5	EUR	European Union 15 plus EFTA countries *Belgium, Denmark, France, Germany, Greece, Ireland, Italy, Luxembourg, Netherlands, Portugal, Spain, United Kingdom (EU), Austria, Finland, Sweden (EU3), Iceland, Norway, Switzerland (EFT)*
6	IDN	Indonesia (IDN)
7	IND	India (IDI)
8	JPN	Japan (JPN)
9	LAT	Central and South America *Argentina (ARG), Brazil (BRA), Antigua & Barbuda, Bahamas, Barbados, Belize, Costa Rica, Cuba, Dominica, Dominican Republic, El Salvador, Grenada, Guatemala, Haiti, Honduras, Jamaica, Nicaragua, Panama, St Kitts & Nevis, St Lucia, St Vincent, Trinidad & Tobago (CAM), Chile (CHL), Bolivia, Colombia, Ecuador, Guyana, Paraguay, Peru, Suriname, Uruguay, Venezuela (RSM)*
10	MNA	Middle East and Northern Africa *Algeria, Bahrain, Egypt, Iran, Iraq, Israel, Jordan, Kuwait, Lebanon, Libya, Morocco, Oman, Qatar, Saudi Arabia, Syrian Arab Republic, Tunisia, United Arab Emirates, Yemen Arab Republic (MEA)*
11	NFT	North American Free Trade Area *Canada (CAN), Mexico (MEX), United States of America (USA)*
12	NIS	Newly Independent States *Armenia, Azerbaijan, Belarus, Estonia, Georgia, Kazakhstan, Kyrgyz Republic, Latvia, Lithuania, Moldova, Russian Federation, Tajikistan, Turkmenistan, Ukraine, Uzbekistan (FSU)*
13	RAS	Rest of South Asia *Bangladesh, Bhutan, Maldives, Nepal, Pakistan, Sri Lanka (RAS)*
14	ROW	Rest of the World *Afghanistan, Albania, Andorra, Bosnia-Herzegovina, Brunei, Cambodia, Croatia, Cyprus, Fiji, Kiribati, Laos, Leichtenstein, Macedonia former Yugoslav Republic of, Malta, Monaco,*

                Mongolia, Myanmar, Nauru, North Korea, Papua New Guinea,
                San Marino, Solomon Islands, Tonga, Turkey, Tuvalu,
                Vanuatu, Vietnam, Western Samoa, Yugoslavia Serbia and
                Montenegro) (ROW)

15 SSA   Sub Saharan Africa
                Angola, Benin, Botswana, Burkina Faso, Burundi, Cameroon,
                Cape Verde, Central African Republic, Chad, Comoros, Re-
                public of the Congo, Democratic Republic of the Congo (for-
                merly Zaïre), Côte d'Ivoire, Djibouti, Equatorial Guinea,
                Eritrea, Ethiopia, Gabon, Gambia, Ghana, Guinea, Guinea-
                Bissau, Kenya, Lesotho, Liberia, Madagascar, Malawi, Mali,
                Mauritania, Mauritius, Mozambique, Namibia, Niger, Nigeria,
                Rwanda, Sao Tome & Principe, Senegal, Seychelles Islands,
                Sierra Leone, Somalia, South Africa, Sudan, Swaziland, Tan-
                zania, Togo, Uganda, Zambia, Zimbabwe (SSA)

Aggregate Regions

1	OECD	ANZ, ECE, EUR, JPN, and NFT
2	Asia	CHN, DAE, IDN, IND, and RAS
3	Other	LAT, MNA, NIS, ROW, and SSA

APPENDIX 8.3 SECTORAL CONCORDANCE FOR THE
LINKAGE MODEL[12]

1 Rice   Paddy rice
                Agricultural & livestock production (paddy rice only): 1110,
                Agricultural services (servicing paddy rice production only):
                1120 (PDR)

2 Wheat   Wheat
                Agricultural & livestock production (wheat only): 1110,
                Agricultural services (servicing wheat production only):
                1120 (WHT)

3 OGrains   Other grains
                Agricultural & livestock production (grains except wheat
                & rice only): 1110, Agricultural services (servicing pro-
                duction of grains, except wheat & rice only): 1120 (GRO)

4 Livst   Livestock products
                Agricultural & livestock production (wool only): 1110,
                Agricultural services (servicing wool production only): 1120
                (WOL), Agricultural & livestock production (other live-
                stock production only): 1110, Agricultural services (ser-
                vicing other livestock production only): 1120, Hunting,
                trapping & game propagation: 1130 (OLP)

5 OAgric   Other agriculture
                Agricultural & livestock production (non-grain crops only):

		1110, Agricultural services (servicing non-grain crops production only): 1120 (NGC), Forestry: 1210, Logging: 1220 (FOR)

6 Coal

Coal
Coal mining: 2100, Manufacture of miscellaneous products of petroleum and coal (briquettes only): 3540 (COL)

7 Oil

Crude oil
Crude petroleum & natural gas production (oil only): 2200 (OIL)

8 Gas

Natural gas
Crude petroleum & natural gas production (gas only): 2200, Petroleum refineries (LPG only): 3530 (GAS)

9 OMining

Other mining
Iron ore mining: 2301, Non-ferrous ore mining: 2302, Stone quarrying, clay and pits: 2901, Chemical and fertiliser mineral mining: 2902, Salt mining: 2903, Mining and quarrying n.e.c.: 2909 (OMN)

10 PrRice

Processed Rice
Grain mill products (processed rice only): 3116 (PCR)

11 MeatProd

Meat Products
Slaughtering, preparing and preserving meat: 3111 (MET)

12 Dairy

Dairy Products
Manufacture of dairy products: 3112 (MIL)

13 BevTob

Beverages and Tobacco
Distilling, rectifying & blending spirits: 3131, Wine industries: 3132, Malt liquors and malt: 3133, Soft drinks & carbonated waters industries: 3134, Tobacco manufactures: 3140 (BT)

14 OFdProc

Other Food Processing
Ocean and coastal fishing: 1301, Fishing n.e.c.: 1302 (FSH), Canning and preserving of fruits and vegetables: 3113, Canning, preserving & processing of fish, crustaceans and similar foods: 3114, Manufacture of vegetable and animal oils & fats: 3115, Grain mill products (except processed rice): 3116, Manufacture of bakery products: 3117, factories and refineries: 3118, Manufacture of cocoa, chocolate & sugar confectionery: 3119, Manufacture of food products n.e.c.: 3121, Manufacture of prepared animal feeds: 3122 (OFP)

15 Textile

Textile
Spinning, weaving & finishing textiles: 3211, of made-up textile goods excluding wearing apparel: 3212, Knitting mills: 3213, Manufacture of carpets & rugs: 3214, Cordage, rope & twine industries: 3215, Manufacture of textiles n.e.c.: 3219 (TEX)

16 Apparel

Apparel, leather, and footwear
Manufacture of wearing apparel, except footwear: 3220 (WAP), Tanneries & leather finishing: 3231, Fur dressing & dyeing industries: 3232, Manufacture of products

of leather & leather substitutes, except footwear and wearing apparel: 3233, Manufacture of footwear, except vulcanised or moulded rubber or plastic footwear: 3240 (LEA)

17 PulpPap   Pulp and Paper
Manufacture of pulp, paper & paperboard: 3411, Manufacture of containers & boxes of paper and paperboard: 3412, Manufacture of pulp, paper & paperboard articles n.e.c.: 3419, Printing, publishing & allied industries: 3420, 3710 (PPP)

18 IronSteel   Iron and Steel
Iron and steel basic industries: 3710 (IS)

19 NFMet   Non-ferrous basic metals
Non-ferrous metal basic industries: 3720 (NFM)

20 RefOil   Refined oil
Petroleum refineries (except LPG): 2530, Manufacture of miscellaneous products of petroleum and coal (except briquettes): 3540 (PC)

21 ChemPlast   Chemical and plastics
Manufacture of basic industrial chemicals except fertilisers: 3511, Manufacture of fertilisers and pesticides: 3512, Manufacture of synthetic resins, plastic materials and man-made fibres except glass: 3513, Manufacture of paints, varnishes and lacquers: 3521, Manufacture of drugs and medicines: 3522, Manufacture of soap and cleaning preparations, perfumes and cosmetics: 3523, Manufacture of chemical products n.e.c.: 3529, Tyre and tube industries: 3551, Manufacture of rubber products n.e.c.: 3559, Manufacture of plastic products n.e.c.: 3560 (CRP)

22 TrpEqpt   Transport equipment
Ship building and repairing: 3841, Manufacture of rail-road equipment: 3842, Manufacture of motor vehicles: 3843, Manufacture of motorcycles and bicycles: 3844, Manufacture of aircraft: 3745, Manufacture of transport equipment n.e.c.: 3849 (TRN)

23 OthManu   Other manufacturing
Sawmills, planing & other wood mills, Manufacture of wooden & cane containers & small cane ware: 3312, Manufacture of wood & cork products n.e.c.: 3319, Manufacture of furniture & fixtures, except primarily of metal: 3320 (LUM), Manufacture of pottery, china and earthenware: 3610, Manufacture of glass and glass products: 3620, Manufacture of structural clay compounds: 3691, Manufacture of cement, lime and plaster:3692, Manufacture of non-metallic mineral products n.e.c.: 3699 (NMM), Manufacture of cutlery, hand tools and general hardware: 3811, Manufacture of furniture and fixtures primarily of metal: 3812, Manufacture of structural metal products: 3813, Manufacture of fabricated metal prod-

*ucts except machinery & equipment n.e.c.: 3819 (FMP),
Manufacture of engines and turbines: 3821, Manufacture of agricultural machinery and equipment: 3822, Manufacture of metal and wood working machinery: 3823, Manufacture of special industrial machinery and equipment except metal and wood working machinery: 3824, Manufacture of office, computing and accounting machinery: 3825Machinery and equipment except electrical n.e.c.: 3829, Manufacture of electrical industrial machinery and apparatus: 3831, Manufacture of radio, television and communication equipment and apparatus: 3832, Manufacture of electrical appliances and housewares: 3833, Manufacture of electrical apparatus and supplies n.e.c.: 3839, Manufacture of professional and scientific, and measuring and controlling equipment, n.e.c.: 3851, Manufacture of photographic and optical goods: 3852, Manufacture of watches and clocks: 3853 (OME), Manufacture of jewellery and related articles: 3901, Manufacture of musical instruments: 3902, Manufacture of sporting and athletic goods: 3903, Manufacturing industries n.e.c.: 3909 (OMF)*

24 Elec — Electricity, gas distribution and water
Electric light and power: 4101, Gas manufacture and distribution: 4102, Steam and hot water supply: 4103, Water works and supply: 4200 (EGW)

25 Constr — Construction
Construction: 5000 (CNS)

26 NCA — All other goods and services
Wholesale trade: 6100, Retail trade: 6200, Restaurants, cafes, and other eating and drinking places: 6310, Hotels, rooming houses, camps and other lodging places: 6320, Railway transport: 7111, Urban, suburban and interurban highway passenger transport: 7112, Other passenger land transport: 7113, Freight transport by road: 7114, Pipeline transport: 7115, Supporting services to land transport: 7116, Ocean and coastal transport: 7121, Inland water transport: 7122, Supporting services to water transport: 7123, Air transport carriers: 7131, Supporting services to air transport: 7132, Services incidental to transport: 7191, Storage and warehousing: 7192, Communication: 7200 (TT), Activities not adequately defined: 0000, Monetary institutions: 8101, Other financial institutions: 8102, Financial services: 8103, Insurance: 8200, Real estate: 8310, Legal services: 8321, Accounting, auditing and bookkeeping services: 8322, Data processing and tabulating services: 8323, Engineering, architectural and technical services: 8324, Advertising services: 8325, Business services, except machinery and equipment rental and leasing, n.e.c.: 8329, Machinery and equipment rental and leasing:8330,

> *Motion picture production: 9411, Motion picture distribution and projection: 9412, Radio and television broadcasting: 9413, Theatrical producers and entertainment services: 9414, Authors, music composers and other independent artists n.e.c.: 9415, Libraries, museums, botanical and zoological gardens, and other cultural services, n.e.c.: 9420, Amusement and recreational services n.e.c.: 9490, Repair of footwear and other leather goods: 9511, Electrical repair shops: 9512, Repair of motor vehicles and motorcycles: 9513, Watch, clock and jewellery repair: 9514, Other repair shops n.e.c.: 9519, Laundries, laundry services, and cleaning and dyeing plants: 9520, Domestic services: 9530, Barber and beauty shops: 9591, Photographic studios, including commercial photography: 9592, Personal services n.e.c.: 9599 (OSP), Public administration and defence: 9100, Sanitary and similar services: 9200,Education services: 9310, Research and scientific institutes: 9320 Medical, dental and other health services: 9331, Veterinary services: 9332, Welfare institutions: 9340, Business, professional and labour associations: 9350, Religious organisations: 9391, Social and related community services n.e.c.: 9399, International and other extra-territorial bodies: 9600 (OSG), Dwellings (DWE).*

Aggregate Sectors

1	LA	Rice, Wheat, OGrains, Livst, OAgric. PrRice, MeatProd, Dairy, BevTob, OFdProc
2	RE	Coal, Oil, Gas, OMining
3	CO	Textile, Apparel, ChemPlast,
4	IM	PulpPap, IronSteel, NFMet, RefOil
5	KA	TrpEqpt, OthManu
6	SH	Elec, Constr, NCA

Notes

* The author would like to acknowledge the efficient and indispensable assistance of Christophe Complainville in the preparation of this chapter. The views and results expressed in this chapter are those of the author and do not necessarily reflect those of the OECD or of any of its Member countries' governments.

1. The Linkage model used for this chapter differs somewhat from the Linkage model used for the OECD's Linkages II study. The main difference is in the regional definition of the model. Otherwise, the model specification and underlying assumptions are identical. A detailed overview of the Linkage model is provided in OECD (1997b).

2. See OECD (1997a) for a full description of the assumptions underlying this high-growth scenario.
3. The aggregate growth rates are weighted using the 1992 market exchange rates, not PPP exchange rates.
4. The population and labour statistics reflect UN projections on international migration (see United Nations, various editions). The model does not allow for international labour movements save through the initial projections.
5. The base data excludes most of intra-regional trade for the aggregate regions. For example, the EU region in the base data, excludes intra-EU trade. The EUR region defined for the purposes of this chapter includes trade between the three separate regions which compose the aggregate region. Therefore, intra-OECD trade is underestimated as a share of total world trade.
6. Note that most of intra-European trade is netted out in the base dataset. The export diversification percentages therefore essentially concern non-European export destinations.
7. Note that the numbers understate the percentage for EUR since, as noted above, it excludes to a large extent intra-EU trade.
8. It is worth noting that these numbers are based on 1992 statistics. Given the rapid growth in both GDP and trade, particularly in the Asian region, it is likely that these numbers have changed perceptibly over the last six years.
9. Note that the numbers in Figure 8.6 and in Table 8.6 include intra-regional trade.
10. For a more complete description of GTAP, see Hertel (1997).
11. GTAP acronym in parenthesis
12. GTAP acronym in parenthesis, and ISIC sectors in detailed description.

References

Armington, P. (1969) 'A theory of demand for products distinguished by place of production', *IMF Staff Papers*, 16, 159–78.

Ballad, C.L., Fullerton, D., Shoven, J.B. and Whalley, J. (1985) *A General Equilibrium Model for Tax Policy Evaluation*, Chicago: University of Chicago Press.

British Petroleum (various years) *BP Statistical Review of World Energy*, London: The British Petroleum Company.

Burniaux, J.-M. and van der Mensbrugghe, D. (1994) 'The RUNS global trade model', *Economic and Financial Modelling*, Autumn/Winter, 161–282.

Burniaux, J.-M., Martin, J.P., Nicoletti, G. and Oliveira-Martins, J. (1992) 'GREEN – a multi-sector, multi-region dynamic general equilibrium model for quantifying the costs of curbing CO_2 emissions: a technical manual', *OECD Economics Department Working Papers*, 116.

Drysdale, P. and Garnaut, R. (1993) 'The Pacific: an application of a general theory of economic integration', in Bergsten, C.F. and Noland, M.

(eds), *Pacific Dynamism and the International Economic System*, Washington, DC Institute for International Economics.

EMF 14 (1995) 'Second round study design for EMF 14: integrated assessment of climate change', Energy Modeling Forum, Stanford University, mimeo.

Francois, J.F. and Reinert, K.A. (1997) *Applied Methods for Trade Policy Analysis: A Handbook*, New York: Cambridge University Press.

Fullerton, D. (1983) 'Transition losses of partially mobile industry-specific capital', *Quarterly Journal of Economics*, 98, 107–25.

Gunning, J.Q. and Keyser, M.A. (1995) 'Applied general equilibrium models for policy analysis', in Srinivasan, T.N. and Behrman, J. (eds), *Handbook of Development Economics*, vol. IIIA, Amsterdam: North-Holland.

Hertel, T.W. (ed.) (1997) *Global Trade Analysis: Modeling and Applications*, New York: Cambridge University Press.

Howe, H. (1975) 'Development of the extended linear expenditure system from simple savings assumptions', *European Economic Review*, 6, 305–10.

International Energy Agency (1996) *Global Offshore Oil Prospects to 2000*, Paris: OECD/IEA.

Lee, H., Oliveira-Martins, J. and van der Mensbrugghe, D. (1994) 'The OECD GREEN model: an updated overview', *OECD Development Centre Technical Papers*, 97, Paris: OECD.

Lee, H., Roland-Holst, D. and van der Mensbrugghe, D. (1997) 'APEC trade liberalization and structural adjustment: policy assessments', *APEC Discussion Paper Series*, 11, APEC Study Center, Graduate School of International Development, Nagoya University and the Institute of Developing Economies.

Lee, H. and Roland-Holst, D. (1995) 'Trade liberalization and employment linkages in the Pacific Basin', *Developing Economies*, 33, 155–84.

Lee, H. and Roland-Holst, D. (1996) 'CGE modelling of trade and employment in Pacific Rim countries', in Taylor, J.E. (ed.), *Development Strategy, Employment, and Migration: Insights from Models*, Paris: OECD.

Lluch, C. (1973) 'The extended linear expenditure system', *European Economic Review*, 4, 21–32.

OECD (1997a) 'The World in 2020: Towards a new global age', Paris: OECD.

OECD (1997b) 'The Linkage Model', A Technical Note, CD/R(97)2, Paris: OECD.

United Nations (various editions) *World Population Prospects*, New York: United Nations.

9 Quantifying the Effects of Labour Sanctions on Trade[1]

John Whalley and Randall Wigle

9.1 INTRODUCTION

In this chapter we present some preliminary and illustrative calculations of the consequences of trade sanctions against low-income countries. The main theme is that the impact of actions against low labour standards (or poor enforcement) have the unintended effect of depressing wages, particularly if actions are focused on labour-intensive sectors. The estimates suggest that these indirect effects can be sizeable, and that impacts on trade and employment can also be significant.

The chapter reflects the debate in the later stages of the Uruguay Round, and following the NAFTA side agreements dealing with labour standards, in which there has been increasing pressure to tie labour issues to trade. The argument is that countries with inadequate protection of workers' rights and safety should be subject to trade sanctions to force change in their policies.

9.2 THE ISSUES

Using trade policy to promote workers' rights and encourage fair labour standards has recently received increased attention. This was first as part of the debate in the USA over whether to grant fast-track authority for bilateral negotiations for a free trade agreement with Mexico,[2] then more recently prior to the signing of the Uruguay Round agreements in Marrakesh in 1994 when the USA and several other developed countries tried to put workers' rights on the agenda of the work programme for the new World Trade Organisation (WTO). This attempt was unsuccessful because of the

199

opposition of developing and newly industrialised countries (NICs), but the issue came up again in the debate on fast-track negotiating authority to be included with the Uruguay Round implementing legislation in the US.[3] These proposals reflect a continuation of a trend in US trade policy as expressed in the 1983 Caribbean Basin Initiative (CBI) and the 1984 extension of the Generalised System of Preferences (GSP). They can be traced as far back as the International Labour Conference in Berne in 1906 and the Havana Charter for the ITO in 1947.[4] Under the CBI, potential beneficiary countries are evaluated according to a number of criteria, including whether workers are given 'reasonable workplace conditions and enjoy the right to organise and bargain collectively'.[5] While this is a discretionary criterion under the CBI, it has been taken seriously by a number of Caribbean countries and has led to commitments to improve workers' conditions in Haiti, Honduras, the Dominican Republic and El Salvador.[6]

As part of the renewal of the US GSP scheme in 1984, Congress also added a fair labour standard to the mandatory criteria for country eligibility. Under the 1984 Act, beneficiaries can be denied preferential treatment if they are not providing internationally recognised workers' rights. These rights generally include 'the right of association, the right to organize and bargain collectively, a prohibition against forced labour, a minimum age for child labour and "acceptable" conditions of work.'[7]

This provision has also been used to re-evaluate, and in some cases deny, beneficiary status on a number of occasions since its implementation. Both Romania and Nicaragua have been denied beneficiary status as a result of a review of labour standards, and in 1987 Chile was removed from eligibility for preferential treatment. Subsequent annual reviews have led to either the re-examination of eligibility, or the suspension of benefits for Burma, the Central African Republic, Israel, Malaysia, Haiti, Liberia, Syria and Indonesia.[8]

Workers' rights and labour issues gained a higher profile during the negotiations for a NAFTA[9] and maintained a high profile throughout the negotiations. When President Clinton took office in January 1993, after the NAFTA negotiations had already concluded, it was announced that NAFTA would not be submitted to Congress for ratification until separate side agreements on labour and the environment had been negotiated.

The labour side agreement reiterates the commitment in the

NAFTA preamble to 'improve working conditions and living standards' in all three countries and 'to protect, enhance and enforce basic workers' rights.' Each country is committed to enforce its own labour laws. Cooperation on labour issues will be achieved through the establishment of a Commission for Labour Cooperation and the establishment of a cooperative work programme. In the event that a country is found to persistently fail to enforce its labour law, an arbitral panel may impose a severe fine.[10] In Canada, the fine would be enforced through the domestic courts, but for Mexico and the USA, failure to pay the fine could lead to trade sanctions. US and Mexican labour organisations recently filed the first complaint under the side agreement. Sony is being accused of obstructing free association of Mexican workers.

The USA has attempted in the past to include the fair labour standards issue in discussions at the multilateral level, both during the Tokyo Round and in the post-Tokyo Round Work Programme, but could not generate enough support for wider involvement. Currently there are no articles or codes in the GATT or the WTO that apply to workers' rights specifically. However, had the Havana Charter for the ITO been implemented, Article 7 on Fair Labour Standards contained in Chapter 2 would have applied. Under this vaguely worded article, members of the ITO recognised the importance of fair labour standards and their mutual interest in improving working conditions. Each member was supposedly to take steps to eliminate such unfair conditions.

9.3 EVALUATING THE EFFECTS OF LABOUR STANDARDS ON TRADE

Here we use a global general equilibrium model to evaluate the possible effects of labour standards on developing country welfare and trade; further details on the model can be found in Nguyen, Perroni and Wigle (1991). The model is an empirically calibrated real trade model which employs the Armington (1969) assumption; that is, goods from different countries are treated as qualitatively different goods.[11] Basic intermediates produced in Canada are thus qualitatively different than those produced in the USA or Japan. Perfect competition and constant returns to scale are assumed throughout. These assumptions are partly motivated by the belief that increasing returns to scale may be less prevalent than others appear to believe (See, for example, Markusen and Wigle, 1990; Nguyen and Wigle, 1992).

Tariffs and non-tariff barriers (NTBs) to imports are applied by all regions in the model, with all revenues redistributed to the domestic consumer. In the case of agricultural commodities, policy measures are represented by producer subsidy equivalents (PSEs).[12] Protection for textiles echoes the MFA: MFA source countries are endowed with quota rights to supply OECD destination countries in our model. The quotas are bilateral, and in many cases are accompanied by tariff barriers. In several of our experiments, liberalisation in textiles means a significant increase in these quotas. A single consumer in each region receives all income and maximises utility by purchasing a bundle of goods (both domestic and foreign). These goods are produced according to nested CES production functions using inputs of capital, labour, and (in the case of agriculture) land.

9.3.1   Commodity and Country Aggregation

The commodity aggregation used in the model is set out in Table 9.1, and the country aggregation used is presented in Table 9.2. The country aggregation was suggested by the relative importance of agriculture in the Uruguay Round discussions. It separates two groups of countries for special attention; namely, agricultural exporters (AGX), and agricultural importers (AGM).

9.3.2   Model Results on the Potential Impacts of Sanctions Against Low Labour Standards

There are many things that importing countries could perceive as low labour standards. This could include 'exploitation' of labour (paying less than a fair or 'living' wage), insufficient protection of worker health or safety and insufficient protection of worker rights (either by industrial relations law or basic law protecting democratic rights). Equally, there are many ways in which sanctions could be taken against these measures. We discuss the potential impacts of trade sanctions via (very stylised) countervailing duties, using the model set out above. The argument is that 'exploitation' or insufficient protection of rights can be seen as an unfair subsidy to manufacturers who employ the labour. We consider duties applied

Table 9.1 Commodity aggregation used in the global trade model

AGR	AGRICULTURE AND FOOD: agriculture, food manufacturing, hunting, trapping
BSI	BASIC INTERMEDIATE: fabricated goods, primary metals, wood products, textile fibres, electrical energy, chemicals NES
MIN	MINING AND RESOURCE EXTRACTION: mining, energy products
LIN	LIGHT INDUSTRIES: clothing, yarn, cloth, furniture
FRF	FORESTRY AND FISHING PRODUCTS: lumber, pulp and paper, fish landings
FCG	FINISHED CAPITAL GOODS: vehicles and parts, machinery and equipment
HTC	HIGH-TECH MANUFACTURES: pharmaceuticals, cosmetics, jewelry, instruments, scientific equipment, electrical machinery
INM	INTERMEDIATE MANUFACTURES: fixtures, electrical equipment, office supplies, printing and publishing
SVC	NON-FACTOR SERVICES: personal services, business services, government services

Table 9.2 Country aggregation used in the global trade model

AGX	MIDDLE-INCOME AGRICULTURAL EXPORTERS: Brazil, Argentina, Indonesia, Thailand, Malaysia, Philippines
AGM	MIDDLE-INCOME AGRICULTURAL IMPORTERS: South Korea, Taiwan, Hong Kong, Singapore
CNP	CENTRALLY PLANNED ECONOMIES: Bulgaria, Hungary, East Germany, Cuba, Mongolia, Poland, Romania, Soviet Union, Czechoslovakia, Yugoslavia, People's Republic of China
OWE	OTHER WESTERN EUROPEAN ECONOMIES: Sweden, Norway, Finland, Switzerland, Austria
USA	UNITED STATES OF AMERICA
CAN	CANADA
EEC	EUROPEAN ECONOMIC COMMUNITY: United Kingdom, France, West Germany, Italy, Holland, Belgium, Luxembourg, Spain, Portugal, Ireland, Denmark, Greece
JPN	JAPAN
ANZ	AUSTRALIA AND NEW ZEALAND
ROW	REST OF THE WORLD: All other countries, notably all of Africa, all of Latin America (except Brazil, Argentina, and Cuba), and all of Asia (except People's Republic of China, Mongolia, Japan, South Korea, Thailand, Indonesia, Malaysia, Singapore, Hong Kong, Taiwan, and Philippines)

by high-income regions against imports of labour-intensive goods from low-income regions in our model.

9.3.3   What is 'Labour-intensive'?

The labour intensity of a sector can be thought of in a number of ways. If one considers that sectors with a high labour:capital input ratio (in value terms) are labour-intensive, then in the developed world, the three most labour-intensive sectors of our model would be the following:

LIN	Light Industry	Includes clothing, yarn, cloth and furniture
FCG	Finished Capital Goods	Includes vehicles and parts, machinery and equipment
INM	Intermediate Manufactures	Includes fixtures, electrical equipment, office supplies, printing and publishing

If, on the other hand, we consider sectors by share of labour costs in total costs, we would rate different sectors as labour-intensive in different countries. In particular, as well as those mentioned above, the following sectors would be considered labour-intensive in some regions:

BSI	Basic Intermediates	Fabricated goods, primary metals, wood products, textile fibres, electrical energy and chemicals NES
HTC	High Technology Manufactures[13]	Pharmaceuticals, cosmetics, jewelry, instruments, scientific equipment and electrical machinery

In this paper we treat LIN, FCG, INM as labour-intensive sectors. We conduct experiments where all developed regions (OWE, USA, CAN, EEC, JPN, ANZ) impose high tariffs (ranging from 25 to 50 per cent in the experiments) on imports of these labour-intensive goods originating from the low- and middle-income regions (AGM, AGX, CNP, ROW).

Table 9.3   Sectoral (labour) employment effects from labour standard trade actions (% change)

	AGR	BSI	MIN	LIN	FRF	FCG	HTC	INM	SVC
AGX	−12.9	1.7	1.9	2.4	0.6	1.0	6.6	−0.4	1.0
AGM	−0.3	0.9	4.2	0.0	1.8	−13.2	16.2	−14.5	0.5
CNP	−0.1	0.1	0.2	−0.4	0.0	0.2	0.3	−0.5	0.1
OWE	0.4	−0.6	−0.5	−0.0	−1.3	1.8	−2.5	2.1	−0.4
USA	0.2	−0.4	−0.8	1.2	−0.4	0.4	−2.1	1.2	−0.0
CAN	0.4	−0.3	−2.1	0.6	−1.4	3.2	−3.0	2.8	−0.1
EEC	0.4	−0.2	−0.3	0.2	−0.2	0.8	−2.6	0.8	−0.2
JPN	0.1	−0.4	−1.4	5.3	−0.6	0.8	−1.2	2.0	−0.1
ANZ	0.8	−0.3	−1.9	0.2	−1.0	1.3	−0.9	1.1	−0.1
ROW	0.3	−0.0	0.4	−0.3	0.0	−1.6	0.9	−0.9	0.0

9.3.4   Employment Impacts

We concentrate on the employment impacts of the central case (duties of 35 per cent). In Table 9.3, we see that employment falls in the INM sector in all regions subject to the tariff. In the other sectors, employment falls in some cases, and even rises in others. The AGM region includes major net exporters of the labour-intensive manufactured goods, so the impact of trade barriers on these goods is sizeable (note the employment reductions of 13.2 per cent and 14.5 per cent respectively for FCG and INM). In the ROW region, employment falls in all of the sectors hit by increased trade barriers abroad.

The increase in employment in the FCG sectors of the AGX and CNP regions is explained by the feature that the trade impacts on these sectors are small (because the initial exports are small). The major influence on employment thus comes from the fact that wages have fallen as a result of the trade barriers having an impact on other sectors hit by the protection. Since this is a full employment model, the decrease in employment in the trade-impacted sectors is matched by an increase in employment in other sectors.

9.3.5   Wage Rates

One of the most important effects of the duties applied is on wage rates. The effects are summarised in Table 9.4. In some cases, wages

Table 9.4   Effects of labour standard duties on wages (% change)

Region	Percentage duty					
	25	30	35	40	45	50
AGX	−1.53	−1.56	−1.58	−1.60	−1.61	−1.63
AGM	−4.04	−4.64	−5.15	−5.57	−5.93	−6.27
CNP	−0.42	−0.55	−0.65	−0.73	−0.80	−0.86
ROW	−0.13	−0.15	−0.16	−0.17	−0.18	−0.19

are significantly reduced. Given that the duties are imposed on the labour-intensive exports of these regions, the general thrust of these results is perhaps not surprising. At the same time, they imply that policies aimed at sanctions against poor protection of labour are not likely to be costless, *even to those the policies are intended to help*.

9.3.6   Trade Impacts

The impacts on the pattern of trade are presented in Table 9.5, for the central case duty of 35 per cent. Exports of all labour-intensive goods by all of the low- and medium-income regions fall, and in some cases by large amounts.

All regions suffer reduced total exports. In the case of the low-income regions, their exports are subject to further protection in high-income markets. The high-income countries also suffer falls in exports as input costs rise and as incomes in their trading partners fall. Total world trade volume falls by 1.6 per cent.

9.3.7   Welfare Effects

The welfare effects of the labour standard trade actions are reported in Table 9.6. As expected, the AGM, CNP and ROW regions lose from the increased protection. The loss is sizeable for the AGM region, since they are important net exporters of the goods subject to tariffs. Unexpectedly, the AGX region gains; this is because they are net importers of the goods subject to increased protection. As a result, they experience a terms of trade improvement from the tariffs. The USA and EEC experience welfare gains from terms of trade improvements. World welfare falls by about $15 billion.

Table 9.5   Trade (exports) effects of labour standard trade actions
(% change)

	LIN	FCG	INM	TOTAL
AGX	–1.36	–50.71	–53.82	–4.64
AGM	–2.87	–61.08	–49.00	–3.71
CNP	–19.14	–43.09	–42.84	–1.18
OWE	–0.34	2.90	9.08	–0.52
USA	–5.38	–1.65	2.76	–3.38
CAN	1.45	4.06	15.82	–0.23
EEC	0.56	0.93	5.06	–1.15
JPN	–12.17	1.95	9.19	–0.65
ANZ	–2.63	2.83	5.34	–1.19
ROW	–4.32	–77.01	–64.26	–0.66

Table 9.6   Welfare effects of labour standard trade actions (35% duty)

	%	$B
AGX	0.3	4.57
AGM	–2.8	–10.74
CNP	–0.2	–11.10
OWE	0.1	.30
USA	0.1	4.70
CAN	0.1	.31
EEC	0.1	3.07
JAPAN	0.1	–.85
ANZ	0.1	.16
ROW	–0.2	–6.03
WORLD	–0.1	–15.53

9.4   CONCLUSIONS

This chapter presents results on the impact of widespread use of
trade sanctions for labour standard purposes. Foremost, and perhaps most straightforward, is that the measures can have the unwanted impact of decreasing wages in countries subject to them.
Further, these attempts to deal with poor standards are likely to
have an impact upon trade volumes and the pattern of trade.

Notes

1. This chapter draws heavily on material in an earlier draft prepared for an UNCTAD/CSIER project aiming to evaluate the impacts of the Uruguay Round on developing countries. The report upon which this chapter is based will appear in a parallel Macmillan volume edited by Harmon Thomas and John Whalley. Wigle gratefully acknowledges financial support from the Social Sciences and Humanities Research Council of Canada.

2. See *Financial Times* (25 March 1991). In an 'action plan' submitted to Congress on 1 May 1991, to generate support for the fast track authority, the Bush Administration pledged to negotiate a joint action plan with Mexico concerning labour issues. It would cover improved working conditions, child labour laws and health and safety measures (*Financial Times*, 2 May 1991, p. 6). Under President Clinton, the USA negotiated side agreements to NAFTA with Mexico and Canada over the environment and labour.

3. Interestingly, the provisions concerning environment and labour issues had to be dropped from the fast-track negotiating authority objectives due to lack of support, especially from the business community. (*Financial Times*, 24 August 1994, p. 1). President Clinton, however, approved legislation which would make observance of workers' rights a condition of the international lending institutions (*Financial Times*, 16 August 1994, p. 1).

4. For the history of international fair labour standards see Charnovitz (1986).

5. Quoted in Charnovitz (1986), p. 61. This criterion was also included in the 1989 CBI-II legislation to extend and expand the CBI preferences.

6. See Charnovitz (1986), p. 66.

7. Charnovitz also notes that while the GSP law does not specifically mention ILO conventions, they are the only comprehensive internationally recognised rights of workers. Others include the Universal Declaration of Human Rights; International Covenant on Civil and Political Rights; International Covenant on Economic, Social and Cultural Rights. See Charnovitz (1986), p. 67.

8. Under the 1990 Review, USTR designated Namibia, Chile, Paraguay and the Central African Republic eligible for duty-free status, while under the 1992 Review, Syria was suspended for 'not taking steps to afford internationally recognized workers' rights'.

9. Vocal opposition to the negotiations came from a coalition of workers' rights groups, environmental groups, organised labour and consumer groups. The Action Plan submitted to Congress on 1 May 1991 by the Bush Administration aimed to address the concerns of these groups and generate support for the negotiations. See *Financial Times* (30 January 1991, p. 4) and *Congressional Quarterly* (4 May, vol. 49, no. 18).

10. The panel may impose a fine of up to US$20 million, for the first year. Government of Canada (1993), p. 94.

11. The model is implemented using the modelling package MPS/GE (see Rutherford, 1988).

12. The PSE is a measure of the financial transfers to the agriculture sector. It includes all types of direct and indirect supports, as well as border measures.
13. It may seem strange to find that high-tech manufacturing is labour-intensive, but this may be because the sector requires large numbers of highly skilled individuals.

References

Armington, P. (1969) 'A theory of demand for products distinguished by place of production', *IMF Staff Papers*, 16, 159–178.

Charnovitz, S. (1986). 'Fair labour standards and international trade', *Journal of World Trade Law,* 20, 61–78.

Government of Canada (1993) *The North American Free Trade Agreement: The NAFTA Manual*, Department of Foreign Affairs and International Trade, Ottawa.

Markusen, J. and Wigle, R. (1990) 'Explaining the volume of North–South trade', *Economic Journal*, 100, 1206–15.

Nguyen, T. and Wigle, R. (1992) 'Trade liberalization with imperfect competition: the large and small of it', *European Economic Review*, 36, 17–35.

Nguyen, T., Perroni, C. and Wigle, R. (1991) 'Model documentation for the Uruguay Round transparency model', *Working Paper*, Wilfrid Laurier University.

Nguyen, T., Perroni, C. and Wigle, R. (1993) 'An evaluation of the Draft Final Act of the Uruguay Round', *Economic Journal*, 103, 1540–9.

Rutherford, T. (1988) *General Equilibrium Modelling with MPS/GE*, De partment of Economics, University of Western Ontario.

Index

Index